FLAMING CLASSICS

D0165316

FLAMING CLASSICS
Queering the Film Canon

A L E X A N D E R   D O T Y

ROUTLEDGE
NEW YORK AND LONDON

Published in 2000 by
Routledge
29 West 35th Street
New York, NY 10001

Published in Great Britain by
Routledge
11 New Fetter Lane
London EC4P 4EE

Cataloging-in-Publication Data is available from the Library of Congress.

To Ben,
grand diva and fellow Dunston fan,
with love and admiration

C O N T E N T S

A C K N O W L E D G M E N T S

A number of people have contributed to this book, in ways they might not even realize, through their encouragement, advice, and friendship: Jean Rosales, Richard Dyer, Rosemary Mundhenk, Bob Mundhenk, Jeff Hendricks, Karen Cole, Corey Creekmur, Henry Jenkins, Carol Laub, Vivien Steele, Kim Silvestri, Barbara Traister, Stephen DoCarmo, Harry Benshoff, Sean Griffin, Tony Bleach, Patty Ingham, Steven Bross, Ellis Hanson, Brian Yowell, Jane Shattuc, Scott Gordon, Andrew Ramos, Bob Jacobs, and Dave Artman.

I also want to thank Stephen Tompkins for his stimulating conversations and proofreading skills; Phyllis Santamaria for her energy, good cheer, and hospitality; Mike DeAngelis for his sharp wit and great heart; Jan Fergus for her interest in my work (although it is a far cry from Jane Austen) and for many memorable nights at the theatre; and the students in my fall 1998 horror film senior seminar, especially Alicia Almeida, Sunny Bavaro, and Joe Dispoto, for making me think more carefully about gender, sexuality, and *Psycho* (among other things).

Additional thanks to the staff of the British Film Institute Library, to Kevin MacDonald for permission to use and to quote from the material in the Emeric Pressburger Collection at the BFI Library, to Linda Williams, and to Bill Germano, whose enthusiasm helped me in the home stretch.

As for Ben Gove, without you things wouldn't have been half as fun or as interesting: here's to Brighton, Ealing, Allentown, Devon, Dublin, Galway, St. Ives, Seattle, Vancouver, Ithaca, Washington D.C., Chicago, Blackpool, Manchester, Liverpool, Edinburgh, Glasgow, Paris, Philadelphia, New York, and all those amusement parks we went to during the Year of the Roller Coaster.

WHAT'S MY INVESTMENT?

I have huge cultural and erotic investments in so-called mainstream and classic popular culture texts and personalities that date from my childhood in the 1950s and 1960s. They gave me as much pleasure as they did pain and bad ideological lessons. For example, Marilyn Monroe was my first sex education teacher. From her emotional and physical struggles with Robert Mitchum in *The River of No Return*, I learned that heterosexuality was about a woman resisting, then submitting to, a man who said he was concerned about her welfare, but who, finally, had to show the woman who was boss by forcing his attentions upon (i.e., raping) her. But it all looked very exciting and erotic to a nine-year-old sissy boy and his eight-year-old sister watching *Saturday Night at the Movies* on television: Monroe's creamy, breathy blondeness crushed up against Mitchum's rough, unshaven darkness. My sister and I performed variations on the film's crucial sex scene for months afterwards, alternating in the Monroe and Mitchum roles. So I guess Monroe also helped me learn about queerness, since I would act out fantasies of desiring her and of being her at the mercy of my butch-acting straight sister.

From the 1980s onward my life within gay, lesbian, and queer cultures reinforced many of my childhood and teenage popular culture investments. To return to the example above, while Monroe continued to be a feminine identification figure, she also became a tragic, misunderstood gay diva; a sexy femme; and the site of bisexual erotics. As these queer understandings of Monroe indicate, classic texts and personalities actually can be more queer-suggestive than "openly" gay, lesbian, or bisexual texts. That is, the coding of classic or otherwise "mainstream" texts and personalities can often yield a wider range of non-straight readings because certain sexual things could not be stated baldly—and still cannot or will not in most mainstream products—thus often making it more difficult to categorize the erotics of a film or a star. Of course, if you aren't careful, this line of thought can begin to sound like an argument valorizing the closet, for understanding queerness as always something "connotated" or suggested (and never really there "denotatively"), for "subtexting," and for "subcultural" readings. But since

I don't see queer readings as any less there, or any less real, than straight readings of classic or otherwise "mainstream" texts, I don't think that what I do in this book is colluding with dominant representational or interpretive regimes that seek to make queerness "alternative" or "sub" straight.

I came to this position gradually as my relationship to classic and otherwise "mainstream" popular culture changed over the years from understanding myself as taking covert, secret, subcultural, "against the grain," co-optive pleasures to deciding my readings and pleasures were no less valid or "there" than those of people who took things straight. What I've discovered is that once you take this unapologetic, nonsubcultural, "not-against-the-grain" stance concerning your queer film and popular culture understandings and pleasures, you encounter much more resistance and hostility than you ever did when your readings and pleasures remained safely "alternative" or "reading into things." Because I want to position queerness inside texts and production, and to think of queer reading practices as existing alongside straight ones, I usually put quotation marks around the term "mainstream"—for me, any text is always already potentially queer. Along the same lines, I now feel that maybe I/we should drop the idea of "queering" something (as in the title of this book), as it implies taking a thing that is straight and doing something to it. I'd like to see queer discourses and practices as being less about co-opting and "making" things queer (well, there goes the title of my first book, too) and more about discussing how things are, or might be understood as, queer.

What I find particularly interesting is that resistance to understanding "mainstream" texts as including the possibility for queer readings often comes from academic and nonacademic gays, lesbians, and other queers. Are these reactions the result of dominant culture colonization? Of not being aware of certain queer codes? Or do they indicate that just because you identify as lesbian, gay, bisexual, or otherwise queer doesn't mean you won't understand something in the same way that a straight person might, outside considerations of colonization or self-oppression? I tend to think that there is often heterocentrist colonization, if not homophobic self-oppression, involved in queer folks' resistance to queer readings of mainstream texts and personalities. To use myself as an example, shortly after finishing a draft of this introduction I went to see *The Blair Witch Project*.[2] It is the story of three filmmaking students shooting a documentary somewhere in Maryland about a supernatural legend. "Wouldn't it have been great if one of the characters was gay, lesbian, or bisexual?" I thought as I left the theatre. It would have been one of those rare films in which queerness wasn't "the issue" because the narrative focuses upon the trio's attempts to make their film and then to survive after getting lost in a forest. Sometime later I realized that I had fallen into one of those heterocentric traps this book attempts to point out: assuming that all characters in a film are straight unless labeled, coded, or otherwise obviously proven to be queer.

After the *Blair Witch* trio realize they are lost, one of the male characters mentions a girlfriend who will be worried when he doesn't return when he said he would. As a means of reassuring himself and the others, he suggests his girlfriend eventually will call the authorities and instigate a search. What struck me as odd on second or third thought is that neither of the other characters (one male, one female) follows suit at this point by talking about an opposite sex romantic interest who also might be concerned about their whereabouts. Why not? Wouldn't it make sense for these characters to say something along these lines at this tense narrative juncture? Of course, each might be straight and happen not to be in a relationship at the moment. Certainly this is the type of understanding we have been culturally trained and encouraged to come to when filling in the narrative blanks about a character's sexuality. But it is just as likely that these two characters aren't heterosexual. They, and the narrative, could be silent on the subject for reasons psychosocial (the closet, homophobia) and/or commercial (potentially higher grosses). For that matter, just because a character mentions he has a girlfriend doesn't rule out the possibility that he could be understood as bisexual. In representation, as in life, you might never know for certain, as silences and gaps in information can be as telling and meaningful as what is said or shown. It is arrogant to insist that all non–blatantly queer-coded characters must be read as straight—especially in cases like *The Blair Witch Project* where all we have is narrative silence on the subject of certain characters' sexuality.

It is also a mistake to decide which characters are straight and which are queer solely with reference to common (stereo)typing. Granted, (stereo)typed coding of queerness and straightness does exist in both dominant and queer cultures. And this coding is based upon how certain queers and straights look and act in real life. However, in an era when only the most insistently ignorant still think all straights or all gays, lesbians, bisexuals, and other queers look and act the same, why do most people still register "queer" only when confronted with visual and aural codes drawn from a narrow (and often pejoratively charged) range?

How Do I Queer Thee? Let Me Count the Ways

As my immediate post–*Blair Witch Project* thoughts illustrate, heterocentric and (stereo)typed ways of thinking can remain stubbornly persistent in relation to acknowledging the queerness in popular culture. Maybe part of the problem is the suggestion of textual essentialism that crops up when one speaks of something being "in" popular culture texts. When the terms of discussion are framed this way, as they usually are, the result is often a cultural battle over what the text ultimately or primarily "means to say." Rarely do such battles produce more rancor than when you are trying to convince people, queer and straight, that a "popular," "mass," "mainstream," "classic" text might be understood queerly.

For one thing, I find that you have to go the extra mile in terms of conducting really close and exhaustive analyses of "mainstream" or classic texts to even begin to get most people to consider the validity of queer, or lesbian, or bisexual, or gay readings. Is it any wonder that by the time I get to the end of these analyses I often find myself in the position of wanting people to see the queerness as being "in" the text, just as I am asked to understand straightness as being "in" the text, when it is just the preferred reading that dominant culture sanctions? Besides, to base queer readings only upon notions of audience and reception leaves you open to the kind of dismissive attitude that sees queer understandings of popular culture as being the result of "wishful thinking" about a text or "appropriation" of a text by a cultural and/or critical special interest group. It often seems as if people think that since you have chosen to read something queerly—as you might be said to choose to be queer—you need to be pressured or patronized into feeling that you have made the wrong or the "less common and therefore easy to undermine or put in its place" choice.

But to think that all the texts produced within dominant capitalist systems are (supposed to be) straight, is pretty naive—and I'm not speaking here just of films, televisions shows, and other popular culture texts that obviously take queerness as their subject, such as *The Children's Hour* or *Victim*.[3] For one thing, and as I mention in the chapter on *Gentlemen Prefer Blondes*, in order to appeal to the largest audience possible it behooves the film and television industries to allow queerness some sort of expression much of the time. I'm not saying that this is always a deliberate or conscious capitalist marketing ploy (although sometimes it is), but there seems to be room for queerness in many "mainstream" films and television programs—and I find it difficult to believe that all this queerness comes from reading practices alone. Straight people aren't the only ones making these movies, television shows, and music videos. Creative queers, including queer-positioned, straight-identifying people, behind the scenes and in front of the camera can also be a source of the queerness that finds its way into the final product. How conscious these queer producers are of their part in queer coding popular culture texts is another question.

This might be a good place to discuss something that precedes the question of where the queerness might be coming from—producers? the text? spectators?—in film and popular culture. Namely, what do you consider to be an expression of queer sexuality or eroticism in life or in representation? I understand the social and political arguments for the view held by a number of queers that only those representations that say the word(s) or show the sexual acts can be considered truly "lesbian," "gay," or "bisexual." After all, it still takes the most graphic sounds and sights to get many people, straight and queer, to consciously or willingly recognize as queer what they see and hear in the "mainstream." But we know that human sexuality and erotic situations are not always expressed so obviously or clearly. In recognizing a wide range of representational codes and reading practices as "queer," I am not attempting to take the sexual aspects out of lesbianism, gayness, or bisexuality. Even though the films I discuss queerly don't offer scenes of same-sex or bi-sexed intercourse, oral sex, nudity, and kissing, or don't have someone say "I'm lesbian," "You're homosexual," or other variations on these phrases, I don't believe that most people reading this book will think that understanding certain non–sexually explicit representations as lesbian, gay, bisexual, or queer means they have nothing to do with the erotic. Queerness is frequently expressed in ways other than by nude bodies in contact, kissing, or direct verbal indicators; the reasons for finding different means of expression are many—psychological (fear, repression), cultural (oppression), and institutional (censorship, commerce). Even aside from the constraints imposed by these considerations, however, queerness is often (and freely) expressed in subtle ways.

Do we, in our roles as queer producers, audiences, or cultural critics, always have to play to, or consider, the segments of the population that prefer "hit them over the head" messages or that only "registers dominant culture's understanding of things." I suppose, as with most things, it comes down to your ideological agenda within a particular situation. Working with classic studio films from 1910 to the 1960s, and hoping to get all sorts of people to consider the queerness of what has been called the "mainstream," leads me to take a less "show me the action/say the word" view of queer representation. Besides, while representation isn't "real life," I think representation can be understood in ways as subtle and complex as those with which we understand real life.

Why should we refine our understanding of the cultural and psychological workings of gender and sexuality in real life only to narrow things down to the perspective of the most limited ideological dictums of dominant culture when we are faced with a "mainstream" popular culture text or personality? The argument that "most people" will understand "mainstream" texts and personalities in these limited ways doesn't wash with me any longer because (a) "most people" aren't "all people"; (b) within the "most people" group are many people who, to differing degrees, have complicated and conflicted relationships to gender and sexuality, even if, on a conscious level at least, they stick to the straight and narrow much of the time; and (c) while it is frequently politically strategic to assume an essentialist position and critically examine how "most people"/dominant culture might understand things, it is also politically important, if queer readings are to stand up as legitimate readings in their own right, to articulate how other people might understand things *without reference to* these dominant cultural readings.

So what has been understood as "queer" in film and popular culture theory and practice? For a conference a few years ago, I put together a list of the ways in which "queer" has been used in film and popular culture studies. While in certain ways this list seems to indicate that "queer" is becoming another social and academic category, it also suggests that the very range of its uses has prevented it from becoming a clear and fixed category. This element of definitional elusiveness can become nervous-making, even to those who frequently invoke queerness in their work. But this is a good thing, as Martha Stewart would say, as it keeps the gender and sexuality dialogue open and complicated.

One caveat about the list below: saying something is queer according to one of these definitions does not necessarily indicate a radical, progressive, or even liberal position on gender, sexuality, or other issues. For example, the queer work a straight person does in writing about a gay- or lesbian-themed film might express a conservative or normative ideological position. Some would like the term "queer" to be reserved for only those approaches, positions, and texts that are in some way progressive. But, in practice, queerness has been more ideologically inclusive. Hence there is a need to discuss the politics of queerness carefully and specifically, and not just assume that to be queer is to represent a position somewhere on the left.

Queer/queerness has been used
1. As a synonym for either gay, or lesbian, or bisexual.
2. In various ways as an umbrella term
   (a) to pull together lesbian, and/or gay, and/or bisexual with little or no attention to differences (similar to certain uses of "gay" to mean lesbians, gay men, and, sometimes, bisexuals, transsexuals, and transgendered people).
   (b) to describe a range of distinct non-straight positions being juxtaposed with each other.
   (c) to suggest those overlapping areas between and among lesbian, and/or gay, and/or bisexual, and/or other non-straight positions.
3. To describe the non-straight work, positions, pleasures, and readings of people who don't share the same "sexual orientation" as the text they are

producing or responding to (for example, a straight scholar might be said to do queer work when she/he writes an essay on Gus Van Sant's *My Own Private Idaho*, or someone gay might take queer pleasure in the lesbian film *Desert Hearts*).[4]

4. To describe any nonnormative expression of gender, including those connected with straightness.

5. To describe non-straight things that are not clearly marked as gay, lesbian, bisexual, transsexual, or transgendered, but that seem to suggest or allude to one or more of these categories, often in a vague, confusing, or incoherent manner (for example, Buffalo Bill in *The Silence of the Lambs* or Katharine Hepburn's character in *Sylvia Scarlett*).[5]

6. To describe those aspects of spectatorship, cultural readership, production, and textual coding that seem to establish spaces not described by, or contained within, straight, gay, lesbian, bisexual, transsexual, or trangendered understandings and categorizations of gender and sexuality—this is a more radical understanding of queer, as queerness here is something apart from established gender and sexuality categories, not the result of vague or confused coding or positioning (I would contend that Jack Smith's *Flaming Creatures* is a queer avant-garde film by this definition).[6]

Given the variety and flexibility of the definitions of queerness, I don't agree with the idea that queer theory has become a rigid academic category and, therefore, has "had its day" politically. Most people in and outside of the academy are still puzzled about what queerness means, exactly, so the concept still has the potential to disturb or complicate ways of seeing gender and sexuality, as well as the related areas of race, ethnicity, and class. Having said this, I think there are more and less dynamic psychosocial and political uses of the term. Using "queer" simply to mean "gay" or "lesbian" doesn't really do much except to give someone's speech or writing a certain contemporary patina. Some uses of "queer" as an umbrella term are more interesting in their attempts to reveal cultural and psychological common ground between gays, lesbians, bisexuals, transgendered, transsexuals and other queers. For me, some of the most exciting deployments of "queer/queerness" are related to the word's ability to describe those complex circumstances in texts, spectators, and production that resist easy categorization, but that definitely escape or defy the heteronormative.

As suggested above, however, just saying that something is "queer" doesn't quite do the trick; because the label is so open, you need to go on and more specifically discuss what you mean, which forces people to present subtler arguments and analyses. So I find "queer," understood as a suggestive rather than a prescriptive concept, far from becoming yet another reified term in cultural studies, or in life. This probably makes many people uneasy, if not threatened, which could be behind some of the "queer theory has had its day" rhetoric. But I suppose even when you say that "queer" refers to a range of currently category-defying positions, you have given these things a label. Is there a way to get around this rhetorically? Maybe using "queer" is one of those steps toward the day when we discuss gender and sexuality not by labels or categories, but on a descriptive case-by-case basis. "Queer" can now point to things that destabilize existing categories, while it is itself becoming a category—but a category that resists easy definition. That is, you can't tell just from the label "queer" exactly what someone is referring to, except that it is something non-straight or non–normatively straight.

Considered in relation to the list of definitions above, this book, taken as a whole, employs one of the umbrella uses of queer to indicate the collection and juxtaposition of a range of distinct non-straight readings: lesbian (*The Women, The Wizard of Oz*), gay (*The Cabinet of Dr. Caligari, The Red Shoes*), and bisexual (*Gentlemen Prefer Blondes*). But some of these chapters also include a range of readings within them or indicate overlapping readings. For example, the *Caligari* chapter briefly discusses lesbian and bisexual elements in the film while focusing most of its attention on the gay (or, to be more accurate, male homosexual) aspects of the film. And then there's *Psycho*. Here we have an example of definition #5, or is it #6? Are the gender and sexuality codes surrounding Norman Bates and Lila Crane in this film unclear or contradictory, and therefore "queer," or might we understand Norman and Lila as queer characters without reference to conventional categories of gender and sexuality—that is, try to read them neither as "straight," "gay," "lesbian," "feminine," "masculine," nor even as some muddled or uncertain combination of these categories?

By and large, the chapter on *Psycho* that follows reads the film with reference to established gender and sexuality identity categories. In discussions of Norman, however, you might occasionally detect my frustrations with these categories—after all, when things are as confusing, incoherent, and contradictory as they often are in *Psycho*'s representation of Norman, why even bother using conventional gender and sexuality labels? In *It's a Queer World*, Mark Simpson speaks to this question when he says:

> Identitism is not my cause. Hence the "queer world" of this collection is not a world of homosexuality...but rather a world put out of order, out of sorts, out of joint; a world of queasy dislocation and general indeterminacy; a drunken world of wayward fun that can be had when you refuse to recognize the sovereignty of sexual identity.... [T]here must be an ever-increasing number of people who feel their sexual identity something of a

fraud perpetuated on them. . . . The queerest irony of all would be a queer world that had no place for queers.[7]

Given *Psycho*'s (and my) cultural and authorial contexts, however, I didn't feel fully comfortable beginning my examination of *Psycho* at that beyond-gender-and-sexuality-categories place Simpson indicates would be the most radical queer position. For one thing, I'm still living in a world where I'm often dealing with heterosexual privilege, homophobia, and gender issues. At present, and as people like Kate Bornstein and Sue-Ellen Case have also suggested, deciding it would be great not to be identified with or limited by established gender and sexuality labels doesn't eliminate the need to help pass nondiscrimination city ordinances that cover "sexual orientation," for example.[8] But this doesn't mean we shouldn't try thinking and understanding apart from given gender and sexuality categories. On the other hand, many of us whose writing and teaching is centered on gender and sexuality shy away from Simpson's "queerest irony" as it seems threatening in so many ways. What will we have to write about, talk about, and teach if academic and other cultural discourses move toward the queerest queerness? Thinking about this concerns me somewhat, too, but it also excites me, so I will keep testing myself and, hopefully, others.

I think one route into the queerest queerness might begin with definition #3, wherein you are positioned outside of the identity categories you have consciously chosen or feel you were born into. While I have most often identified myself as "gay" and "feminine," working through the chapter on "lesbian" sitcoms in *Making Things Perfectly Queer* and on the *Wizard of Oz*, *The Women*, and *Gentlemen Prefer Blondes* chapters in this book have made it clear that I'm not always gay or feminine in my gender and sexuality positioning. But this doesn't mean I "become" lesbian, bisexual, or masculine either just because I am writing about these things, or watching films in certain non-gay or non-feminine ways. What does it mean? This is where definition #3 comes in handy. While thinking about, taking pleasures in, and writing about certain texts, I am in a queer zone—no longer "being" or positioning myself as gay or feminine, and also not "being" or positioning myself fully within the other remaining gender and sexuality labels, including "straight."

How can anyone say queerness has had its day as long as it continues to have the ability to indicate the indefinable (yes, paradoxically through certain of its definitions) and gesture toward the complexities of human feeling, understanding, and behavior? Sometimes, though, it is difficult to decide when and how to use the term, in any of its definitions. How careful are we in considering the possible philosophical and ideological stakes when we use "queer," and not some other term(s), to discuss gender and sexuality? I

recently found myself in a descriptive and ideological dilemma while thinking about the Michael Powell and Emeric Pressburger film *A Canterbury Tale*.[9]
There is a character in the film who pours glue into women's hair at night in
an attempt to keep them inside, and, by this strategy, to encourage the soldiers stationed nearby to come to his lectures on local history instead of
going out on dates.

Initially I thought of using "queer" to describe "the Glueman," as he is
called. Then I felt that maybe a more accurate description would be the narrative suppression of male homosexuality or gayness. But I was loathe to label
this character "gay" or "homosexual" as it might appear that I was basing my
reading on certain cultural stereotypes about gay men hating straight women
and being their rivals for straight men. So perhaps "queer" might really be
more ideologically sound in this case. By using this term, I could not only
resist reinforcing stereotyped cultural decoding practices, but "queer" would
suggest that the character and the narrative, finally, had no intention of "coming out" as homosexual. However I also felt that, stereotyped or not,
repressed/suppressed or not, this character's coding is connected to male
homosexuality, not to something less specific or more amorphously non-
straight. So why not just call him/it "gay" or "homosexual"? I'm still not certain what I'll do when I finally write about the film.

I had a similar definitional and ideological crisis in writing the chapter
in this book on *The Red Shoes*. At one point, I paused over a line I had written that called the collaborative efforts of the male characters on the screen,
and of the men behind the screen, "queer expressiveness." Why not call these
collaborations "gay," or examples of "non–normative straight masculinity"?
But, then, maybe the shared collaborative space might be called "queer" as
these gay and straight men were meeting on the culturally feminine and gay
grounds of the ballet and the art film. However, even if these grounds are usually considered feminine and homosexual by dominant, normative straight
culture, do they necessarily need to be gendered and sexualized in these
ways? So where is the "queerness" in the collaboration of these male characters and filmmakers if we reject dominant culture's feminization and
homosexualization of the ballet and the art film?

Perhaps the queerness would be in our rejection of such gendering and
sexualization, and the supposed tensions that result from the lack of gender
or sexuality alignment between a certain sexed person and an activity. Following this line of thought, what happens when men do ballet and art films
is not so much the queer mixing of the masculine and the feminine, or of the
homosexual and the straight, as it is a queer resistance to dominant culture's
idea that certain pursuits or attitudes are necessarily masculine or feminine,
straight or homosexual. But does this more radical understanding and use of

queerness as ignoring or transcending traditional gender and sexuality clas-
sifications really work when you're discussing a 1948 film made by a group
of men, and some women, within the British studio system? You can find my
final thoughts, for the moment at least, about the film and its makers in relation to queerness, gender, and sexuality, in the *Red Shoes* chapter.

HOW TO BE A SCHOLAR-FAN

Some readers who have made it to this point may have found certain things
I mention in the preceding pages cringe-inducingly autobiographical in the
context of a "serious" film book. Or the tone of the material may sometimes
seem too "conversational" for an academic tome. Looking over sections
such as the introduction's opening, I'm still not fully comfortable myself. But
why is this? Why shouldn't readers know something about a critic's personal
and cultural background and training? Why is hiding or suppressing information like this still considered more professional and scholarly by most people? Is it part of a general 1980s and early 1990s backlash against the kind
of confessional "consciousness-raising" and "reclaiming our lives and our
histories" work that was done in the late 1960s and in the 1970s as part of
the women's liberation, gay/lesbian liberation, and civil rights movements?
Or, perhaps, it was the rise of "scientific" poststructuralist and psychoanalytic
discourses in film and media studies that began in the mid-1970s but really
took hold in the 1980s, that encouraged academics and other serious writers to bury the traces of their personal and cultural histories by employing
more "objective" theoretical and rhetorical approaches. This suppression
seems especially urgent, I suppose, if you are working on something like film
or popular culture. After all, you want the academy and the world at large to
respect you even though you are writing about, or teaching, *Casablanca*, *Letter from an Unknown Woman*, or *The Birds*.[10]

The result of a couple of decades of ignoring or hiding personal and cultural investments in our (post–contemporary theory) academic writing,
however, has been to squeeze much of the life out of it in many senses, often
relegating our investments in, and enthusiasms for, film and popular culture
to the realm of hidden pleasures. It's as if showing too much interest in what
we are writing about somehow undermines our credibility as intellectuals.
My concerns and complaints here aren't new ones. But I think many of us are
still struggling with the concept of writing and teaching as "scholar-fans."
Tucked away at the end of Andrew Ross's excellent introduction to *No
Respect: Intellectuals and Popular Culture* is "[f]inally, a word from [him]self
as an erstwhile Scot."[11] In this roughly page-long section, Ross tell us that,
in the chapters that follow,

I have tried not to overlook my own prejudices, tastes, and affections for this or that idea, image, film, music, writer, critic, or artist. Although it may not always be evident, research is always autobiographical, and in this case, was bound up with the larger project of self-criticism that the book encourages on behalf of intellectuals engaged with the popular.[12]

If, as Ross suggests here, our personal and cultural baggage and agendas are always going to be there in our intellectual writing, why hide them, or, in this case, why only quickly and briefly mention all this at the end of the introduction—and then make it largely implicit in the rest of the book? Something Ross mentions earlier gestures toward one possible reason he—and most of the rest of us—still curtail, or eliminate altogether, things autobiographical in our writing and teaching. Dicussing the recent history of American cultural studies, Ross finds that it has "rejected the more celebratory, native tradition of gee-whizzery," by and large.[13] This is also true of film and popular culture studies. And, wouldn't you know it, an important part of this tradition's "celebratory" approach is placing your personal enthusiasms and histories front and center in your writing and teaching. As mentioned earlier, what replaced this tradition for most academics and other intellectuals was a tradition rooted in poststructural, psychoanalytic, and postmodern theories. Certainly the perspectives these theories provide have been a valuable corrective to the uncritical, universalizing practices of the celebratory tradition. But is there really little room for autobiographical or fan elements in rigorous, intelligent critical work, whether it is being done inside the academy or not?

For those of us who believe there is room for autobiography, including our fan enthusiasms, the question is then how to introduce this into our work/teaching without losing the respect of the reader/student by coming off as embarrassingly egotistical or gee-whiz celebratory. It's not an easy task, as some of the writers who contributed to the anthology *The Madonna Connection: Representational Politics, Subcultural Identities, and Cultural Theory* discovered.[14] One of the contributors, Laurie Schulze, points out that while some of the articles in the collection were trashed by both the conservative and the left-leaning popular press as attempting to dignify studying Madonna by using difficult theoretical jargon, other pieces were criticized as desperate attempts by "academic wannabes" to look cool when they were really being "mercenary, overcelebratory, or just plain silly."[15] Schulze goes on to suggest some of the tensions and dilemmas faced by academics, and other intellectuals, who want to give their work a more autobiographical touch:

I'd always felt awkward about studying Madonna and her fans (as if I wasn't one of them). Sometimes I worried that my job as an academic cultural critic disqualified me from real fandom; I never expected that Madonna fans would think of me as one of them or be particularly happy about my work on Madonna and Madonna fandom. I also knew that being a Madonna fan in the context of the academy, especially as I was working on Madonna, would for some, disqualify me as a member of the real academy—that "real" academics would not think of me as one of their own or my work on Madonna as truly scholarly.[16]

So what's a scholar-fan to do? Both Schulze and Ross point to work by academic music critic Simon Frith, who, though he says he sees "no clear binary division between fans and academics. . . . I mean academics can be fans and fans can be academics," also mentions the "very complicated relationship between work and pleasure" that many academics, "particularly [those in] cultural studies," must negotiate in their teaching and writing.[17] Though he doesn't comment further on this work-as-pleasure, pleasure-as-work situation, part of what I see as a complication here is that academics and other intellectuals who write about popular culture can feel guilty about "getting paid to look at and talk about movies," or other popular culture material. As a result, we can feel that we should play down or eliminate our fan excitement and play up our more serious role as theoretically savvy analyst. Of the chapters that follow, the one on *The Wizard of Oz* most self-consciously reveals my attempts to negotiate how much and what kind of personal and cultural autobiographical elements might be introduced into a "serious" piece of critical analysis. It was originally written for an anthology, *Hop on Pop: The Pleasures and Politics of Popular Culture*, coedited by Henry Jenkins III, one of the most ardent American proponents of finding effective ways to write and teach as a scholar-fan.[18] While the editors directed me to write something that clearly indicated my interests in the subject I chose, I found myself unable to take the plunge. My first draft, consisting of a standard close textual reading, was returned with a letter saying the reading was all well and good, but it didn't reveal the investment(s) I had in the film that led me to such a reading—or that led me to choose to write about this film in the first place.

You'll find the answer to the editors' "What's your investment?" question in the opening and closing pages of the *Oz* chapter. I felt a mixture of embarrassment and vulnerability when I returned the revised article—and I still wonder if people need, or want, to know everything I've revealed in these sections. But maybe these are risks that need to be taken every once in a while on the path of scholarly fandom. As it is, the personal and cultural autobiographical materials in the *Oz* chapter are still only the frame for a close reading, which could indicate I have a way to go in thoroughly integrating and balancing the scholar and the fan in my writing—but this chapter is a start.

OF CLASSICS, CANONS, AND QUEERNESS

What is the fascination with and appeal of certain classic and otherwise "mainstream" texts, genres, and personalities for queers? I don't know if within the confines of this introduction it is possible to say something that would cover all, or even most, of the pleasures, and sometimes perverse unpleasures, lesbians, gays, bisexuals, and queers get from film and popular culture. One thing that might be worth thinking about is that taking lesbian, gay, bisexual, and queer pleasures in these "mainstream" works constantly reinforces the idea that queer is everywhere. For some people, it might also be something like having sex with (or yourself becoming) a married person, a priest, a nun, a cop, a jock, or someone in the military. Of course, the politics of this—whether taking queer pleasure in a "mainstream" text or with a representative of a dominant culture institution (or becoming part of these institutions)—is not necessarily progressive. I suppose this is why some people criticize those who take pleasure in, help produce, and/or write about "mainstream" products: they see this as always already being seduced by, or buying into, normative values on some level.

I have to agree with B. Ruby Rich, however, when she said that the "Cinema of the Sons" (the avant-garde) is just as suspect as the "Cinema of the Fathers" (classical narrative cinema) in most respects.[19] Granted, openly gay, lesbian, bisexual, and queer filmmakers have had a somewhat better time of it in the avant-garde and, later, in independent filmmaking. But in the 1960s wasn't there a call to purge what some saw as homosexual threats to the aesthetic purity of American avant-garde cinema? It took me a long time to realize that the avant-garde, as a whole, is not as progressive about gender, sexuality, race/ethnicity, or class as legend would have it. The one thing avant-garde film could do that traditional narrative film couldn't or wouldn't (at least until relatively recently) is to show explicit queer sexual activity, although not without frequent censorship challenges from within and without. So, in its sexual explicitness, the avant-garde can represent queerness differently than traditional narrative film, aside from porn, usually does. But, fundamentally, I don't think there is the sort of privileged relationship between queerness and the avant-garde that many people seem to think is there. When you look at gay, lesbian, and queer avant-garde history, you will find that many directors take their inspiration from the "mainstream," even if they are being critical of it. Kenneth Anger, George Kuchar, Jack Smith, Andy Warhol, and Su Freidrich are among those who have all been influenced by "mainstream" film culture in some way. Even lesbian avant-garde pioneer Barbara Hammer has revealed an interest in "mainstream" film and media in some of her more recent works.

As recent queer films about kids such as *Dottie Gets Spanked*, *Trevor*, and *Ma Vie en Rose* remind us, "mainstream" films and other popular culture texts and performers, for all their potential to alienate, have been, and continue to be, positive formative influences for many lesbians, gays, bisexuals, and other queers.[20] Films and videos such as *Remembrance*, *Forbidden Love: The Unashamed Stories of Lesbian Lives*, *Dry Kisses Only*, and *Meeting [of] Two Queens* reveal that popular culture fandom remains undiminished for most adult queers, even though we often experience shocks and disappointments from what we see and hear.[21] I find all this an interesting contrast to straight culture's frequent representation and understanding of film and popular culture as dystopic, kid-corrupting, soul-stealing, and mind-numbing.

For most of the century, "mainstream" texts and canons of classics like *The Wizard of Oz* were all most queers had access to, whether as scholars, fans, or teachers. But, as suggested earlier, there are differences of opinion about the relationship of queerness to "mainstream" texts and film canons. Do scholar-fans and the general queer public co-optively or subversively "queer" certain films in established straight canons in order to place them in their own, subcultural, queer canons that challenge straight canons? Or do queer scholar-fans and the queer public articulate queer readings of canonical classics in order to suggest that these films are not the exclusive property of straight culture—that these films are as queer as they are straight, and that there is no need for queer canons that are marked as alternative or subcultural because queerness can be anywhere, in any canon you care to set up. I suppose that most queers, individually and as a group, have been both subcultural subversives and nonsubcultural "it's as queer as it is straight" readers at different times in their encounters with classic, "canonical" films.

Taken together, these two general queer approaches to "mainstream" films and the idea of film canons complicate any discussions of what constitute queer canons or queer films. Historically certain films have accumulated more queer cultural currency than others. Most of the films I discuss at length in this book are in this category, and have been considered central to queer canons. Some of these films, like *The Wizard of Oz*, *Psycho*, and *The Red Shoes*, are also often placed within straight, dominant culture film canons. Other films, like *The Women* and *Gentlemen Prefer Blondes*, are only considered canonical in queer cultures. Then there are films like *The Cabinet of Dr. Caligari* that have been on dominant culture lists of the greatest films of all time for decades, but as far as I can tell have never been considered queer classics.

Just to show you that no film is safe—I use this word in response to someone who implied I was "recruiting" texts for queerness—I'm going to end this introduction with brief discussions of two heretofore non-queer canonically classic films that, like *Caligari*, I have come to queerly appreciate only recently: *Intolerance* and *Citizen Kane*.[22] Can we consider these queer films? Might they become a part of a queer canon of classics?

Intolerance: Perhaps having three of the four stories in this multinarrative epic set in the past allowed director D.W. Griffith's queerer impulses a freer rein. At the center of the massacre of the Huguenots narrative is a classic dominating mother–effeminate son relationship. Scary Catholic diva Catherine de Medici forces her fey dandy of a son, Charles IX, to sign a proclamation allowing for the wholesale slaughter of the Protestant Huguenots, who are sympathetically represented by the romantic straight couple, Prosper Latour and Brown Eyes. The modern story also casts queerness as an evil threat to heterosexual couples and families when it has the dykey spinsters who fund and run a reform movement take the child of "The Dear One" even as her husband is unjustly jailed.

As a counterbalance to these homophobic sections is the glorious Babylonian story. To start at the top, we have the camp and mannered King Belshazzar and his fiancée, Princess Beloved. But while they often loll around or strike poses with members of their court in "decadent" polysexual splendor, the king and the princess also show their mettle when war comes. Princess Beloved directs incredible displays of anger at the invading troops, while Belshazzar dons his armor and leaves to fight, with his muscular aide at his side. Introduced in an intertitle as "The two-sword man...Mighty Man of Valor," our first shot of the king's loyal aide is strictly beefcake, as he stands in his skimpy uniform pulling one of his two swords in and out of its holder. We are left to speculate where (or what) his other sword is. For me there is no doubt about this other "sword," as what precedes the beefcake, sword-pulling shot of the Mighty Man of Valor is a shot of Belshazzar dreamily lounging on a divan. We know all about those ancient soldier-lovers, don't we? As Babylon falls, we are treated to tender scenes between the king and his aide before they both die in battle.

Another soldier in the Babylonian story who adds to the queer positive dimensions of this section is also the most fabulous dyke, or maybe bisexual, in silent film history: the Mountain Girl. When her abusive father puts her on the marriage auction block, the Mountain Girl dissuades all potential husbands. Freed by the king, she decides to serve him from afar. Does she fall in love with the king, or does he become some kind of role model for her with his balancing of masculine and feminine characteristics? Maybe a little of both. Given his position, he's a safe, not to mention a rather queer, romantic attachment for this peasant woman–turned–soldier. In any case, her devotion to the king encourages the Mountain Girl to continue rejecting the romantic advances of her feminized suitor, the Rhapsode, as well as to disguise herself as a man in order to get into the army. She becomes, in effect, the Mighty Woman of Valor, spying, fighting, and dying for Belshazzar and the queerness that is Babylon—at least Griffith's Babylon.

If you've been counting, there is one section of *Intolerance* left to discuss: the Judean story, which chronicles the adult life of Jesus Christ, or the "Man of Men—The Nazarene" as he is called here. It is the least developed of the four stories, so my queer account of it will be likewise brief, and it is a reading that could fit most film representations of Christ. Jesus, perhaps particularly as portrayed by Howard Gaye (I will resist an obvious wisecrack here) in *Intolerance*, is hardly anyone's idea of a "man's man," is he? On second thought, maybe he is. At least that's Kenneth Anger's take on Jesus and his apostles in *Scorpio Rising*.[23] And let's not forget his non–heterosexually conceived virgin birth, close relationship with his mother, and general lack of romantic interest in women. The central miracle Jesus performs in *Intolerance*'s account of his life is changing water into wine in order to save a heterosexual marriage reception. Do I have to point out that assisting heterosexuals, especially helping couples get and stay together, is one of the primary roles for "good" queers in traditional narrative films? Just look at Greg Kinnear's character in *As Good as It Gets* or Nancy Blake in *The Women*.

Citizen Kane: Perhaps the major queer element in this film is the relationship between Jed Leland and Charles Foster Kane. Or, to be more precise, Leland's feelings toward Kane, as it doesn't appear that Kane is as romantically taken with Leland as Leland is with Kane. Leland has followed Kane from school to school when the latter gets kicked out, and then becomes, by his own choice, the theatre critic on a newpaper Kane runs. Hero worship mixes with desire as Leland stands by his man—that is, until he is asked to write a favorable review of Susan Alexander Kane's disastrous opera debut. At this point it becomes clear to Leland that Kane's obsession with Susan and her career leaves him little time for anything, or anyone, else.

It seems appropriate that Leland narrates those portions of the story devoted to Kane's marriage to Emily Norton and his affair with (and later marriage to) Susan Alexander. These are the romantic and sexual parts of the story—the parts that would be most interesting to a queer guy who is himself in love with his friend. Given Leland's artsy bent, it also makes sense that the most spectacular moment of overlapping stories in the film should come with Leland's and Susan's accounts of her operatic debut. Here and elsewhere, Susan and Leland are narratively positioned as rivals for Kane's attention and affection, but also as being connected in their "feminine" artistic interests.

With some telling word choices, Laura Mulvey describes Leland as "function[ing] more as a raconteur than as a straight witness" to Kane's life.[24]

From my queer perspective, I couldn't agree more. Mulvey finds Leland character and narration of central importance within *Citizen Kane*'s overall structure:

> While the narrative is roughly, with some inconsistencies, developed by the linear unfolding of Kane's story, structurally it divides into two parts that cut across the chronological biography with a broad, dominating, binary opposition. Kane's rise and decline separate the two parts narratively, but his relation to male and female worlds separates the two parts thematically. Bernstein tells the story of Kane's dramatic rise to triumphant success; Susan's flashback tells the story of his disgrace and withdrawal. Bernstein's story is set in the competitive, public, male world of newspaper reporting; Susan's is set in the spectacular, cultural and feminized world of the opera and Xanadu. The turning point comes in Leland's narration, which deals with Kane's love life and his political life and the increasingly inextricable connection between the two. . . . [Leland] has to solve all the problems that accumulate in the middle of the narration.[25]

It makes sense that a queer man provides the bridge in this film between art and politics, love/sex and career, and, more generally, those aspects of the traditionally feminine world and those of the traditionally masculine world. When we leave Leland he is in a nursing home making feeble jokes about the attractiveness of the nurses in a weak attempt to cast himself as a geriatric ladies' man, even while he is being flirtatiously charming to the male newsreel reporter sent to interview him.

While the queerness in *Citizen Kane* is most essentially and extensively worked out through the character and narration of Jed Leland, there are many other queer characters and situations in the film to consider. Both Mulvey and David Lugowski point to the librarian at the Thatcher Library as perhaps the first of the film's queer characters. Mulvey describes the librarian as "a woman without the slightest vestige of femininity, dressed in a severe suit and with an equally severe, repressive manner,"[26] while Lugowski finds that she more specifically "evokes the 'mythical mannish lesbian' type."[27] Lugowski's account of the queerness of/in *Kane* uses the dyke librarian and her "sissy" security guard as the jumping off point to queer the entire film and almost everyone in it, moving from the librarian and guard to Walter Parks Thatcher himself (a prissy, "fussbudget" bachelor), to Kane (his intense mother attachment, being raised by queer bachelor Thatcher, his most enduring relationships being with men, his inability to sustain relationships with women), to his friends Leland (see above) and Bernstein.[28] As an aside, Lugowski also mentions there is a "flamboyant Italian queer," Matiste, who is Susan's voice coach.[29]

As you might expect by this point, even Kane's famous dying word, "Rosebud," can be part of a queer reading. A straight reading might consider the word as connected to Kane's lost "normal" family life back in Colorado (Rosebud is the name of his childhood sled), or as being related to his love for Susan Alexander (there is a cut between one of the newsreel men saying "Rosebud, dead or alive" and a shot of a poster with Susan's face on it) or, more specifically, her genitals (via the story that "rosebud" is what Kane's real-life model, William Randolph Hearst, called mistress Marion Davies's genitals). As Lugowski points out, however, "Rosebud" is also associated with the librarian and the guard, and, therefore, with queerness:

> Thompson [the newsreel reporter], still wondering about the meaning of Kane's mysterious last word, addresses the portrait of Thatcher with a flip, cynical wisecrack, "You're not rosebud, are you?" He then tries the librarian, and finally asks the guard, "And your name's Jennings?" Considering two men, and a mannish woman, as possibly being "rosebud" operates queerly on two levels. One is that the term is a gay slang expression for the anus. Another, though, would have been known much more widely in U.S. culture at the time, namely that calling men by the names of flowers, or speaking of flowers even indirectly in connection with men, was enough to suggest that they might be effeminate queers.[30]

I would add to this that even within its straight association with Kane's lost childhood and family in Colorado, "Rosebud" maintains a queer connection, if we consider Kane's Oedipal relationship with his mother can have queer "mama's boy," as well as straight, cultural associations. With some degree of heavy-handed psychoanalytic symbolism, Kane's sled Rosebud is finally shown hidden among the items he's inherited from his mother's home—items which Kane has stored deep within his basement among the art he's been collecting. The queer Oedipal "mama's boy" connection between Susan and Kane's mother is most strikingly made by the glass globe containing a rural snow scene that Susan owns, as it recalls the winter sequence in which young Kane is separated from his mother and taken to live with Thatcher. As Susan and Kane talk about mothers, you can first spot the globe on Susan's dressing table near a picture of her own mother. One wonders if one reason Kane becomes attracted to Susan so quickly is that she understands what it means to be devoted to one's mother.

I hope it is clear at this point that queerness offers a valuable line of pursuit in answering the newsreel chief's question "Who, or what, is Rosebud?" and, therefore, in discussing the psychosocial and psychosexual enigmas of Charles Foster Kane and *Citizen Kane*. Now that the American Film Institute's "Greatest American Film," as well as the top film in *Sight and Sound*'s 1962,

1972, 1982, and 1992 once-a-decade international critic's survey, has been given its queer due, it's time to move on to other flaming classics.[31]

NOTES

1. This introduction owes a great debt to Brett Farmer's incisive questions in "Seeing Queerly: Going to the Movies with Alexander Doty," *Critical inQueeries* 2:1 (June 1998): 1–12. Indeed, large chunks of the material in the introduction can be found in my responses to Farmer's questions.
2. *The Blair Witch Project* (1999, Haxan Films: Daniel Myrick and Eduardo Sanchez).
3. *The Children's Hour* (1961, Mirisch-Worldwide/United Artists: William Wyler); *Victim* (1961, Allied Film Makers: Basil Dearden).
4. *My Own Private Idaho* (1991, New Line: Gus Van Sant); *Desert Hearts* (1986, Samuel Goldwyn: Donna Deitch).
5. *The Silence of the Lambs* (1991, Orion: Jonathan Demme); *Sylvia Scarlett* (1936, RKO: George Cukor).
6. *Flaming Creatures* (1963: Jack Smith).
7. Mark Simpson, *It's a Queer World* (London: Vintage, 1996), 21–22.
8. Kate Bornstein, *Gender Outlaw: On Men, Women and the Rest of Us* (New York and London: Routledge, 1994); Kate Bornstein, *My Gender Workbook* (New York and London: Routledge, 1998); Sue-Ellen Case, "Tracking the Vampire," *differences* 3:2 (1991): 1–20.
9. *A Canterbury Tale* (1944, Archers: Michael Powell and Emeric Pressburger).
10. *Casablanca* (1942, Warners: Michael Curtiz); *Letter from an Unknown Woman* (1948, Republic: Max Ophuls); *The Birds* (1963, Universal: Alfred Hitchcock).
11. Andrew Ross, *No Respect: Intellectuals and Popular Culture* (New York and London: Routledge, 1989), 13.
12. Ibid., 14.
13. Ibid., 7.
14. Cathy Schwichtenberg, ed., *The Madonna Connection: Representational Politics, Subcultural Identities, and Cultural Theory* (Boulder, Co.: Westview Press, 1992).
15. Laurie Schulze, "Not an Immaculate Reception: Ideology, *The Madonna Connection*, and Academic Wannabes," *Velvet Light Trap* 43 (Spring 1999): 37.
16. Ibid., 47.
17. Simon Frith, "The Cultural Study of Popular Music," in *Cultural Studies*, ed. Lawrence Grossberg, Cary Nelson, Paula Treichler (New York and London: Routledge, 1992), 183–84.
18. Henry Jenkins III, Tara McPhearson, and Jane Shattuc, ed., *Hop on Pop: The Pleasures and Politics of Popular Culture* (Durham, N.C., and London: Duke University Press, 2000).
19. B. Ruby Rich, "In the Name of Feminist Film Criticism," in *Issues in Feminist Film Criticism*, ed. Patricia Evens (Bloomington and Indianapolis: Indiana University Press, 1990), 269.

20. *Dottie Gets Spanked* (1994: Todd Haynes); *Ma Vie en Rose* (1997, WFE/RTBF/Haut en Court/La Sept Cinema/TFI Film Production/Freeway Film: Alain Berliner); *Trevor* (1994: Peggy Rajski).

21. *Dry Kisses Only* (1990: Jane Cottis and Kaucyila Brooke); *Meeting [of] Two Queens* (1991: Cecila Barriga); *Forbidden Love: The Unashamed Story of Lesbian Lives* (1992, National Film Board of Canada, Aerlyn Weissman and Lynn Fernie: Weissman and Fernie).

22. For a queer reading of another canonical classic, *2001: A Space Odyssey* (1968, MGM: Stanley Kubrick), see Ellis Hanson, "Technology, Paranoia, and the Queer Voice," *Screen* 34:2 (summer 1993): 137–61.

23. *Scorpio Rising* (1962–63: Kenneth Anger).

24. Laura Mulvey, *Citizen Kane* (London: British Film Institute, 1992), 40.

25. Ibid., 40.

26. Ibid., 48.

27. David Lugowski, "Queering the (New) Deal: Lesbian, Gay and Queer Representation in U.S. Cinema, 1929–1941," Ph.D. dissertation, New York University, 1999, 53.

28. Ibid., 53–56.

29. Ibid., 57.

30. Ibid., 53.

31. *Citizen Kane* placed sixth on a list of "Top Ten Films of All Time" voted on by 200 lesbian and gay filmmakers, video makers, curators, and critics. This poll was conducted by Jenni Olson and can be found in the book she edited, *The Ultimate Guide to Lesbian and Gay Film and Video* (New York and London: Serpent's Tale, 1996), 6. The top film on the list was *Vertigo* (1958, Paramount: Alfred Hitchcock).

Render unto Cesare:
The Queerness of Caligari

Neither Carl Mayer nor I ever contested the fact that we were both the legitimate parents of the brainchild "Caligari": I the father who planted the seed,
Mayer the mother who carried it to fruition.

Hans Janowitz[1]

Much has been written about it, and many people have a vague idea that it
is a slightly diseased and disreputable cinematic freak.

Bosley Crowther[2]

Let's begin with *The Cabinet of Dr. Caligari's* notorious framing story. The one
that many people involved in the film's production and criticism have dis-
credited over the years as having been forced onto the body of the film. I will
suggest in my analysis below that part of the outrage over *Caligari's* frame
might, at some level, have to do with its potential to queer the narrative within
the frame. In its opening moment, the film reveals a young man and an
older man sitting on a bench in a bleak and strangely designed park. The older
man has the first lines: "Everywhere there are spirits.... They are all around
us.... They have driven me from hearth and home, from my wife and children."[3] That is, the "spirits" have driven him from a cozy normative heterosexual life to this encounter with a young man in a bizarre park.[4] The young
man, whom we later know as Francis, looks uneasy—as if he doesn't really
want to hear the older man's story yet feels compelled to sit there and listen.

The appearance of a woman who seems as if she is sleepwalking causes
Francis to stare "with a mixture of anxiety and admiration."[5] "That is my
fiancée," he tells the older man, as the woman (Jane) moves past them and
offscreen, "What she and I have experienced is yet more remarkable than the
story you have told me. I will tell you...."[6] Thus, by the end of the frame
opening, Francis attempts to reverse the other man's narrative, moving it
from an older man–younger man cruising scenario back to a normative

A cruise in the park interrupted by Francis's (Friedrich Feher) somnambulistic "fiancé," Jane (Lil Dagover).

heterosexual one with allusions to marriage ("my fiancée") and a shared history as part of a straight couple ("she and I have experienced"). Yet as the shot of the two men, now more intimately huddled together on the bench, irises to black, it is difficult not to think that Francis's assertion of his heterosexual credentials as a means of establishing a straight narrative is more than a little suspect. For one thing, his "fiancée" is a traumatized and detached figure who takes no notice of him.

This reading of *Caligari's* opening moments as establishing a disturbed and disturbing queerness is not only the product of contemporary cultural and academic reading practices, but is an understanding some post–World War I viewers might have brought to the film, particularly in the context of its original release in Germany. As is widely known, postwar Germany (particularly the larger cities) supported an increasingly public homosexual culture, in spite of the law known as Paragraph 175 (passed in 1871), which made homosexual acts criminal offenses. Berlin, especially, was a hotbed of queer social, cultural, and political activity that was the talk of Germany, Europe, and the United States. "That traditional definitions of gender were in crisis during the Weimar years can hardly be disputed," notes Patrice Petro, going on to link this with a "contemporary fascination with notions of sexual ambiguity."[7] But the 1920s was a decade of gender and sexuality "crises" for most Western countries, with Germany, possibly, leading the pack in terms of striking cultural displays of gender and sexual queerness.

Richard Dyer finds that the only films made between 1919 and 1931 that feature "homosexuality centrally, unambiguously and positively" were made in Weimar Germany—*Anders als die Andern* (1919) and *Mädchen in Uniform* (1931)—though he also notes there were a number of other films produced during the Weimar period that represented homosexuality, often negatively.[8] Made the same year as *Caligari*, *Anders als die Andern* "opened in one of the major Berlin cinemas . . . and was fully reviewed in the press, where it was recognised as another of the highly successful run of Aufklarungsfilme" ("enlightenment films" that usually dealt with "social, mainly sexual, 'problems' ").[9] The film was also a commercial success, in part, perhaps, because of its immediate notoriety: disrupted screenings; walkouts; a public forum of doctors, scientists, and writers discussing the film; exhibition bans in Vienna, Munich, and Stuttgart.[10] Because of the controversy, many people, especially in Germany and Austria, who never saw *Anders als die Andern* at the time of its release did end up hearing about it through the press and gossip.

Anders als die Andern's narrative follows the story of violinist Paul Korner, who falls in love with a pupil, Kurt Sivers. While walking through a park, Paul and Kurt encounter Franz Bollek, whom Paul had once picked up at a dance and taken home. Later, Franz tries to burglarize Paul's apartment, but is caught by Kurt. Paul arrives as Franz calls Kurt Paul's "paid boy." Upset by the encounter, Kurt leaves Paul. Thinking back over his life, Paul recalls visits to a supportive sex researcher, to a hypnotist who tries to cure him of homosexuality, and to the dance where he met Franz. He also recalls his discovery that Franz is a blackmailer, as well as the time he and Kurt's sister Else went to a lecture by real-life sex researcher and political activist Magnus Hirschfeld. After these recollections, Paul discovers that Franz has been to the police, and both of them are arrested and brought to trial. Franz is sent to jail for blackmail and Paul is imprisoned for homosexuality under Paragraph 175. Once out of jail, Paul finds himself without friends or work and commits suicide. Kurt learns of Paul's death and, falling over Paul's body, threatens to kill himself, but a doctor convinces him to join the fight for repeal of Paragraph 175 instead.[11]

From this plot synopsis it is clear that while *Anders als die Andern* is generally sympathetic to Paul's plight and finds the legal and social systems at fault, it also suggests that Paul's cruising of Franz at the dance is in part to blame for his downfall. "[I]t would be as easy to take the film as showing that it is gay lust itself that causes, or simply is, the problem," Dyer notes.[12] This ambivalent and potentially negative aspect of the otherwise supportive *Anders als die Andern* is echoed and expanded upon in many representations of homosexuality—and other forms of gender and sexual queerness—in the next decade of German film. The sense one gets from most Weimar films that treat queerness is that producers and audiences want to use it as a marker of their sophistication, while also attempting to contain and marginalize it as decadent or comic. So while more and more homosexual and otherwise queer signs were circulating in 1920s German culture, particularly urban culture, the context for understanding these signs was often less than celebratory.

Caligari opened following much publicity on February 26, 1920, at the Marmorhaus Theatre, Berlin. *Anders als die Andern* opened before this on May 24, 1919. So the period of *Caligari's* greatest success in Germany and the rest of Europe came just after the time *Anders als die Andern* had stirred up talk. With their close publicity and exhibition dates, it is not too much to imagine that these successful and controversial films could have been discussed in the same breath. But these films might have been thought of together for more specific reasons than just the proximity of their theatrical runs, the heated critical debates that surrounded them both, and the public fascination or outrage that followed in their wake. Certain scenes echo each other: Francis and the older man in the park in the framing story/Paul and Kurt meeting Franz in the park; the head of the asylum (who is, in Francis's fantasy, the sideshow hypnotist Caligari) declaring at the end of the film he can now "cure" Francis/Paul's remembered visit to a hypnotist to cure him of his homosexuality; scenes in which a grieving man (Caligari, Kurt) falls over his male lover's dead body. But the most compelling specific connection between the two films is the actor Conrad Veidt, who plays Paul in *Anders* and Cesare in *Caligari*. Theodore Price gets right to the point about the queer effect that Veidt's casting in *Anders als die Andern* can have on readings of *Caligari*: "Thus, we have, so to speak, Cesare himself in the role of a homosexual."[13] Actually, it worked the other way around for original audiences as they might recall that Cesare was being played by the actor who had starred as a homosexual character in *Anders*. Veidt himself was homosexual, and his screen image combined the sinister and the seductive for most audiences, then and now. Dyer finds that this "duality" in Veidt's image works well for such roles as Paul in *Anders als die Andern* and Cesare in *Caligari*, as it makes the characters at once "handsome" and disturbing.[14]

I would contend that, for many people from the 1920s to the present, part of the disturbing yet compelling quality of Veidt's performance of these roles has to do with what could be understood as their "feminine," and therefore homosexually inflected, aspects. At the time these films came out, these feminine qualities might have been connected with "third sex" notions of male in-betweenism, particularly in relation to the figure of the androgyne and the Tante ("auntie") style within gay culture.[15] But while the femme Tante was often denigrated within and outside gay culture, the image of the feminine gay man as androgyne was often celebrated—and Veidt's playing of Paul and Cesare contains suggestions of the Tante and the androgyne. In the decades since the 1920s, similar tensions between many viewers' understandings of the image of the queeny gay man and that of the queerly androgynous man would keep Veidt's Paul and Cesare figures caught between audience desire and aversion. Even in an otherwise heterocentric reading of *Caligari*, David Robinson finds that "[d]ominating all is the performance of the androgynous and sexually fascinating Veidt."[16]

It is Veidt's Cesare who offers the clearest visual key to *Caligari's* queerness through his appearance in the final section of the film's frame. An iris out moves us from the end of the story Francis has been telling the older man to a shot of them still sitting on a park bench. "And from that day on the madman had never left his cell," a saddened Francis remarks, as the older man rises and gestures for him to follow. Francis, in an imitation of Jane's trancelike state at the beginning of the film, walks off with the older man. An establishing shot reveals the interior of an asylum, with a blankly staring Jane sitting frame left, while the person we know as Cesare is walking up and back across from her, frame right, tenderly holding and stroking a bunch of flowers. As soon as Francis enters with the older man he becomes agitated at the sight of Cesare, who is languidly leaning against a wall behind them. As he warns the older man against Cesare, we are shown closer shots of Cesare looking melancholic and caressing his flowers. The older man casts a disturbed look at Francis and leaves the shot to Francis and Cesare. A moment later, Francis looks off frame left, smiles, extends his arms, and exits. Francis enters the next frame and approaches Jane, asking her to marry him "at last." Maintaining her frozen, trancelike demeanor, Jane replies: "We queens are not permitted to follow the dictates of our hearts."

There is more to the final section of the framing story, but let us pause here to discuss Cesare's crucial queer functions. For one thing, the final section tells us that the horrible thing hidden in the coffinlike "cabinet" in Francis's story has been modeled upon the harmless figure of a feminine gay man—a Tante. In a queer reading, Francis's reconfiguration of the benign Tante into the threatening, yet fascinating, androgyne in the cabinet is one very important indication of the "homosexual panic" and denial of homosexual desire that pervades Francis's fantasy narrative. In light of this, it makes sense that as soon as he enters the asylum after his tentative cruising interlude with the older man, Francis immediately focuses his hysterical attention upon Cesare. It is only after he has warned the older man against Cesare that Francis notices the supposed object of his desire, Jane. But Jane, as we discover, is unattainable—and therefore a safe object for Francis. To complicate matters, however, Francis's selection of Jane as his "fiancée" may link him to homosexuality as much as to heterosexuality.

What if Jane is a lesbian who, like Francis, is attempting to repress and deny her queer desires? She just might be, as certain signs are there: her initial passage through the frame ignoring her supposed fiancé; her rigid demeanor and its conventional associations with sexual "frigidity" and, therefore, possible lesbianism; her outrageous excuse for exempting herself from heterosexual affiliations ("We queens are not permitted to follow the dictates of our hearts"). Understood this way, Jane is Francis's perfect counterpart: she, too, is denying her homosexuality with a straight cover story. No wonder he chooses her for his potential beard. But however you read Jane's sexuality, the idea that Jane is Francis's "fiancée," and that, therefore, there is a central normative heterosexual couple in the film, clearly is as much a delusion as the one that casts the homosexual inmate as the monster.[17]

However, while the final section of the narrative frame reveals that the homosexual is not the monster, it does code him/her as mentally ill. The homosexual as neurotic (or even psychotic) is a position that was in line with conservative, orthodox psychiatric opinion until the 1970s—and it is still a position that, to varying degrees, influences much popular opinion to this day. Cesare, fondling and stroking his flowers, is a figure of pathos, but he is also an asylum inmate, as is distant, glacial Jane. Francis actually seems the most dangerously volatile figure, yet he is the one whom the film, in its final moments, suggests is capable of being "cured" of his "mania." Maybe this is because Francis attempts to be "masculine" or, rather, more the "Bube" or "Bursch" counterpart to inmate Cesare's Tante and Jane's femme.[18] The final intertitle reveals that Francis's condition is somehow related to his mistaking the head of the asylum for "that mystic Caligari," but the events of the final section of the frame point as insistently to other symptoms: Francis's delusion that the mild-mannered homosexual inmate "Cesare" (if that really is his name) is Caligari's monstrous somnambulist; his conviction that Jane is his fiancée.

But let's begin a queer inquiry into the long fantasy narrative Francis tells the older man by using the film's final suggested psychological point of entry: Francis's casting the head of the asylum as Caligari. To be perfectly accurate, Francis's fantasy casts the head of the asylum as someone who is both an asylum head and a fairgrounds sideshow exhibitor who calls himself Dr. Caligari after an eighteenth-century mystic who traveled around exhibiting a somnambulist named Cesare whom he compels "to perform acts which, in a waking state, would be abhorrent to him." While in his fantasy Francis attempts to position himself as the active heterosexual Oedipal hero, especially when he unmasks the paternal asylum head as the villainous Caligari, the final section of the film reveals Francis's actual position is more like that of Cesare (whether the one in the fantasy narrative or the one in the asylum). Francis, like Cesare, is under the control of "Caligari," someone he believes can make men perform "abhorrent" acts. This parallel also recalls Francis's position vis-à-vis the older man he tells his story to in the park: after recounting how Caligari has compelled Cesare to do his bidding, Francis follows the older man with trancelike obedience.

While most of the discussions in this chapter will consider Cesare's functions as one of Francis's homosexual doubles, there is also a good case to be made for Cesare's representing a bisexual option for Francis. It is an option that is only a little less negatively presented in the fantasy, however. Jane's fascinated and horrified reaction to Caligari's revelation of Cesare in his cabinet (compositionally placed between Caligari and Jane) might be understood as the homosexual figure's defiant "I possess him" gesture to the straight woman. As Theodore Price puts it, Cesare is "the sleepwalker, the 'slave,' whom the homosexual master has seduced and taken for his own."[19] The film's fantasy narrative could be said to represent Cesare as a bisexual man by referring to two conventional cultural tropes: the bisexual as the "passive" partner, the one who has to be seduced into homosexual (and sometime any sexual) activity; and the bisexual as androgynous.[20]

Yet the cabinet-opening sequence also evokes a striking and an exciting connection between Cesare and Jane that suggests an element of erotic attraction. In a bisexual reading of *Caligari*, this suggestion would be borne out by the sequence in which Cesare has been sent by Caligari to kill Jane—that is, sent by the older homosexual man to kill his straight female rival for the younger bisexual man. Under Caligari's hypnotic influence, Cesare is initially prepared to stab Jane, but the sight of Jane sleeping in her filmy bedclothes breaks the homosexual spell. Upset by Jane's panicked reaction upon awakening, the stereotypically "confused" bisexual carries her off looking for a place where they can escape the influence of Caligari (homosexuality) and of Jane's father (heterosexuality).[21] But there is no place to hide, and an exhausted Cesare drops Jane, with fitting symbolism, on the middle of a bridge. He dies a few moments later. In the final section of the framing story, the inmate Cesare, now more unambiguously representing feminine homosexuality, is placed opposite Jane in one shot. After moving from homosexual Cesare to heterosexual Jane, Francis finds himself standing in the middle of the frame in a hysterical panic at the sight of the head of the asylum (his "Caligari"). He is now in the position of the fantasy Cesare, visually and (bi)sexually. It is a frustrating position marked as both central and as untenable.

To return to more homosexual readings of the film, Theodore Price situates the queerness of the Cesare and Caligari pairing within the doubles or Doppelgänger motif of Weimar Expressionist filmmaking: "Caligari and

Cesare are *homosexual* Doubles, with Caligari the Active Double, Cesare the Passive, doing whatever Caligari tells him to do."[22] As these figures are actually part of someone's fantasy, however, they finally (re)double Francis. In fantasy-dream coding, then, Francis positions himself as both the passive "son" ("I couldn't help it, he forced me to do it") and the active "father"—and makes their activities both thrilling and evil, as befits his conflicted attitudes towards homosexuality. So while the framing story and the fantasy find Francis attempting to assert a heterosexual masculinity, it is consistently troubled by his Doppelgänger connections to Caligari and Cesare, who become expressive of his homosexual fears and repressed desires.[23]

As Paul Coates suggests, Caligari's and Cesare's positions as "simultaneously double[s] and other[s]" may also represent certain German cultural fears and desires regarding Italy.[24] With their Italian names, Caligari and Cesare represent the country "located beneath Germany on the map . . . its unconscious."[25] Also, one might add, its "bottom." Over the years, one strand of ethnic and nationalist stereotyping in Germany (and England and the United States, for that matter), has associated Italianness with passivity, femininity, and a sexual openness that includes bisexuality and homosexuality. These are qualities that have been simultaneously scorned and desired in German (popular) cultural discourses over the last couple of centuries. This state of cultural affairs could explain, in part, the particular form Francis's fantasy doubles/others take in *Caligari*.

Even Jane, the major figure in Francis's (and the filmmakers') attempts to heterosexualize the narrative, is implicated in the network of homosexual doubles, and not just because she might be read as a lesbian. While she has been most frequently understood as a conventionally victimized straight female narrative counter between straight men and monsters, the framing story reveals she has placed herself outside of Francis's (and the film's) heterosexualizing grasp. Jane's trancelike appearance in the film's framing sections is a far cry from the lively and expressive Jane of Francis's fantasy. Indeed her appearances in the framing sections suggest that she is one of the original models for the somnambulist Cesare—the other model being the gentle homosexual inmate who strokes flowers. Francis appears to have synthesized a (possibly lesbian) woman and a gay man to create his androgynous sleeping monster of repressed and denied homosexual desire. Put in other terms, he has taken the figure of his false public heterosexuality and combined it with the figure of his denied homosexuality to come up with a compelling, yet threatening, androgyne whom he houses in a coffinlike cabinet that becomes the central symbol of Francis's sexual dilemma. For him, expressions of homosexuality (the inmate Cesare) are connected with femininity (Jane), and both of these together are associated with death and destruction (the androgynous Cesare), just as they often are in patriarchal dominant culture.

In Francis's fantasy, violence and death will function both as substitutes for forbidden gender and sexual expressiveness, and as the representation of the psychic cost of these repressions. In my queer reading of *Caligari*, Francis goes mad because he represses (or, rather, feels forced to repress) his "feminine" homosexual desires and enacts (or feels compelled to enact) the role of heterosexual suitor to Jane. As Francis's fantasy doubles, the team of Caligari and Cesare carry out desires perverted by internalized homophobia in the form of violent acts, most spectacularly violence directed against Francis's homosexual best friend, Alan, and his hyperfeminine "fiancée." The first murder in the film—of an officious town clerk who humiliates Caligari—would seem unrelated to the sexualized violence later in the film. But recall that Caligari has come to see the clerk for a permit to exhibit Cesare—that is, to open his cabinet and display the young man whom he compels to perform "abhorrent acts." The town clerk's condescension and rudeness about the exhibition seals his doom. With this representative of the law out of the way, the display and enactment of forbidden sexualized thrills in Francis's fantasy can begin.

In this tenuously heterosexualized fantasy, Francis and his friend Alan are rivals for Jane's love. But take a look at Alan. The published script describes him as "a young man of aesthetic pursuits ... [h]e affects the style of the Nineties aesthete—a loosely-tied, flopping bow-tie and hair parted in the centre in the style of Aubrey Beardsley."[26] Alan's style and his languid demeanor code him as homosexual for many viewers—even those who otherwise would not read the film as queer. So placing Alan in the position of rival for Jane's love is yet another way Francis throws into question attempts to establish a conventional heterosexual narrative. Indeed, Alan appears to be Francis's real object of desire.

In Francis's fantasy, a homosexually coded Alan is the one who convinces a "reluctant" Francis to go to the fair, where arm-in-arm they stroll over to Caligari's tent. With a little more persuading, Francis follows Alan into the tent to see the twenty-three-year-old (roughly their age) somnambulist who "will awaken from a death-like sleep" (Francis's denied homosexual desires?) for his "master" Caligari. Cesare's awakening seems painful—he seems to be in shock and fearful of facing the gaping crowd.[27] As Caligari uses his phallic walking stick to gesture across Cesare's body, Alan becomes nervously excited, and even Francis betrays signs of interest. When the audience is invited to ask Cesare a question, because he "knows every secret," an agitated Alan volunteers, despite Francis's attempts to stop him. "How long do I have to live?" Alan asks. "Till dawn tomorrow" is Caesar's reply. As Alan becomes hysterical, Francis gazes at Cesare in fascination. That night, Cesare slips into Alan's room, and stabs Alan to death in his bed with a very long knife—an event represented by the play of shadows on the wall.

These early scenes involving Alan might be understood as the not-so-heavily translated representation of the source of Francis's sexual fears and desires. Alan is presented as the more "out" of the two men in his looks and attitudes. He is eager to see the forbidden object in the cabinet, and to ask it a question about his own "secrets." Francis first presents himself as someone who feigns disinterest in the somnambulist, then as someone fearful of the secrets Cesare might reveal, and finally as a person mesmerized by what Cesare reveals about Alan. The secret revealed ostensibly involves Alan's death, but this death scene is sexualized, like much of the violence in *Caligari*—Alan thrashes about in his bed before being pierced by Cesare's stiletto. That we only see Cesare and the stabbing as shadow play on the bedroom wall adds to the sense that this event might be standing in for another one that Francis can't bring himself to represent.

A production still included in the published script suggests what this unrepresentable thing might be as it shows Cesare, with his knife upraised, climbing into bed as Alan lifts his arms to fend off (or embrace) him.[28] In other words, in his fantasy, Francis has his more openly homosexual friend Alan make the connection with his younger double Cesare at a fair, and then has the two enact a sex scene translated into a murder scene, which is in line with Francis's disturbed understanding of his desires. Sex with Alan seems to be something Francis wants but cannot bring himself to admit to, let alone to act upon, so in his fantasy he has Cesare attack Alan in bed. If you look carefully at his scenes with Alan's landlady, Francis reacts with shock *before* she tells him of the death, and, at the murder scene, he looks rather shifty and conscience-striken. While he shouts that Alan's death fulfills "The prophecy of the somnambulist!" the death is actually the fulfillment of Francis's own troubled desires. The next sequence finds Francis reenacting the murder for the police, pantomiming the somnambulist's stabbing of Alan with particular animation.[29]

Alan's murder early in the story seems to free Francis of having to deal with his feelings for his friend, while it also appears to clear the way for establishing a central heterosexual couple. But Alan's murder less clinches the heterosexual couple than it sends Francis off on an investigation that finds him becoming more deeply involved with his homosexual doubles. Intriguingly, just as Francis sets out with Jane's father to question Caligari and examine Cesare, he concocts what appears to be a narrative digression or excess. Crosscut with the visit to Caligari are scenes involving a man who is caught brandishing a large knife after attempting to kill someone. Taken to the police station, the criminal is placed where Francis stood earlier, while the knife is passed around by police officers. At one point, the police chief holds the knife in the position of an erect penis as he questions the man.

Accused of Cesare's stabbings, the man is arrested and thrown into a cell that Francis will later insist upon visiting to make certain the prisoner is "safe." Spying through the cell peephole, Francis sees the prisoner sitting at the center of a white "X" on the floor in much the same way Francis will occupy the center of a white sunburst pattern on the floor of the asylum before the asylum director's ("Caligari"'s) appearance makes him try to hide behind two women inmates. The parallels and associations Francis's fantasy sets up in relation to the would-be killer are compelling within a queer understanding of *Caligari*, in particular within the context of homosexuality in Weimar Germany under Paragraph 175. Francis connects the criminal to both himself (the positioning in the police station and the cell/asylum) and Cesare (the long knife, the murder/attempted murder). Considering Cesare's role as one of Francis's homosexual doubles, a provocative associative series arises—Cesare: monster: homosexual: murderer: criminal: Francis: madman. This series encapsulates the most negative cultural associations with homosexuality in Weimar Germany as well as in the West from then until now.

Granted, the attempted murder is of a woman, but, then, a woman, Jane, plays an important part in Francis's repressed homosexual fantasy life as the figure connected with heterosexual pressures, femininity in both its straight and male homosexual form, and, perhaps, femme homosexuality. Jane is the object of the fantasy's second spectacular act of violence when Francis has Caligari send Cesare off to murder her, and not, as it turns out, so that Francis can have himself rush in and save her from the "monster" in accordance with heterosexual narrative convention. While Jane is being attacked and carried off by Cesare, Francis has himself watching Caligari sleeping next to what turns out to be a dummy of Cesare. His fantasy has a pair of servants—an older and a younger man who sleep in the same room—hear Jane's cries and go off to save her.

The multiplication here of older-younger male pairs who sleep together is interesting considering the prototype for these couples: Francis and the older man huddled together on a bench in the park. Remember that Francis's story seems to be as much a response to the older man's "from heterosexuality to homosexuality" tale as it is to the sight of his supposed fiancée, Jane, sleepwalking her way through the scene and ignoring him. So in the sequence cited above, Francis has himself voyeuristically monitoring the central older man–younger man homosexual pairing (they are also his doubles) to make certain that they don't do anything untoward—or maybe, as he suspects them of wrongdoing, hoping to see something "abhorrent." While this is happening, Francis's younger double goes over to his fiancée's house to enact his conflicted feelings about her and his own sexuality.

Initially sent to stab Jane—a fantasy translation of Francis's frustrating attempts at heterosexual union—Cesare looks at Jane sleeping amid layers of gauzy white material and drops his knife. Something about her touches him. Perhaps it is the homosexual's connection with the feminine? Both the inmate Cesare and the androgynous somnambulist Cesare are feminine-coded in certain ways. And recall that there are two models for the monstrous Cesare: the inmates Cesare and Jane. But as Cesare the somnambulist bends down to touch Jane, she awakens screaming. He struggles with her before finally carrying her off. The brief moment of potential connection between the young homosexual man and the woman (whether she is read as femme lesbian or not) has been broken by Jane's fright at the "horror" she sees before her.

It is a horror first revealed to her in Caligari's tent, where she goes looking for her father. Instead she is shown the terrible secret in the coffinlike cabinet: Cesare, the young slave of the old doctor. In this context, Dr. Caligari and Cesare's "monstrous" pairing suggests itself as a parallel to Jane's "heterosexual" relationship with her doctor father. That is, Francis's fantasy codes them both as falling outside normative heterosexuality: one homosexual, one incestuous. Recall along these lines that after Jane has been kidnapped, Francis has her father fall weeping over her bed just as he has the asylum director ("Caligari") throw himself over Cesare's dead body. In the cabinet-opening scene, Jane is alternately fascinated by Cesare and repelled by him, as she feels a connection with him, yet is appalled by the sexual secrets he represents. Among other possible reasons, Francis's fantasy sends Jane to see Caligari and Cesare in order to shock her, to reveal both his and her sexual secrets through his doubles so that she might break with him and end their "normal couple" heterosexual charade.

But her first encounter with Cesare doesn't seem to do the trick, so Francis sends Cesare to remove Jane from his fantasy in another way. As mentioned earlier, Francis/Cesare's inability to murder Jane suggests either stereotypical bisexual confusion or a possible connection through femininity between Francis's androgynous somnambulistic double and his sleeping straight girlfriend. However, Jane's horrified reaction at being confronted by a "monster" might be said to return the narrative to more traditional homosexual man vs. straight woman conventions. Unable to kill the straight woman as his older homosexual master has directed, the young homosexual man resorts to carrying her off. But where can they go since queer and straight patriarchs control the world around them? A confused Cesare stumbles about with Jane for a while before he suddenly drops dead from exhaustion. Jane is left to be saved by that pair of servants who may be the most benevolently represented older man–younger man couple as they act as the helpers of heterosexuality (albeit incest-coded) by returning Jane to her father.

Catherine B. Clement, Patrice Petro, and Mike Budd are among those contemporary critics whose interest in Jane's functions in *Caligari* have provided a feminist retort to years of criticism and analysis focusing upon straight male Oedipal, "masculinity in crisis" understandings of the film.[30] While this feminist work is also straight, and none of it consistently remembers that the bulk of the narrative is Francis's fantasy, some of it is queerly suggestive. Besides discussing Caligari and Cesare as "narcissistic" older-younger doubles, Clement focuses on the doubling of Jane and Cesare in the fantasy: "The male somnambulist, almost androgynous in Caligari's manipulations, is the equivalent of the female hysteric: they exchange the same look, a pure stare, detached from its object, the space where desire passes, an obscure desire."[31] That this "obscure desire" of the hysteric(s) might involve queerness is suggested in an earlier comment about the scene in which Caligari reveals Cesare to Jane:

> In the opening of the box, there is something of a ritual unveiling, like the hermaphrodite unveiling a male sex under women's clothes. In all the anxieties that produce the fantastic, of waiting, of fright, of surprises, are found the echo of this gesture, the repetition of this ritual, which takes up again the very question of the hysteric: "Am I man or woman?"[32]

But the hysterical queerness, or queer hysteria, Clement suggests in regard to the Jane and Cesare doubling, is actually an expression of Francis's hysteria. It is his fantasy that pairs Cesare and Jane in this way, and their queer hysteria presages his own at the end of the film when faced with the inmate "Cesare" and the head of the asylum ("Caligari").

Petro takes Clement to task for setting her discussions of the Jane-Cesare doubling within a too-simplistic "allegory of seduction and hysteria (father and daughter)," wherein Caligari is the exhibitionist who "exposes his 'thing'" (Cesare) to Jane.[33] Following the lead of Linda Williams's essay "When the Woman Looks," Petro is interested in placing "affinity between monster and woman" at the center of her analysis of *Caligari*. But while she agrees with Clement that Jane's encounters with Cesare "reveals a slippage of conventional gender roles—a fundamental confusion regarding gender definition and identification," Petro's analysis of the Jane-Cesare pairing also flirts with queerness without ever clearly committing to it.[34] So while (après Williams) Petro says Jane and Cesare are "the site of a different kind of sexuality (the monster as the double for the woman)," that "Cesare recognizes in Jane his own difference from the other male characters in the film," and that the woman and the monstrous man "share a similar status—and similar fate—within patriarchal ways of seeing," the overall critical position of the essay, like that of Clement, remains straight.[35]

Also concerned with the question of women's position in patriarchal narratives, Mike Budd finds that while "Jane's trancelike appearance seems to prompt Francis's story as an explanation," her story is displaced by Francis's search for Alan's murderer, and, in the final framing section, by Francis's "insane outburst."[36] For Budd, Jane has a "supporting role" in the film, with "the final explanation of her psychology submerged under that of the central male character, just as the initial question about her was a means toward 'his' ends."[37] Looked at as a conventional straight narrative, Jane does play a secondary part in *Caligari*. She functions largely as women do in most traditional films: passive or hysterical spectacle. But read as a queer fantasy, with Francis's and the filmmakers' attempts at heterosexualization exposed, Jane has a much more important role in *Caligari*. For one thing, the sleepwalking Jane is linked with the somnambulist Cesare, the queer heart of the film, and their first meeting is perhaps the central symbolic dream event of the fantasy narrative. Initiated by Jane's leaving home, then orchestrated by the older homosexual Caligari, the now-active woman and the awakening "monster" gaze at each other in a sexually charged and disturbing moment that represents the excitement and terror that the culturally despised combination of femininity and male homosexuality (or bisexuality) have for the repressed Francis—and for many viewers.

Of course being the representative of femininity in a fantasy of male homosexual desire and denial doesn't exactly make Jane the main character, but it certainly makes her a much more important figure than she is in most straight readings of *Caligari*. The femininity she is the first model of finds its expression in Cesare, Caligari, Alan, Francis, and some more minor male characters—granted mostly as moments of fainting, "overemotionalism," or passivity. Queerly speaking, Jane's initial appearance does in part encourage Francis to tell his fantasy to the older man, but less because she is the inspiration for a conventional heterosexual narrative than because her overdetermined guise of hyperfeminine, zombielike passivity prods the nervous Francis to tell his potential cruising partner a fantasy story that on its manifest level seems heterosexual, but which is actually about his ambivalence toward femininity and homosexuality/bisexuality. If nothing else, Jane's excessive and strange appearance warns viewers not to take Francis's narrative "straight" even before the revelations of the final scenes. If we also understand Jane as a femme lesbian, then she becomes even more central to a film finally concerned with the oppression and repression of homosexuality and femininity. Besides, with Jane as a repressed lesbian, the film's final moments would no longer be only about Francis and his psychosexual "problems," but could be said to be about what is "wrong" with her as well.

Budd's only gesture toward queerness in his discussion of Jane is a comment he makes connecting her to the film's legendary mise-en-scène: "Yet of the 'normal' characters, only she carries the mark of expressionism, the sharp, angular lines across the front of the dress she wears when meeting Alan and Francis and later, when Caligari 'exposes' Cesare to her."[38] Extrapolating from Budd's ideas here, Jane's expressionist outfit makes her the link between the "normal" major characters in Francis's fantasy—Alan, Jane's father, Francis himself—and Caligari and Cesare. In this reading, *Caligari's* expressionist style is connected in Francis's fantasy with the "abnormal" and the monstrous. But since what is monstrous comes to include homosexuality, bisexuality, incest, and female (sexual) initiative, the "mark of expressionism" finally touches all the main characters: that is, they are all "abnormal" in some way. For most viewers, then, the revelation that Francis is considered mad would really come as no surprise, considering the style in which his tale is told.

Even at the time of the film's release, its visual style was considered suspect by a number of groups.[39] In Germany, many found the film's expressionism "a mystification rather than a revelation, a symptom of pathology rather than insight."[40] French commentator Blaise Cendars, writing "the most famous hostile commentary" of the film in *Cinea* on June 2, 1922, found that *Caligari* "is a film that casts discredit on all modern Art. Because it is hybrid, hysterical, unwholesome."[41] Within a more general sociopolitical context, "[f]or many people there appeared to be the eloquent affinities between the seeming irrationality of abstract art, or the excesses of Expressionism, and the political instability, economic crises, and collapse of moral values during the Weimar Republic."[42] In the United States, the initial response to the film by the press and public, especially those who knew the film was German, included a fair share of complaints that *Caligari* was "morbid, degenerate, or unhealthy."[43]

Within the range of possible readings of *Caligari's* queerness, however, I can understand how the film's mise-en-scène could encourage viewers to understand the style as one expressing a "degenerate, unhealthy" state of mind: either that of Caligari and Cesare in the fantasy, or that of Francis once his "madness" is revealed. After all, the final intertitle does talk about curing a disturbed Francis. Poor Francis, his attempt to fool the old man and us with a conventional heterosexual narrative was queered by the (to most viewers) bizarre and strangely disturbing visual style in which it is represented. The tension of the effete "fine arts imagery on the surface of a familiar narrative structure," is one that has struck a number of (re)viewers from 1920 to the present—even if it is not always consciously understood within the queer and/vs. (quasi)straight terms I am using here.[44]

Theodore Price proposes another queer approach to Caligari's style:

> However else the unusual, distorted, Expressionistic decor, costume, and exaggerated facial expressions may function in the film, *Caligari*, this film of sex and murder, has the appearance and air of campiness. The young, tall, slim Conrad Veidt in his skin-tight, ballet dancer leotards, and with his garish mascara-like eye makeup, looks more like a beautiful boy than a handsome man.[45]

Taking their cue from the film's stylistic excesses, camp readings are certainly one way to queer *Caligari*—and one imagines this was as true in the 1920s as during later periods. But camp readings of *Caligari* can take many forms, from condescending "look at this funny silent movie" understandings to humorous appreciations of the pretentious audacity of the film's visual conception, including its performances. I have to admit that there are times when I watch the film in a mood to appreciate *Caligari*'s camp qualities—and that many of these pleasures revolve around the Expressionist appearance and performances of a heavily made-up, leotard-clad Cesare/Veidt and the diva Jane/Lil Dagover. But, for me, it is always a case of camp readings alternating with, or standing beside, non-camp queer appreciations of the film.

Whether understood as a sign of degeneracy, camp or something else, the use of expressionist style in the framing story creates certain complications in understanding *Caligari*'s Expressionism as only representing queerness as monstrousness or madness. Granted, in order not to give away the twist ending, the opening of the frame perhaps needs to be visually in line with the story that follows, but what explanation is there for continuing to use a visual style linked with fantasy and mental illness in the closing section of the frame? Danny Peary makes an interesting point when he says, "common sense tells us that men who wanted to promote expressionism wouldn't represent it as the visualization of madmen."[46] So while many people understand *Caligari*'s style as expressive of madness, the use of Expressionism in the film's final section allows a reading of the film that makes it less a film about queerness as an illness that must be cured, than a film about how a person can become mentally ill by succumbing to cultural pressures to lead a traditional straight life by repressing and denying homosexual (or bisexual) desires.

From this position, Expressionism is being used by "creative, quite sane minds" to tell the story of how a repressive culture incarcerates those who are different and subjects them to "cures" by benevolent patriarchs.[47] Knowing something about *Caligari*'s original cultural context, it is easy to understand why Francis might turn the head of the asylum into a mystic and hypnotist in his fantasy while also maintaining his medical position. The asylum chief is like those conservative psychiatrists and hypnotists in the 1920s, and later, who offered cures for homosexuality—like the person Paul visits in *Anders als die Andern*. One of the benefits of this "homosexual positive" reading is that it maintains the "antiauthoritarian" theme *Caligari's* scriptwriters and subsequent critics felt was compromised by the addition of the framing story. *Caligari* is still an antiauthoritarian film, as long as you are prepared to see Francis as a repressed queer and the chief doctor as not all that benevolent.[48] As more than one critic has pointed out, "it's difficult to trust [actor Werner] Krauss's asylum director at the end."[49] David Robinson elaborates:

> In an era of endemic skepticism in the face of authority, a fin-de-siècle audience does not so easily accept the ending at face value. A modern viewer can readily interpret the ending of the film from a position that Franzis's [sic] story is true and that he is not mad, but that the seemingly benign director... has used his wiles to have him incarcerated as a madman.[50]

For one thing, the director's grandiose pronouncement that he can now cure Francis seems a bit premature. After all, he hasn't heard/seen everything the old man and the viewer has. And just what does he plan to cure Francis of, exactly? The vagueness of the film on this point encourages viewers to become "Sherlock Freuds" and go back to decode Francis's fantasy looking for answers. As noted earlier, the final intertitle suggests that the director wants to cure Francis of the delusion that he (the director) is Caligari. But what does this mean, exactly? In a queer reading, what the doctor wants to cure Francis of is a case of hysterical projection: that is, to cure Francis of seeing the straight doctor as the actively homosexual Caligari. But while the director might see the cure as an elimination of homosexuality, we can understand Francis's turning him into Caligari as indicating that he wants the director to be like Caligari and open Francis's psychosexual cabinet by curing him of his internalized homophobia, even though he is consciously resistant to this process.

However, to the end, and like its main character, *Caligari* remains deeply conflicted and incoherent about its queerness. It is just as easy to read the final moments of the film as supporting the good doctor's plans to cure Francis of his queer "mania." This is certainly the position of the epilogue of a staged prologue and epilogue that framed the film's framing story during its initial New York run at the Capitol Theatre. Set in the home library of a man named Cranford (who turns out to be the older man to whom Francis tells his story), the epilogue has Cranford pick up on the the final intertitle of the film, "...and now I also know how to cure him":

> And he did! Francis Purnay is today a prosperous jeweler in Edewald, happily married, with a couple of healthy, normal children. . . . He is like a man suddenly awakened from a bad dream.[51]

Implicitly indicating that what Francis has been cured of is some form of queerness, Cranford's words provide a clear, conventional heterosexual happy ending to Francis's story.[52] But queerness will out, and the staged frame leaves us with the spectacle of the young auditor of Cranford's story, provocatively called Janes, "comfortably sprawled out in his chair." Both men are shadowy figures outlined by the moonlight streaming in through a window, as the fire in the fireplace "has banked down to glowing embers."[53] What's their story?

Another aspect of the end of the film that might indicate Francis's cure is a good thing is the parallel created between the image of a straightjacketed Francis and the last shot of his fantasy, in which Caligari is put into a straightjacket after he hysterically throws himself over Cesare's dead body. One possibly disconcerting effect of having this striking comparison close both the fantasy and framing narratives is that instead of offering evidence for the argument that Francis's problem is internalized homophobia (as Francis's hysterical reaction to the benign figure of the inmate Cesare does a bit earlier), the parallel straightjacketing shots seem to reinforce the idea that homosexual (or bisexual) desires are signs of a dangerous mental illness.

On the other hand, the image of Francis in a straightjacket might remind us that Caligari really only went "mad" at the sight of his lover's dead body. The final shot of the framing story lacks one element to make it an exact parallel to the scene of Caligari's breakdown: the body of Francis's lover, his Cesare. It is a crucial, telling, and poignant absence—and one that brings us back to Alan. Why is Alan the only major figure from Francis' fantasy not to reappear in the asylum? Could it be because he has come to represent what is intolerable for both Francis and dominant culture: the possibility of homosexual desire? This desire becomes the structuring absence in Francis's "mania," in the asylum director's plans to "cure" Francis, in *Caligari*'s narrative as a whole, and in the many straight critical commentaries on the film.

In Francis's fantasy this hidden desire, not surprisingly, is brought to light via a diary. Late in the fantasy, Francis and a group of doctors at the asylum are transfixed by the director's diary. As they read certain entries, these entries are visualized in flashbacks: the asylum director's ecstatic examination of the reclining Cesare when the latter is first brought to him ("The irresistible passion of my life is being fulfilled. . . . Now I shall learn if it's true that a somnambulist can be compelled to perform acts abhorrent to him. . . ."); the director staggering around outdoors "in the grip of an obsession" ("I must penetrate the heart of his secret. I must become Caligari"). At the end of the

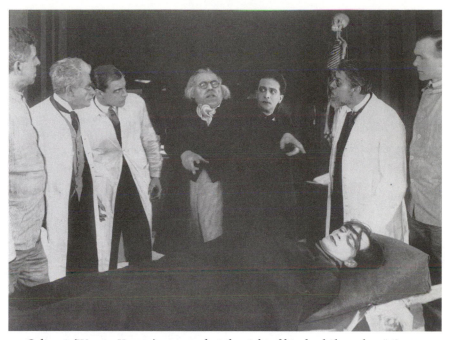

Caligari (Werner Krauss) goes mad at the sight of his dead "love slave" Cesare (Conrad Veidt), as Francis and the asylum doctors look on in dread and fascination.

last flashback, the scene returns to the asylum, where we realize, if we haven't already, that Francis is "penetrating" the "heart of [Caligari's and Cesare's] secret" even as he occupies the director'/Caligari's chair. More than this, as the secret of the director and Cesare is being revealed, a young doctor (an Alan substitute?) is standing behind Francis's chair and moving his arms down toward Francis. Francis has "become Caligari." It is at this point that a man rushes in to announce Cesare's dead body has been found. After the sight of Cesare's body forces the director/Caligari to "come out," he goes mad, like many a film homosexual, and is then taken offscreen, leaving the frame to Francis and Cesare. Justice has been served in the fantasy: an eye for an eye, a lover (Cesare) for a lover (Alan). But Francis also gives himself away as he takes Caligari's place—he has always been Caligari, really.

For its original release, *Caligari* was publicized in Berlin with "a new catch-phrase, 'You must become Caligari.' For weeks this mysterious command shrieked out at one from every kiosk, jumped out from the pages of all daily papers."[54] I have understood this command as a call to queerness, but it is a queerness that can be placed within a range of conflicting readings that alternately or simultaneously encourage fear and loathing, ambivalence, or sympathy. The final image of Francis suggests he has "become Caligari" and has given himself over to the hysterical expression of a culturally repressed queerness. But he is also in a straightjacket and in the hands of the asylum's "Caligari," who is ready to "cure" him both of being Caligari and of thinking the director is Caligari.[55] Francis is Caligari, the asylum chief is Caligari, "You must become Caligari": the thrill and terror of queerness seemed to be everywhere in the art and popular culture of Weimar Germany, as it still is for anyone willing to forego more obvious heterocentric readings of *Caligari* and take the plunge into the troubled heart of queerness the film's *mise-en-abyme* ending gestures toward.[56]

NOTES

1. Hans Janowitz, "*Caligari*—The Story of a Famous Story," in *The Cabinet of Dr. Caligari: Texts, Contexts, Histories*, ed. Mike Budd (New Brunswick, N.J., and London: Rutgers University Press, 1990), 224. For a discussion of the (homo)erotics of male collaboration, see material in the chapter on *The Red Shoes* later in this book.
2. Bosley Crowther, "The Cabinet of Dr. Caligari," in *The Great Films: Fifty Years of Motion Pictures* (New York: G.P. Putnam's Sons, 1962), 21.
3. *The Cabinet of Dr. Caligari* (1919, Decla-Bioscope: Robert Wiene). All quotes are taken from intertitles in Kino's 1996 restored video print of the film, which provides English translations of the original title cards done in the graphic style of those in the original film.
4. In the staged prologue and epilogue that framed the film's framing story during its initial run at New York's Capitol Theatre, the older man is called Cranford. Seated in a comfortable home library, Cranford is telling a young man the story of Caligari as he heard it from Francis. Both men are shadowy figures outlined by moonlight that is streaming through a window. While this staged prologue ignores the fact that the older man is himself an inmate, it does duplicate the older man–younger man dynamics of the film's opening park cruising scene. Cranford's overheated monologue here also readily lends itself to (homo)erotic, if also homophobic, interpretations. Describing his approaching rendezvous with Francis, Cranford symbolically evokes a scenario of anal sex that expresses the combination of desire and disgust that characterize Francis's (and the film's) ambivalent relationship to queerness:

> I cannot express to you in words the intense distaste that grew on me the nearer I drew to my goal. There was something positively malignant and unnatural in the density of the twisted creepers and shrubbery.... I continued to force my way through the dark, green foilage.... As I struggled on in the tangled thicket suddenly the green wall in front of me parted easily to my touch and I plunged breathless, confused and shivering with a nameless dread.

Meeting Cranford on the other side of the wall is "a young man who appeared in no wise surprised at my advent, but more as if he has been expecting me."

Cranford's description of Francis as "tall and slender, with haunted eyes set in a sad and sensitive face," evokes a comparison between Francis and the homosexuals in Francis's fantasy, Alan and Cesare. Material quoted above from the Capitol Theatre prologue and epilogue are taken from Mike Budd, "The Moments of *Caligari*," in *The Cabinet of Dr. Caligari: Texts, Contexts, Histories*, ed. Mike Budd (New Brunswick, N.J., and London: Rutgers University Press, 1990), 64–69.

5. Robert Weine, Carl Mayer, Hans Janowitz, *The Cabinet of Dr. Caligari*, ed. R.V. Adkinson (New York: Simon and Schuster, 1972), 41.
6. David Robinson translates the intertitle referring to Jane as "That is my bride." *Das Cabinet des Dr. Caligari* (London: BFI Publishing, 1997), 62.
7. Patrice Petro, *Joyless Streets: Women and Melodramatic Representation in Weimar Germany* (Princeton, N.J.: Princeton University Press, 1989), 36.
8. Richard Dyer, *Now You See It: Studies on Lesbian and Gay Film* (London and New York: Routledge, 1990), 7. Films cited: *Anders als die Andern* (1919: Richard Oswald); *Mädchen in Uniform* (1931, Deutsche Film-Gemeinschaft: Leontine Sagan).
9. Ibid., 8, 10.
10. Ibid., 10.
11. This summary of the film is indebted to the synopsis from *Jahrbuch fur sexuelle Zwischenstufen* reprinted in Dyer, 11–12.
12. Dyer, 14.
13. Theodore Price, *Hitchcock and Homosexuality: His 50-Year Obsession with Jack the Ripper and the Superbitch Prostitute—A Psychoanalytic View* (Metuchen, N.J., and London: Scarecrow Press, 1992), 349.
14. Dyer, 14, 16.
15. For a more detailed discussion of male in-betweenism and the Tante style in Weimar Germany, see Dyer, 17–22.
16. Robinson, 29.
17. The 1962 "remake" of *Caligari*, entitled *Cabinet of Caligari* (Twentieth Century-Fox/Lippert: Roger Kay), makes Jane the central character. This Jane is also marked as being (hetero)sexually inhibited or frigid, while sharing Francis's homophobia. As with Francis in the original, the remake suggests that Jane's homophobia, as well as her "frigidity," might be read as a sign of denied and repressed homosexuality, as in her fantasy she simultaneously rejects men while homosexualizing and demonizing both Caligari and his female assistant, Chris(tine). "What sort of a monster are you?" Jane shouts at Chris, wondering how Chris can live with a "beast" like Caligari. Chris explains that she isn't Caligari's mistress, but that they "love the same things." "You love sadism, bestiality, perversion," Jane retorts. Later, deciding that Caligari's secret is that he's "impotent," Jane asks his male colleague, "What would such a superman do if it became known he wasn't a man after all?"

To complicate, or muddle, psychosexual matters, the remake finally uses the hints at incest in the original (between Jane and her father) when it reveals that the young man who tries to make love to Jane during the course of her fantasy is her son. When this son comes to pick Jane up after her release from the sanitarium, he's driving the open-top sports car Jane pictured herself wildly driving in her bare feet at the beginning of her fantasy. In retrospect, this ride becomes an emblem of her desire for sexual adventure: "A fever was on me. For once I responded to it. Be free. Be free as the wind." Finally, the remake suggests that Jane's "adventure" involves some combination of repressed incestuous desires and denied lesbianism. More conventionally, the film allows a reading that understands all of Jane's desires for nonnormative sexual freedom as detrimental as they prevent her from functioning as a "normal" heterosexual woman.

18. Not that Francis is all that successful in masculinizing himself. See Dyer, 20, on the Bube/Bursch figure in German gay culture.

19. Price, 332.

20. Examples of the "passive" bisexual can be found in many fictional works such as Joe Orton's play *Entertaining Mr. Sloane* (1963), which was made into a film (1969, Pathe/Canterbury: Douglas Hickox) and the films *Cabaret* (1972, ABC Pictures/Allied Artists: Bob Fosse) and *Sunday, Bloody Sunday* (1971, United Artists/Vectia: John Schlesinger). *Caligari* carries Cesare's passivity to the point of infantalization in a scene in which Caligari is spoon-feeding Cesare—one wonders if he also has to wipe his ass? A good single source for further discussions of both the cultural trope of the passive bisexual and the connections between bisexuality and androgyny is Marjorie Garber's *Vice Versa: Bisexuality and the Eroticism of Everyday Life* (New York: Touchstone, 1995).

21. In the original script, the description of Cesare's confrontation with Jane reads like the scenario for a heterosexual rape, as Cesare's "merciless stare of bestial stupidity gives way to a lecherous grin" at the sight of Jane in bed. Cesare grabs Jane's hair, "savouring its perfume, then with a greedy hand strokes Jane's body, which quivers profoundly" (Robinson, 70). As David Robinson points out, in the filmed version of this scene, Cesare "seems like some docile animal angered by sudden fear rather than the lecherous rapist suggested by the script" (70).

22. Price, 318.

23. In an interesting straight reading of the doubles in the film, Thomas Elsaesser writes:

> What, then, is Francis' story, and why does he go mad? It is, essentially, the tale of a suitor who is ignored or turned down.... Cesare is Francis' double: he kills the rival and abducts the bride, thus acting out Francis' secret desires. The fact that throughout the rape/abduction scene both Francis and Caligari sit stupidly in front of Cesare's dummy, not only accentuates the gesture of disavowal, it also establishes a parallelism of desire between Francis and Caligari.... The investigation of the series of crimes thus culminates in the visual statement that the criminal is the alter ego of the detective, the story of Oedipus in other words. ("Social Mobility and the Fantastic: German Silent Cinema," in *Fantasy and the Cinema*, ed. James Donald [London: BFI Publishing, 1989], 35.)

24. Paul Coates, *The Gorgon's Gaze: German Cinema, Expressionism, and the Image of Horror* (Cambridge: Cambridge University Press, 1991), 36.

25. Ibid., 36.

26. Wiene, Mayer, and Janowitz, 44.
27. In the original script, this awakening is also clearly feminized and (homo)sexualized, here and there reminding one of what we see of the inmate Cesare:

> Caesare [sic] stands motionless for a few seconds. Under the piercing gaze of Calligaris [sic], who stands beside him, he now becomes quite tender and something like expression enters his face! His eyes blink, now quite gentle and distant...with slightly opened mouth, he struggles for air. The rock-like rigidity of the body gives way to a sudden violent shaking of the limbs. The dangling arms are raised...as if to embrace something. With his gradual awakening, whose climax is evidently an intense physical process, he seems to become suddenly helpless and begins to topple forwards. At this moment the grinning Calligaris catches him... (Robinson, 63).

28. Wiene, Mayer, and Janowitz, 40.
29. The original script contained a scene outside the graveyard after Alan's funeral in which he returns as a ghost to look "affectionately" at Jane and Francis as the latter leads the former away "silently and protectively." This is one of a handful of heterosexualizing moments that were dropped in the final film (Robinson, 67).
30. The touchstone for straight male readings of the film is, of course, Siegfried Kracauer's anaylsis of the film in *From Caligari to Hitler: A Psychological History of the German Film* (Princeton, N.J.: Princeton University Press, 1947). Kracauer discusses the film in the context of what he sees as Wiemar cinema's central theme of authoritarian father figures controlling a powerless populace. While Clement, Petro, Budd, and others set themselves up to some extent as working outside of Kracauer's sociopolitical male Oedipal critical approach, their discussions of *Caligari* in relation to Jane's functions stay within straight critical and theoretical paradigms.

    Thomas Elsaesser's work on the film in "Social Mobility and the Fantastic: German Silent Cinema" (in *Fantasy and the Cinema*, ed. James Donald [London: BFI Publishing, 1989], 23–38), acknowledges Kracauer's reading while suggesting a more open approach to understanding *Caligari*: "It would appear that in *The Cabinet of Dr. Caligari* a visual form and a mode of narration has been found where several different 'versions' or narrative perspectives converge or superimpose themselves...creating entry points for a number of distinct and different spectator-fantasies, centering on male and female Oedipal scenarios" (35). Possible queer scenarios (Oedipal or not) don't enter Elsaesser's critical line of sight, however.
31. Catherine B. Clement, "Charlatans and Hysterics," in *The Cabinet of Dr. Caligari: Texts, Contexts, Histories*, ed. Mike Budd (New Brunswick, N.J., and London: Rutgers University Press, 1990), 197–98.
32. Ibid., 197.
33. Patrice Petro, "The Woman, the Monster, and *Caligari*," in *The Cabinet of Dr. Caligari: Texts, Contexts, Histories,* ed. Mike Budd (New Brunswick, N.J., and London: Rutgers University Press, 1990), 209–10.
34. Ibid., 210.

35. Ibid., 210–11, 213.
36. Mike Budd, "The Moments of *Caligari*," in *The Cabinet of Dr. Caligari: Texts, Contexts, Histories,* ed. Mike Budd (New Brunswick, N.J., and London: Rutgers University Press, 1990), 11.
37. Ibid., 48–49.
38. Ibid., 48.
39. David Robinson suggests that Expressionistic style may have been used in *Caligari* to "titillate" the public—that is, it was used in a conscious effort to commercially exploit the style as daringly trendy: the "strange distorted images could be explained away as the fantasy of a diseased mind" (Robinson, 45–46).
40. Budd, 54.
41. Quoted in Robinson, 51–52.
42. Frank Whitford, "The Triumph of the Banal: Art in Nazi Germany," in *Visions and Blueprints: Avant-Garde Culture and Radical Politics in Early Twentieth Century Europe*, ed. Edward Timins and Peter Collier (Manchester: Manchester University Press, 1988), 266, as quoted in Budd, 54.
43. Budd, 58, 82.
44. Budd, 103. For a more detailed discussion of the relationship of the fine arts, and art films in particular, to cultural notions of homosexality and queerness, see my chapter on *The Red Shoes*. Within its own cultural context, *Caligari* was one of a number of art films the German film industry produced during the Weimer period as part of certain "progressive strategies which involved targeting new audiences and entering the realm of 'high culture' by drawing on contemporary art movements" (Werner Sudendorf, "Expressionism and film: the testament of Dr. Caligari," in *Expressionism Reassessed*, ed. Shulamith Behr, David Fanning, and Douglas Jarman [Manchester and New York: Manchester University Press, 1993], 95).

   In the same way the film's visual "mark of expressionism" comes to queer all the main characters, *Caligari*'s narrative finally becomes thoroughly queered as what we took to be the (straight) reality of the film is revealed as the fantasy of the main character who is in an asylum. But the framing story is also dominated by our "mad" queer character until the very end, and the film leaves us rather uneasy about the vague "cure" the Caligari–look-alike director has in store for our queer hero.
45. Price, 318.
46. Danny Peary, *Cult Movies 3* (New York: Simon and Schuster, 1988), 50.
47. Ibid., 50.
48. With his analysis of *Rope* (1948) in "The Murderous Gays: Hitchcock's Homophobia," Robin Wood provides a model for how more "homosexual positive" (or perhaps more "homosexual sensitive") readings might be done of films that seem to traffic in homophobia. While not denying the possibility of understanding the film as reinforcing certain negative cultural ideas about homosexuality (that it is sick, that it leads to violent crime), Wood also considers the film in its postwar context and offers a reading that positions the attitudes and crimes of the main characters in relation to the repressive and oppressive society in which they

live (*Hitchcock's Films Revisited* [New York: Columbia University Press, 1989], 336–57; rpt. in *Out in Culture: Gay, Lesbian and Queer Essays on Popular Culture,* ed. Corey Creekmur and Alexander Doty [Durham, N.C.: Duke University Press, 1995], 197–215).

49. Peary, 51.
50. Robinson, 33.
51. Budd, 67.
52. By a strange coincidence (or is it, considering dominant culture's heterocentric desires?), the original script opened with a sequence that found Jane and Francis married. Francis tells some guests "a dreadful tale" that involved him and his wife some twenty years earlier (Robinson, 60). That this prologue is not in the finished film seems yet another indication of its creators' queer impulses.
53. Budd, 67.
54. Article in *Die Kinematograph* (March 3, 1920), as quoted in Kristin Thompson, "Dr. Caligari at the Folies-Bergere, or The Success of an Early Avant-Garde Film," in *The Cabinet of Dr. Caligari: Texts, Contexts, Histories,* ed. Mike Budd (New Brunswick, N.J., and London: Rutgers University Press, 1990), 138.
55. The final scenes in the original script more neatly contain the film's queerness as they reestablish heteronormativity. After Caligari has gone mad at the sight of Cesare's body, there is a shot of him strapped to a cot in a hospital cell. This is followed by a shot of Jane and Francis standing before a plaque that reads, in part, "Here stood the cabinet of Dr. Calligaris [sic]. Peace to his victims. Peace to him!" (Robinson, 73).
56. Paul Coates sees the ending of *Caligari* as "introducing an ambiguity that destroys the notion of sense completely, leaving one in a state of vertigo" (33n). As I hope is clear by this point, I would understand the ending of the film as destroying the notion of a stable, conventional heterosexual narrative "sense," leaving the narrative in a state of queerness that may be vertiginous as the film leaves viewers profoundly confused about what to make of this queerness.

"My Beautiful Wickedness": The Wizard of Oz as Lesbian Fantasy

Like many of you reading this, I have a long and tangled history with *The Wizard of Oz*.[1] For the past thirty-five years or so, *Gentlemen Prefer Blondes*, *I Love Lucy*, and *Oz* have been the popular culture touchstones for understanding my changing relationship to gender and sexuality. It all started in the 1960s with the annual televising of *Oz*. Watching as a kid, I loved Dorothy, loved Toto, was scared of, but fascinated by, the Wicked Witch, felt guilty for thinking good witch Glinda was nerve-gratingly fey and shrill, thought the Tin Man was attractive and the Scarecrow a big showoff. But I was really embarrassed by the Cowardly Lion. The supporting cast in Kansas was boring, with the exception of the sharp-featured spinster Almira (which I always heard as "Elvira") Gulch. Only the cyclone could equal this grimly determined bicyclist and dog-snatcher for sheer threatening power.

Looking back, it all makes sense. I was a boy who had a girlfriend who I liked to kiss and to play Barbies with, while also looking for chances to make physical contact with her older brother through horseplay in the pool. I was in love with and wanted to be Dorothy, thinking that the stark Kansas farmland she was trying to escape from was nothing compared to the West Texas desert our house was built upon. The Tin Man might stand in for my girlfriend's older brother (and subsequent crushes on older boys): an emotionally and physically stolid male who needed to find a heart so he could romantically express himself to me. During my first phase with the film, I saw Dorothy's three male companions (on the farm and in Oz) as being like friends or brothers. Well, maybe my heterosexual upbringing had me working to construct some sort of love interest between Dorothy and the showoff Scarecrow. But Dorothy and the Tin Man? Never. Hands off, girl, he's mine! Without my being aware of it, these latter responses to *Oz* were signs that I was moving into what would become my initial place within straight patriarchy: as straight woman rival and wannabe.

Then there was that Cowardly Lion who was teaching me self-hatred. From between the ages of about five and fifteen, I was actually far less disturbed by the Wicked Witch than I was by the Cowardly Lion. When he sang about how miserable he was to be a "sissy," I cringed. Because I was a sissy, too. At least that's what certain boys at school and in the neighborhood called me when I'd play jump rope or jacks with the girls—or even when I'd go over to talk with the girls during recess or after school. At this stage, "sissy" seemed to be a gender thing. It meant being like a girl, liking what they liked. However, in my case, this included boys. But I also liked a girl. While watching *The Wizard of Oz* each year, my gender and sexuality turmoil reached its peak when Dorothy and the Cowardly Lion emerged from their Emerald City beauty treatments with nearly identical perms and hair bows. And then this ultrasissified lion dared to sing "If I Were the King of the Forest"! I would sit in front of the television set paralyzed: my desire for and identification with Dorothy battling my loathing for and identification with the Cowardly Lion.

Between my late teens and my early thirties I found my desire for Dorothy cooling as I became a "Friend of Dorothy." Early on in this process of identifying as gay, I was still embarrassed by the Lion. I hadn't come out to anyone, and he seemed to be too out: flamboyant, effeminate, and self-oppressive. Not a very good role model, I thought, even though in the privacy of my room, cocktail in hand, I would dramatically lip-synch and act out "Over the Rainbow" with Dorothy. Dorothy newly endeared herself to me by her concern for the big sissy she was saddled with. She became my first image of the friendly, caring straight girl/woman. Later someone told me these girls/women were called "fag hags"—a term I thought was mean. I was also told all about Judy Garland. The story of her career and personal struggles intensified my identification with Dorothy as a heroic figure.

Sometime in my twenties, I became aware of butches and of camp, both of which fed into my developing "gay" appreciation of *The Wizard of Oz*. Camp finally let me make my peace with the Cowardly Lion. He was still over-the-top, but no longer a total embarrassment. Oh, I'd get a little nostalgic twinge of humiliation now and then (I still do), but by and large I found him fabulously outrageous. King of the Forest? He was more like a drag queen who just didn't give a fuck. Because of this, he seemed to have a bravery the narrative insisted he lacked. Camp's appreciation of the excessive also led me to reevaluate Glinda. She wasn't just *like* a drag queen, she was one! Artifice surrounded her like that pink (but of course) gossamer gown she wore. Who better to guide Dorothy along the road to straight womanhood, I thought. I saw this as a great ironic joke on all those straights who claimed the film as theirs.

And who better to try and prevent Glinda's plans for Dorothy than some horrible, predatory butch dyke? At this point, the only lesbians I could (or would?) recognize as lesbians were butches. To be honest, sight recognition was about as deep as my interaction with butches went, as the gay society I was keeping from the mid-1970s through the early 1980s did not encourage gay and lesbian mingling. You would have thought that Stonewall, with its frontline drag queen and butch dyke fighters, had never happened. So I enjoyed the Wicked Witch of the West as another camp figure: she was a scary, tough butch dressed in black whom I could also laugh at.

The more extensive political and social coalitions formed between gays and lesbians beginning around the mid-1980s, in large part in response to the AIDS pandemic, gave me opportunities to get to know lesbians beyond the tentative looks and "hellos" we'd exchange at bars and on the street. Needless to say, what I learned from them gave new meaning to many popular culture texts. Besides recognizing butches, I might also be on the lookout for femmes—and butchy femmes and femmy butches. And just as with gay leathermen, I learned that not all butches are tough and scary. And not all femmes dressed or behaved as they did in order to "pass" in straight culture. Add to knowledge like this my encounters with academic gender and sexuality theory and criticism during the same period, and you have someone who was beginning to see many of his favorite pop culture "classics" in a very different light. Not that all of the ways in which I previously understood these texts were wiped out. Aspects of certain readings and pleasures I let go, but other parts remained to complement or supplement my later interpretations. It now seems to me that heterocentricity and sexism limited and perverted much of my earlier straight, bisexual, and gay readings of *Oz*. Actually, returning to *Oz* again and again in recent years has helped me to do battle with some of the remaining limitations and perversions of my straight upbringing. So I'm in love with *The Wizard of Oz* all over again, and, as with any (re)new(ed) love, I feel compelled to publicly count the ways that I now love *Oz*.

I'm feeling especially compelled to do this because of the continuing and pervasive influence of heterocentrism and/or homophobia and/or sexism upon both queer and straight understandings of popular culture. To refer to the case at hand: here is a film about an adolescent girl who has an elaborate dream-fantasy in which there is not a whisper of heterosexual romance—not even displaced onto other figures. Uh, could this girl possibly not be interested in heterosexuality? Well, according to far too many people I've encountered, including a fair share of gays, lesbians, and straight women, this is not really possible. This cannot be a film about a teenaged girl who is having a rite-of-passage dream in which she fantasizes about the possibility of a choice outside of heterosexuality. Tell me, then, where *is* the heterosexuality in this fantasy?

In terms of heterosexual readings of *The Wizard of Oz*, the fantasy, my friends, is not all up there on the screen. Caught within the spell of hetero-centrism (and, for some gay and straight men, sexism), viewers of all sexual identities persist in seeing heterosexuality where it ain't. I say it's wishful reading into the text. Or, if not that, it's a subtext. If anything, a heterosexual reading of *The Wizard of Oz* is appropriative, and could be considered subordinate to lesbian readings. Do you need some behind-the-scenes proof that points to the queer intent of those working on the film? Documented in John Fricke, Jay Scarfone, and William Stillman's *The Wizard of Oz: The 50th Anniversary Pictorial History* are producer Arthur Freed's demands that various scripts develop a tighter narrative built around Dorothy and Aunt Em as well as Dorothy and the Wicked Witch.[2] One important result of Freed's demands was the gradual elimination of all the heterosexual elements in earlier script drafts. These elements included a princess and prince pair (Sylvia and Florizel, who in Kansas are *Mrs.* Gulch's niece Sylvia and her boyfriend Kenny), a farmyard romance between Lizzie Smithers and Hickory (who becomes Oz's Tin Man), an attempt by the Wicked Witch (aka Miss Gulch) to force Princess Sylvia to marry her son Bulbo, and even a flirtation between Dorothy and Hunk (who becomes the Scarecrow in Oz). Granted, traces of the latter pairing might be said to remain in the finished film with Dorothy's pronouncement that she'll "miss [the Scarecrow] most of all" when she leaves Oz. But how refreshing in a classical narrative to have heterosexuality become the repressed thing whose trace returns!

Even with my remarks above, I certainly don't want to suggest that queer readings should just replace straight ones in some hierarchy of interpretation. But I'm constantly being pissed off at the persistence and pervasiveness of heterocentric cultural fantasies that, at best, allow most lesbian, gay, bisexual, and queer understandings of popular culture to exist as appropriative of and subsidiary to taking things straight.

What I find particularly disheartening is that this heterocentrism (and, sometimes, homophobia) often plays itself out in academic and nonacademic arenas as some sort of contest between straight female or feminist approaches and queer approaches to understanding popular culture. While the following cases in point involve straight women, as they come from my recent experiences surrounding the material in this essay, in another context I could just as easily have illustrated the pop culture territoriality of many gays, lesbians, and other queers. First example: I was discussing stardom with a graduate student, when she asked me to name some gay cult stars besides

Judy Garland. As I began to rattle off a list, she stopped me at one name. "Wait!" she said, "Don't take Bette Davis away from us, too!" Before this, I hadn't thought of gay culture—or gay cultural studies—as taking anything away from anyone. Nor had I wanted to believe that anyone apart from white, straight patriarchal types would think that stars and texts were commodities to be owned by one group of cultural readers or another. Was I ever naive: I guess most people out there really are lifting up their leg or squatting to mark their popular culture territory. Regarding the subject of this paper, there was one student at a college in Louisiana who let me know through her friends that she would not be attending my talk because she didn't want to have *The Wizard of Oz* "ruined" for her by all my dyke talk about the film. Something similar happened in class during a discussion of *Thelma and Louise*.

One final example: after reading a draft of this essay, a feminist academic (speaking for herself as well as for a group of editors) was concerned that I "[did] not acknowledge that this is an appropriative reading—[a] move from a women-centered film to a lesbian film." Well, (1) a lesbian film is also "women-centered," just not *straight*-women-centered, and (2) my move from reading *Oz* as straight-women-centered to understanding it as a lesbian narrative was an act of revelation, not appropriation. I don't see the process of queer interpretation as an act of "taking" texts from anyone. Just because straight interpretations have been allowed to flourish publicly doesn't mean they are the most "true" or "real" ones. *The Wizard of Oz* is a straight narrative for those who wish it so. As I suggested earlier, if anything, I would now see straight understandings of *Oz* as "appropriative."

Related to the issue of "appropriation," the editor(s) also "would like [me] to discuss more directly the process of reading an externally 'straight' text as 'queer'." Oh, yes, and while I'm at it, since my "reading will probably outrage many in the straight community," could I "address that anger?" Well, I think I'll address this kind of straight anger by suggesting that any offended straights address the heterocentrism (and, yes, sometimes the homophobia) that is at the heart of much of the incomprehension, defensiveness, or shock they register in the face of gay, lesbian, and queer readings of popular culture. Oh, and they might also mull over the following, from Terry Castle's *The Apparitional Lesbian*:

> When it comes to lesbians...many people have trouble seeing what's in front of them. The lesbian remains a kind of "ghost effect" in the cinema world of modern life: elusive, vaporous, difficult to spot—even when she is there, in plain view, mortal and magnificent at the center of the screen.... What we never expect is precisely this: to find her in the midst of things, as familiar and crucial as an old friend, as solid and sexy as the proverbial right-hand man, as intelligent and human and funny and real as Garbo.[3]

One of the joys of working with popular culture as a scholar-fan is that you never know when or where you'll find material for your current project. It can jump out at you from a scholarly piece you are reading "just to keep up with things," it can pop up during an evening of television watching or magazine scanning, or it can be waiting for you on a shelf in a store. During a vacation in Provincetown, a largely lesbian and gay resort at the tip of Cape Cod, I found myself browsing in a "Last Flight Out" store. I was looking at a display of t-shirts celebrating famous women aviators, when I was struck by a shirt at the center of the display. On the shirt was a drawing of old-fashioned flight goggles, and within one lens were the ruby slippers from *The Wizard of Oz*. The inscription on the shirt read: "Dorothy had the shoes, but she didn't have the vision. Take the controls. Women fly."

In the essay that follows I want to argue that Dorothy really did "have the vision," if you consider that everyone and everything in Oz is a construction of her fantasies. But I understand the frustration with Dorothy expressed by the t-shirt's inscription. Because, at least on the face of it, it seems Dorothy's vision of flying—with all its classic pop Freudian dream symbol references to the expression of sexual desire—is focused on a pair of pretty ruby slippers rather than on the film's more obvious fetishized object of flight, the Wicked Witch's broomstick.[4] I guess for the t-shirt designer, Dorothy unwisely chooses the spectacularized, objectified feminine fetish over its active, phallicized counterpart. But those shoes have their own power, too, even if it is less clearly defined for most of Dorothy's fantasy than is the power of the Wicked Witch's broomstick. And I think the power represented by both the slippers and the broomstick is dyke power.

I know that I can't be the only person who understands the Oz sequences of *The Wizard of Oz* as the fantasy of a teenaged girl on the road to dykedom. But from everything about the film in print or on television, you'd think (as I did once) that Oz can only be either a classic heterosexual rite of passage narrative or a gay campfest.[5] If lesbianism enters into straight and queer readings, it is in relation to understanding Dorothy's connections with straight women protectors (Glinda, Aunt Em) as saving her from predatory, pedophilic dykes (the Wicked Witch, Miss Gulch). Dorothy herself is never, ever anything other than straight. At most, one finds Dorothy/Judy Garland being understood as a "fag hag"-in-the-making, skipping down the road with her rather queer male friends.[6]

But even children understand that the energy-center of Oz has something to do with Dorothy and Miss Gulch/the Wicked Witch—while everyone else, even Toto, is caught up in their passions and desires. Almost every year the telecast of *The Wizard of Oz* inspired my siblings and me to stage an impromptu version of the film using the sidewalk around the block as the

Yellow Brick Road. At each of these performances there were only two essential props: one sister's sparkling red plastic high heels and a suitably messy old broom. My sisters and I would then argue about who would play the two star parts—leaving the loser and our two turned-out-to-be-straight brothers to play Glinda and whatever male roles they fancied.

I have already admitted that at the time, and well into my adult years, I understood some of my pleasures in the film as women-centered but not necessarily as queerly lesbian-centered. Like many gay men, the enjoyment I derived from the woman-woman intensities I found in *The Wizard of Oz* had more to do with what I took to be the spectacle of straight women's antagonism, or with "translating" these women's exciting expressiveness to suit my gay needs. I just didn't consider that the women in the film might be desiring outside of straight or gay contexts. I suppose the inability of most people to consider that Dorothy might be (or be becoming) lesbian can be attributed to that general cultural heterocentrism (to which sexism is sometimes added), affecting straight and queer alike, that considers all fictional narratives and characters heterosexual unless denotatively "proven" homosexual.

This attitude puts the burden of proof on nonheterocentric fans and/or academic commentators, who find that they must develop their skills in exhaustive close reading if they are going to make any serious impression at all. Without the weight of close readings, it is all-too-easy for nonheterocentric and queer comments of any sort to be dismissed outright or to be patronizingly embraced as "fun" or "provocative." Thank goodness that decades of popular culture fandom prepared me to do these "close readings"—otherwise known as watching a film (television show, etc.) over and over, examining and raving about every little detail of the text to anyone who will listen, and then using all these details to get someone else to "see the light" about the film (television show, etc.).

In the context of a heterocentrist (homophobic, sexist) culture, close reading often becomes a social and political strategy: perhaps through overwhelming details and examples we can make what is invisible to so many visible and what is denied possible. Yes, this is usually a reactive position: I often wish I could just go on and on about my queer popular culture enthusiasms without self-consciously presenting the material with a resistant or hostile listener or reader in mind. But I rarely have this luxury. The straightforward pleasures most fans, academics, and scholar-fans get in talking or writing about the cultural objects of their affection are almost always heavily mixed for me.

Certainly people can find themselves in the position of defending their popular culture readings and enthusiasms, but I am often made to feel as if I am also defending my identity or my existence. Or as if I am being chastised for being too visibly gay or queer, and for "recruiting" straight texts as part of some nefarious or misguided plan for a queer takeover of (supposedly) heterosexual popular culture. Or, at the very least, as if I'm about to be caught out for trying to pull a fast one by "reading an externally 'straight' text as 'queer.'" For some reason, queer and nonheterocentrist interpretations of things are never "just another way to see things" for most people, but something akin to delusional experiences, no matter how many examples you provide.

Having said all this, I will soon proceed with another of my Grand Delusions and justify my queer love for *The Wizard of Oz* in glorious detail, including juicy bits of behind-the-scenes production factoids and gossip (aka "archival and field work") that no academic fan piece is complete without. I'll probably have to work even more overtime than usual on this close reading because the tendency toward heterocentrism becomes even more pronounced when people consider characters like Dorothy (and actual persons) who are under eighteen: any signs of homosexual desire and/or lesbian, gay, or queer identity in children and adolescents usually remain unacknowledged or are dismissed as evidence of psychosexual "confusion."[7]

In the case of *The Wizard of Oz* we also have to remember that for millions of straight and queer people this film is a sacred text of their childhood, and, therefore, one that is not to be sullied by discussions of sexuality—particularly queer sexuality. Is it any wonder that the idea of twelve-year-old Dorothy Gale (played by seventeen-year-old Garland) as a developing dyke hasn't exactly been at the center of public or academic readings of *The Wizard of Oz*? But the more I look at the film, the more I am convinced that a lesbian angle is essential to interpreting Dorothy's dream-fantasy. Considering this approach seems particularly vital in the face of the plethora of "compulsorily heterosexual" and gay public, journalistic, and academic readings of Dorothy and the film that I mentioned earlier.[8]

For example, in one of the first attempts to use psychoanalytic theory to explain *Oz*, Harvey Greenberg makes a sharp case for the importance of Dorothy's closeness to her Aunt Em on their matriarchally run farm. Rather than celebrate this intense bond, however, Greenberg sees it as a "pathological dependency upon Em-Mother" that Dorothy needs to get over in order to grow up, which in this context means to move on to a heterosexual relationship with someone like Hunk, the farmhand who becomes the Scarecrow in Dorothy's Oz fantasy.[9] What Greenberg doesn't seem to recall is that during his (psycho)analysis of Dorothy's fantasy he also admits that the men in Kansas and Oz are "presented as weak and damaged in some fashion, while the women are far more capable."[10] So, following Adrienne Rich's line of thought in "Compulsory Heterosexuality and Lesbian Existence," why *should*

Dorothy want to break her connection with Aunt-Mom-women and realign herself with Uncle-Dad-men?[11]

Salman Rushdie's reading of the film is more self-consciously feminist—in at least a couple of ways. He "rehabilitate[s]" the Wicked Witch by suggesting she "represent[s] the more positive of the two images of powerful womanhood on offer" in Oz—the other being that of Glinda, the Good Witch of the North—because in her rage at her sister's death the Wicked Witch shows "a commendable sense of solidarity."[12] Rushdie also understands that Oz doesn't have a traditional male hero and that "[t]he power center of the film is a triangle at whose points are Glinda, Dorothy and the Witch."[13] And at the center of this triangle lies the magic of the ruby slippers. The power of the Wizard "turns out to be an illusion," Rushdie continues, so the film reveals that "[t]he power of men . . . is illusory; the power of women is real."[14] But all this talk about reclaiming "wicked" witches, the absence of a male hero, and the powerful triangular relationship between women in Oz only flirts with the sapphic. Finally the feminist elements in Rushdie's take on *The Wizard of Oz* remain within the rhetoric of straight sisterhood.[15]

A more consistently straight feminist reading of the film is Bonnie Friedman's "Relinquishing Oz: Every Girl's Anti-Adventure Story." What is fascinating to me about this analysis is the number of times it suggests contiguous, and even common, ground between straight feminist and lesbian approaches. While she employs a mother-daughter paradigm to discuss the film, as Greenberg does, Friedman's reading more directly addresses the issue of woman-woman erotics. "The story is a mother-romance," Friedman says near the end of her piece.[16] And while she makes a compelling case for the film as a straight mother-romance—Dorothy returns home to become companion to and replacement for Em-as-mother—Friedman suggests the possibility of queering her own reading when she remarks that in the witch's castle Dorothy is "like a girl who leaves home for erotic love and can't come back."[17] So for all her attempts to connect Aunt Em and the Wicked Witch as harsh straight mother figures, Freidman can't help but see the two women as offering very different options for Dorothy. While the tenor of the article as a whole asks us to read this "erotic love" as heterosexual, it just doesn't make sense when we consider the film context for Friedman's statement, which invites us to see the contrast as that between an "erotic love" that is related to Dorothy's encounters with the witch and a "home" that is connected to fulfilling a heterosexual wife-mother role.

Friedman's article provides a useful starting place for developing a more pointedly lesbian reading of Oz. Indeed, Friedman begins her article by wondering if she "shouldn't have hated that witch so much" as a child because she really represents nonnormative female desire and power.[18]

Rushdie is also high on the Wicked Witch of the West. Describing her as "lean and mean" in her "slimline black" outfit, Rushdie is on the verge of calling the Wicked Witch "butch," particularly in contrast with Glinda, whom he finds "a trilling pain in the neck" in her "frilly pink."[19] A quick look at *The Wizard of Oz*'s production history reveals that the Wicked Witch's butchness was to a great extent consciously developed—if not, perhaps, called "butch" by the film's collaborators (but you never know). In early versions of the script by Noel Langley, the Witch has been married and has a son, Bulbo. This mother-son relationship is developed to suggest the classic overly protective mother and gay son stereotype: "There, my darling boy, mother'll kiss it better! Bulbo musn't cry now; he's going to be King of the Emerald City, and Kings never cry!"[20] Reinforcing this gay rather than lesbian context for the Wicked Witch was the initial casting of Gale Sondergaard in the role. It was producer Mervyn LeRoy's idea to have *Oz*'s Wicked Witch look like the Evil Stepmother in Walt Disney's *Snow White and the Seven Dwarfs* (1937).[21] The result was the Wicked Witch as glamorous diva, with Sondergaard made up "wearing green eye shadow and a witch's hat made out of black sequins."[22]

But as the script changed—particularly with the work of the gay man–straight (I think) woman team of Edgar Alan Woolf and Florence Ryerson—so did the image of the Wicked Witch. It was sometime during the period of making the witch less glamorous that Sondergaard, concerned with maintaining her image, dropped out of the project. Enter Margaret Hamilton and a plainer look for the Wicked Witch. One production still shows Hamilton with her own unaltered features, sans obvious makeup, and with a de-sequined black hat over a near-shoulder-length flip hairdo.[23] But no one was satisfied with this middle-of-the-road approach. It was probably during gay director George Cukor's stint as production consultant on *Oz* that the Wicked Witch got her final look: a sharp nose and jawline, green face and body makeup, a scraggly broom, clawlike fingernails, and a tailored black gown and cape.[24] This is the witch as creature, as alien, as monster, and as what straight, and sometimes gay, culture has often equated with these—butch dyke.[25]

This big bad butch witch, who is loud, aggressive, violent, and wears an obvious "uniform," had been developed by the time of the final script to function on one level as a contrast to good witch Glinda. However, Glinda presents complications for lesbian readings of *The Wizard of Oz*, complications that relate to Rushdie's "trilling pain in the neck" complaint. For Glinda seems to be one of those images of femmes in popular culture that are coded to be able to pass as heterosexually feminine in the eyes of certain beholders.[26] This is the kind of cultural coding/representation I will call "femme-inine" in the rest of this essay. But look at Glinda again: there's more than a touch of camp excess here that finally seems expressive of lesbian femmeness rather than of the straight feminine. And let's not forget that while Glinda may look like a fairy godmother, she *is* a witch, and is therefore connected to the Wicked Witch and to centuries-long Western cultural associations between witchcraft and lesbianism.[27] So what we have set before us in *The Wizard of Oz* is the division of lesbianism into the good femme-inine and the bad butch, or the model potentially "invisible" femme and the threateningly obvious butch.

Into this sexual terrain comes Dorothy, a sixteen-year-old girl just off the farm.[28] Or, rather, it is Dorothy who constructs this sexual fantasyland after being hit on the head by a flying window frame during a cyclone. The distinction between Oz as a "real" place and Oz as a fantasy is one that the film seems to do its best to blur, however. So while almost every commentator and fan has criticized the film's final framing device, which, in contrast to the Frank L. Baum novel, makes Dorothy's adventures in Oz a "dream," *The Wizard of Oz's* movement from sepia cinematography in the short opening Kansas sequences to brilliant Technicolor during the more lengthy Oz sequences, and back to sepia again in the brief Kansas coda, serves to make the Oz material more vivid and vital. In a very important sense, then, the Oz narrative seems as "real" to the film audience as it is to its adolescent hero. Put another way, the affect of the Oz sequences in *The Wizard of Oz* is true to the perceptions of most teenagers. As one teenaged girl quoted in an essay on *Oz* says: "[F]antasy *is* real, necessary, and . . . home is not always the best place to be."[29]

Home down on the farm in Kansas during the latter years of the Great Depression would certainly "not always be the best place to be" for many garden variety heterosexual adolescents, let alone for lesbian, gay, and otherwise queer teens. Among many other sources, Greta Schiller and Robert Rosenberg's documentary film *Before Stonewall* and Allan Bérubé's book *Coming Out under Fire* reveal how the particularly repressive atmosphere of rural and small town America before World War II worked to force most queer women and men either into an imitation of straight life, into closeted homosexual furtiveness, or out into urban centers.[30] The first and third of these responses are important to understanding Dorothy's farm and fantasy lives in *The Wizard of Oz*. Dorothy, told by her Aunt Em to "find yourself a place where you won't get into any trouble," translates this into "[s]omeplace where there isn't any trouble," thereby placing the blame on normative rural culture, not upon herself. Deciding there is such a place, but that "[i]t's not a place you can get to by a boat or a train," Dorothy launches into "Over the Rainbow." While the Land of Oz is most generally this "over the rainbow" place, we discover late in Dorothy's Oz fantasy that at the heart of Oz lies it fabulous capital, Emerald City, through which Dorothy and her friends are conveyed to their beauty makeovers in a carriage pulled by the hue-changing "Horse of a Different Color."[31]

Before letting Dorothy and her gay companions reach what initially appears to be an urban paradise for queers, however, we need to go back to the start of her fantasy, as it is here that the film establishes the terms for its simultaneous expression and disavowal of lesbianism.[32] Two things are central to this expression and disavowal, witches and ruby slippers. To repeat a bit from an earlier section: the distinction Dorothy's fantasy makes between the Witches of the East and West and the Witch of the North turns out to be that between two types of witches—wicked butch and good femme—not the one between fairy godmother and evil witches that the fantasy appears to be presenting with its visual and aural iconography.

The film most strikingly reveals its use of witch = lesbian cultural coding, as well as its butch = bad lesbian associations, during the portion of Dorothy's fantasy that takes place inside the cyclone. At one point, Dorothy's Kansas nemesis, the spinster (as with witch, read "lesbian") Almira Gulch, comes riding by—or, more accurately, is imagined by Dorothy to be riding by—on her bicycle. The original dyke on a bike, Gulch almost immediately transmogrifies into a shrieking witch flying on her broomstick: spinster = witch = evil butch. Less apparent is how the cyclone episode also sets up the femme-inine woman as the positive model. As the published script puts it: "An OLD LADY in a rocking chair sails past. She is knitting busily and rocking, seemingly unaware that she is no longer on her front porch. The old lady waves as she floats out of sight."[33] So where Gulch's spinster harshness is made the clear model for the Wicked Witch of the West's butch badness (reinforced by the fact that the same actress plays both parts), the relationship between Aunt Em and Glinda as images of femme-inine goodness is more obliquely established through the old lady (who looks very much like Aunt Em) floating in front of Dorothy's bewildered eyes, much as Glinda will soon float down toward an equally astonished Dorothy in Munchkinland.

This less obvious, more heavily translated, connection between Aunt Em and Glinda falls squarely within the film's sexuality politics, which, at least on the surface of things, opposes butch and femme, demonizing the former for being loud and obvious (the shrieking laugh, the grotesque green makeup, the black uniform), while humanizing the latter with a name (Glinda) and the ability to pass as a nonwitch. Recall along these lines that Dorothy doesn't initially allow herself to recognize Glinda as a witch. "I've never heard of a beautiful witch before!" she effuses to a smiling Glinda, who replies, "Only bad witches are ugly." But what can we expect of Dorothy's fantasy when the most readily available cultural images are of "ugly," bad butch spinster-witches? Even after she learns there are "beautiful" witches, how-ever, the term "witch" is used almost exclusively in Dorothy's fantasy to pejo-ratively label the "ugly" butch variety.

What's happening here in terms of Dorothy expressing her dyke desires through her Oz fantasy is complicated. Faced with her own nascent les-bianism, as well as the cultural taboos surrounding the open, positive acknowledgment of these desires, Dorothy's fantasy most clearly represents lesbianism in the conventional form of the evil, yet powerful, butch dyke witch. As she sings to the Munchkins by way of explaining her cyclone adventures: "Just then the witch / To satisfy an itch / Went flying on her broomstick thumbing for a hitch." It appears the "itch" the Wicked Witch wants to satisfy is somehow connected to hitching a ride from Dorothy, who has warily watched said witch from her *bedroom* window.[34] And all of this happens deep within the swirling vortex of a cyclone, which becomes in this context a rather outrageously heavy-handed symbolic representation of the classic dangerous butch stereotype: they possess and desire female genitalia (the vortex) while identifying with heterosexual ("phallic") masculinity (how the cyclone *externally* takes the shape of a funnel). Put it all together and you have a destructive force that sweeps through the conservative heart-land of America, separating a young girl from her family. While presented as threatening and predatory, however, the sexualized ("To satisfy an itch") image of the butch dyke in the cyclone is the only one Dorothy constructs here that will carry over into Oz.

Even before we hear the suggestive lines in Dorothy's song, however, the fantasy image of the Wicked Witch has been (homo)sexualized by its pointed visual connection, through that special effects dissolve, to a dyke Dorothy is already acquainted with: the spinster Almira Gulch.[35] There are also moments in the Kansas sequences that suggest everyone knows about Gulch, includ-ing a lot of bizarre talk about Dorothy "biting" Miss Gulch, Dorothy's calling Gulch a "wicked old witch," and Aunt Em's "For twenty-three years I've been dying to tell you [Gulch] what I thought of you . . . and now . . . well—being a Christian woman—I can't say it!"

As you might expect, the image of spinster-turned-butch-witch is one that Dorothy feels culturally compelled to distance herself from—at least in the "public" spaces (that is, on the manifest level) of her fantasy. So Dorothy also constructs the type of woman she can more safely admire, be in awe of, and, perhaps, desire: a glamorous witch whom she, and most of the audience, can take to be the epitome of straight femininity. Dorothy's Glinda is both witch and not conventionally witchlike, both lesbian femme and "straight acting and appearing" (to borrow a phrase from certain gay personal ads). Perhaps the ability to pass is the reason Glinda seems a less powerful and compelling figure than the Wicked Witch of the West in this particular lesbian fantasy. But this was not always the case. One Noel Langley draft script suggested the erotic power of Glinda's femmeness as it has her plant a "magic kiss" on Dorothy which protects her from the wiles of the Wicked Witch.[36] However, while the kiss survives in the film, it has lost its magic power.

Given the tangled and conflicted impulses toward lesbianism expressed in Dorothy's fantasy, it comes as no surprise that she both suggests and denies her connection to witches on first meeting Glinda. When a puzzled Glinda asks the tomboyish yet gingham-dressed Dorothy if she "is a good witch—or a bad witch" (a femme or a butch) Dorothy denies being any kind of witch, because, as culture has told her, all witches are old and ugly. It is here Dorothy's fantasy reveals that Glinda is also a witch, thereby establishing a model through which she can begin to explore and come to terms with her own lesbian desires under cover of witchy femme-ininity. But while Glinda provides her with a safe, because straight appearing, outlet for lesbian expressiveness, Dorothy invests the Wicked Witches of the East and West with the most power and fascination of anyone in her fantasy.

When she first meets the Witch of the West in Oz, Dorothy tries to convince her that the death of her sister, the tyrannical ruler of the Munchkins, was "an accident."[37] While there are no "accidents" in fantasies, it is clear that Dorothy has the farmhouse, and all it represents culturally, really kill the butch Wicked Witch of the East. She doesn't mean to kill (or want to kill) the witch—something that is reinforced in the later "accidental" death of the Wicked Witch of the West by water. So even while she has the Munchkins and Glinda praise her as a "national heroine" by singing "Ding Dong, the Witch is Dead," Dorothy distances herself from the killing of the butch witch by picturing herself as being trapped within that Kansas farmhouse (and its normative ideology) at the time of the death. But it would appear that the cultural pressure on Dorothy is such that she still feels she must contrive to set herself up in opposition to butch witches. Therefore the Wicked Witch of the West remains unconvinced by Dorothy's protestations of innocence: "Well, my little pretty, I can cause accidents, too!"

However, Dorothy establishes her connection to witches and with witchcraft—including the butch variety—by dreaming up what has become, along with *Citizen Kane*'s sled Rosebud, the most fabulous fetish item in film history: the ruby slippers.[38] There is probably no need to rehearse at any length what the sequined blood-red slippers "stand for": teenaged Dorothy's physical entrance into adulthood (the start of menses), as well as her subsequent sexual explorations. It is their particular place within Dorothy's fantasy narrative that gives them their dyke associations. As Salman Rushdie puts it, "Glinda and the Wicked Witch clash most fiercely over the ruby slippers"—and, as Dorothy dreams it, over her body once it wears the coveted slippers.[39] This symbolic dyke fantasy is elaborated upon in the sequence

Dorothy (Judy Garland) and her safe, femme role model Glinda, the Good Witch of the North (Billie Burke), in Munchkinland.

where the witch turns over a large hour glass with blood red sand to mark the period (in both senses of the word) Dorothy has before she must relinquish her ruby slippers to the witch. "Surrender, Dorothy," indeed!

Given the "bad butch—good femme" dynamics of the Oz fantasy, however, the ruby slippers come to indicate Dorothy's sexualized genitalia even while disavowing any "obvious" lesbian desire: the butch Wicked Witch can't even touch the femme-inine shoes while they are on Dorothy's feet without getting a shock. However, when they are first placed upon her feet, the shots of the ruby slippers are clearly presented within the narrative as a spectacular display for the Wicked Witch's benefit. While Glinda says to the Wicked Witch, "There they are, and there they'll stay," we are offered a close-up of the slippers being modeled by Dorothy against the backdrop of Glinda's pink gossamer gown: the femme displaying herself for the butch? Or, perhaps, the tomboy-in-gingham trying femmeness on for size in front of a potential mentor and a dangerous, yet exciting, butch spectator.

The initial appearance and functions of the ruby slippers in Dorothy's fantasy also work to connect all the major female figures in Oz under the sign of witchcraft. What is particularly fascinating about the ruby slippers in this respect is how they manage to mix together the femme and the butch, suggesting that while there are butch and femme styles and attitudes, they need not work in tension with each other, nor are they necessarily the only ways to be expressive as a dyke. Dorothy herself is the perfect person to wear these slippers, as, perhaps until her Emerald beauty treatment, she seems to combine butch and femme qualities as a young girl on the (yellow brick) road to discovering what type of "witch" she is. Ultimately, the uses of the ruby slippers in Dorothy's fantasy suggest that dyke magic resides neither with butchness or femmeness exclusively, but within all sorts of lesbianism.

The tyrannical Wicked Witch of the East first wears the powerful, supposedly incongruous, femmy ruby slippers. But femme Glinda can use her magic to whisk the glitzy shoes off the dead butch witch's feet and onto Dorothy's (despite a noticeable size difference). Oddly enough, however, the formidable butch Wicked Witch of the West seems powerless to remove these slippers, although otherwise her magic seems far more potent than Glinda's. To confuse the butch-femme power issue even more, Salman Rushdie points out that Glinda's knowledge about the shoes in these early scenes is "enigmatic, even contradictory," as she initially says she is ignorant about the shoes' power, even while warning Dorothy to "never let those ruby slippers off your feet for a moment, or you will be at the mercy of the Wicked Witch of the West."[40] Good advice, because, as we all know, they never respect you after they have gotten hold of your ruby slippers!

Glinda's advice about the shoes is just what you'd expect Dorothy to have the "straight acting and appearing" femme tell her at this stage of her fantasy. At this point, it is impossible for Dorothy's Glinda to admit to full and clear knowledge of the magic power contained in a pair of femme slippers owned by some butch witch—and desired by her even more butch sister. Glinda is only allowed to impart this formerly unspeakable knowledge as/at the climax of Dorothy's dyke rite of passage, which includes a progression through the vaginal-shaped hallways of Castle Oz, which are colored "Wicked Witch green," as is everything else in the Emerald City. So even while Dorothy's fantasy narrative contrives to separate the Wicked Witch from the Emerald City—as it also separates the Wicked Witch and Glinda—imagery like the ruby slippers and greenness in this same fantasy reveal that the agents of butch "evil" and femme(-inine) "good" are really related after all. However, within the terms of the manifest fantasy narrative, it is only after Dorothy once again "accidentally" dispatches the "threat" of butchness with that famous badly aimed bucket of water, as well as suffers the failure of patriarchy to help her (after she brings the Wizard of Oz the burnt remnants of the butch witch's "phallic" broom), that she lets femme Glinda come forward to declare that she does know something about the special powers of the butch's femme ruby slippers after all.

Actually, what Glinda says is that Dorothy has always had the "power" within her to activate the ruby slippers, but that she had to "learn it for [her]self." And what does Dorothy learn that allows her to use the power of the fetishized ruby slippers?: "[I]t's that if I ever go looking for my heart's desire again, I won't look any further than my own backyard." Dorothy's lesson returns us, in part, to Greenberg's point about the crucial role Aunt Em plays in her life. If we divest his reading of its pathologizing and heterocentrism, Greenberg makes a compelling case for Aunt Em as orphaned Dorothy's "heart's desire."[41] In many ways Aunt Em is the object of Dorothy's fantasy, for it is her desire to return to Aunt Em in particular, rather than to her life in Kansas in general, that is emphasized time and again in the script. Commenting on early scripts in a lengthy memo to Noel Langley (dated April 30, 1938), Oz's production assistant Arthur Freed advises the scenarist to concentrate more on what he feels is the film's emotional center:

> [I]t is our problem to set up the story of Dorothy, who finds herself with a heart full of love, eager to give it, but through circumstances and personalities, can apparently find none in return.... She finds escape in her dream of Oz. There she is motivated by her generosity to help everyone first before her little orphan heart cries out for what she wants most of all (the love of Aunt Em).... We must remember at all times that Dorothy is only motivated by one object in Oz; that is how to get back home to her Aunt Em, and every situation should be related to this.[42]

Considering all this, it's no wonder that the last face Dorothy sees in Oz is Glinda's (the good witch-mother), and that the first face Dorothy sees at the end of her fantasy of dyke discovery is that of Aunt Em, her mother substitute. But while there is a strong mother-daughter aspect to the lesbian erotics represented in Dorothy's fantasy in "a land that [she] heard of once in a lullaby," it has its limits as *the* explanation of this fantasy's dyke dimensions. Recall that it is Aunt Em who tells Dorothy to find a place where she won't "get into trouble." So a temporary separation from Aunt Em seems as important to Dorothy's development at this point as maintaining the bond with her.[43] Also recall that it is Glinda (Oz's Aunt Em figure) who puts it into Dorothy's head that her goal should be to go back home. But consider this: if Dorothy was so hot to immediately go home to Aunt Em, why does her fantasy repress the fact that she can use the power of the ruby slippers to transport herself back to Aunt Em from the start? Clearly Dorothy wants to be constantly reminded of the importance of her bond with Aunt Em, but she also wants to experience the thrills her fantasy will concoct for her with the Wicked Witch of the West.

Far from being a case of lesbianism as simply a regressive "return to mother," then, Dorothy's fantasy represents the complicated process by which she returns home to renew maternal bonds, but only after she has matured through dealing with the dangers and pleasures of becoming lesbian, which involve both the blatant butchness represented by the Wicked Witch of the West and the femme allure of Glinda and the ruby slippers. Clearly, Dorothy's fantasy is as much structured around a series of exciting flights from and encounters with the shoe-coveting Wicked Witch as it is developed around the return to Aunt Em. As it turns out, these are really two sides of the same psychosexual narrative coin.

The sequence that most strikingly illustrates all this is the one in which Dorothy is imprisoned in the Wicked Witch's castle with her dog, Toto. When the witch threatens to drown Toto, Dorothy is ready to exchange the ruby slippers to save his life. It is here her fantasy finally contrives a compelling excuse for her to surrender the ruby slippers (with their accumulated fetishistic charge) to the butch witch even though "the Good Witch of the North told [her] not to." But Dorothy still shrinks from any direct physical contact. For after offering to give up her ruby slippers, Dorothy has the shoes give the Wicked Witch a shock as she reaches out to grasp them. "I'm sorry. I didn't do it," Dorothy says at this point, thereby adding one more item to the long list of painful "accidents" her fantasy has developed to deal with her ambivalence about butchness (or "obvious" lesbianism). By having her death be the only way for the Wicked Witch to possess the ruby slippers, Dorothy's fantasy also stages a moment that echoes one tragic way many teenagers deal with the pressures and confusions of becoming queer.

After the Wicked Witch leaves to consider how to kill Dorothy, as "these things must be done delicately," a weeping Dorothy approaches a giant crystal ball in which the image of her aunt appears. But just as Dorothy says "I'm trying to get home to you, Auntie Em!" her aunt's face begins to fade and is replaced by that of the Wicked Witch, who mockingly imitates Dorothy's words: "Auntie Em, Auntie Em! Come back! I'll give you Auntie Em, my pretty!" In a way, the witch *does* "give her" Auntie Em, because the crystal reveals that in some way the witch and Auntie Em are related in Dorothy's mind. At one point in the film's history, this sequence was much longer. Scripts indicate that this longer version contains many elements that reinforce the fantasy connections between the Wicked Witch and Aunt Em, as well as more clearly establish the relationship between the witch and the fulfillment of Dorothy's desire to find a place "where the dreams that you dare to dream really do come true."

In this extended version, after the witch's mocking imitation of Dorothy's cries to Aunt Em, the sequence continues with the witch forcing Dorothy to

"All in good time, my little pretty": Dorothy faces the predatory, butch Wicked Witch of the West (Margaret Hamilton), who covets her ruby slippers.

perform Kansas-like domestic chores. As she scrubs and mops, Dorothy finds herself singing "Over the Rainbow" again, even as the witch is concocting a "Spell for Rainbows" in her cauldron: "All the brilliant colors found in the prism are reflected upward into [the witch's] face from the bubbling mass." From the liquid in the cauldron, the witch constructs "The Rainbow Bridge," which the script describes as "a beautiful sight," even though it is to be the means of Dorothy's death. It is the power of the ruby slippers, which "seem to come to life with an iridescent glow," that Dorothy has save her by allowing her literally to go "over the rainbow" made by the witch and off to continue her journey of sexual awareness.

Straight, heterocentric, and homophobic readings (not always the same things) might understand what is happening in the long or short version of this sequence as either the expression of a fear of lesbianism destroying heterosexual-homosocial women's bonds, or as the expression of "how intimately bound together is the Good Mother and the Bad" in the mind of a heterosexual teenage girl.[44] Within the reading I am proposing, however, this sequence becomes the central paradigm for the film's incoherent attitudes about lesbianism. For one thing, the attraction-repulsion aspects of Dorothy's fantasy regarding butch witches are fully on display here, particularly in the longer version of the sequence. The butch witch is both the potential source of fulfilled desires as well as the potential source of physical danger. In addition, the merging and confusion of Aunt Em and the Wicked Witch in the crystal ball suggests that the developing lesbianism Dorothy's fantasy struggles to express requires that she face up to, and work through, her culturally fostered fears, embodied by the figure of the butch dyke, so she can return to her Aunt Em as a more sexually mature young woman—or, to be more precise, a more sexually mature young lesbian. Will Dorothy become a butch, a femme, or remain "in-between" after she wakes up from her fantasy? I think the film leaves this open to some degree, though her strong identification with the ruby slippers and her glamorizing beauty treatment near the end of the film make me think Dorothy enjoys being a femme.

On the other hand, the question of what kind of witch/dyke Dorothy will become might seem unresolved when you consider that her return to Kansas to look "for her heart's desire . . . in [her] own backyard" will actually involve two yards: Aunt Em's and Almira Gulch's. For if her fantasy has revealed that part of Dorothy's lesbian desires have to do with her relationship with her Aunt Em, this same fantasy has also revealed that other aspects of these desires have something to do with Miss Gulch. It is easy to forget that what initiates both the Kansas and Oz narratives is Dorothy's antagonistic relationship with Gulch, or Gulch-as-Wicked Witch. This has all begun, it seems, because Dorothy's relaxed vigilance has allowed Toto to sneak into Miss Gulch's yard more than once to chase her cat. Pleading that "Toto didn't mean to" do what he did and that "[h]e didn't know he was doing anything wrong," Dorothy sets up the first of many "accident" scenarios involving herself (or in this case her canine sidekick) and butches. Just as when she allows the Wicked Witch to take (or try to take) the ruby slippers in order to save Toto, Dorothy's dealings with Miss Gulch over Toto make it appear that Dorothy can only allow herself to satisfy her curiosity about butch dykes (whether spinster or witch) in indirect, and contentious, ways. So time and again in Kansas and in Oz, Dorothy becomes involved in "accidents" that she allows to happen, whether it's letting Toto get into Gulch's garden, "killing" the Wicked Witch's sister, or having the slippers shock the witch. Bonnie Friedman points out that when one of the farmhands suggests that Dorothy avoid trouble with Miss Gulch by finding an alternate route home, Dorothy replies, "You just don't listen," and lets the subject drop.[45] Is it too

In Kansas, Dorothy and Toto are caught between femme Aunt Em (Clara Blandick) and butch Miss Gulch, as Uncle Henry (Charley Grapewin) looks on helplessly.

much to imagine that Dorothy is forced to stage these encounters as antagonistic because of internalized homophobic cultural interdictions warning little girls to stay away from eccentric spinsters and other "witches"?

So while Oz initially appears to be the place where "the dreams that you dare to dream really do come true," my understanding of the much-maligned "no place like home" finale is that Dorothy comes to understand by the end of her fantasy that her daring dyke dreams will really only "come true" when she returns to those two yards in Kansas and works out her feelings toward both Aunt Em and Miss Gulch. Dorothy's last two speeches already indicate how things are sorting themselves out for her, for while she exclaims "And...oh, Auntie Em! There's no place like home!" to conclude the film, her penultimate lines reveal what Rushdie sees as signs of "revolt" after Aunt Em gently tries to dismiss Dorothy's attempt to explain about Oz:[46]

> Aunt Em: Oh, we dream lots of silly things when we...
> Dorothy: No, Aunt Em, this was a real truly live place. And I remember
> that some of it wasn't very nice—but most of it was beautiful!

For a moment before she turns back to praise the virtues of home and Aunt Em, Dorothy rallies to validate her experiences in Oz. Although she doesn't consciously realize it, Dorothy's words here pay tribute to that other key figure in her journey to dykedom, the Wicked Witch of the West, who, with her final breath, half-surprised and half-impressed, exclaims, "Who would have thought that a good little girl like you could destroy my beautiful wickedness!" Dorothy's words, like the witch's, reveal that, to the end, *The Wizard of Oz* remains ambivalent and incoherent about its relationship to lesbianism. It is something that has been, at once, a "not very nice" and a "beautiful" part of Dorothy's fantasy about Oz.

Actually, it was partly through the witch's declaration of her "beautiful wickedness" that I was led to my queer appreciation of the film's lesbian narrative. I'm with Derek Jarman who said that from childhood he "often thought" about the Wicked Witch of the West, and "after [his] initial fright, grew to love her."[47] The Manchester, England, group Homocult ("Perverters of Culture") has presented this gay and lesbian rewriting of the Wicked Witch more boldly by using a publicity still picturing Dorothy in the farmyard, one finger pointing upward, under which they have written "GOOD WAS WRONG, EVIL OUR FRIEND ALL ALONG."[48] My growing affection for the Wicked Witch became one of the keys to understanding that a great deal of my enjoyment of *The Wizard of Oz* is dyke based. Actually, I've noticed that many of the pleasures I take in popular culture representations of strong women, in women icons, and in women-centered narratives have taken a decidedly dyke turn. My cross-gender identificatory investments in reading certain women characters, stars, and narratives as being femininely straight, are now often supplemented or supplanted by the queer-bonding investments and pleasures I have in understanding these women and texts as lesbian. Sometimes I find I'm combining a lesbian angle on popular culture with other approaches, or I discover that certain pleasures and investments I have in lesbian popular culture personalities, texts, and images become the catalyst for questioning conventional gender and sexuality categories: should I call these pleasures and investments "queer," "bisexual," or "unconventionally gay"?

For example, *Oz*'s Wicked Witch encouraged me to reevaluate my enthusiasms for her animated sisters: the Evil Queen (*Snow White and the Seven Dwarfs*), Cruella de Vil (*101 Dalmatians*), and Ursula (*The Little Mermaid*).[49] All of these characters now seem to be wonderful combinations of straight diva, drag queen, and formidable dyke. Another example: I have come to realize that I am one of those "femme" gays who find certain butch and androgynous dykes and dyke icons (real and fictional, actual and performative) very hot: k.d. lang, Katharine Hepburn as "Sylvester" Scarlett, model Jenny Shimuzu, Annie Lennox, Vanessa Redgrave as Vita Sackville-West,

Grace Jones, the Patricia Charbonneau character in *Desert Hearts*, Margarethe Cammermeyer, Glenn Close as Cammermeyer, and a host of butches I've spotted on the streets, at meetings, and in bars. So—to return to *Oz*—while I haven't fully abandoned all of my previous pleasures and investments in popular culture, the sissy lion, the "hunky" Tin Man, (straight) Judy Garland–as–gay icon, and the kitschy decor in Munchkinland now stand alongside, and sometimes mingle with, the butch witches, "spinster" Almira Gulch, femme Glinda, and "baby dyke" Dorothy in my understanding of and enjoyment in *The Wizard of Oz*.

Not surprisingly, it was Dorothy, or, more accurately, a female impersonator performing Judy Garland singing "Over the Rainbow" for a largely lesbian audience, who became another impetus for my re-viewing *Oz*. Before this drag show I would have been among those who would have categorized *Oz*, Garland, and "Over the Rainbow" as "gay things." Perhaps the overwhelmingly gay public claims on Garland, the song, and the film have kept lesbian appreciations in the shade. Or maybe publicly expressing enthusiasms like these has been considered as not being distinctly "dyke" enough in popular culture fandom within lesbian culture at large, although Michael Bronski has pointed out that lesbian folk singer Holly Near was the one to dub "Over the Rainbow" the "gay national anthem."[50] Whatever the case, that night in a Bethlehem, Pennsylvania, club left no doubt in my mind that Judy, "Over the Rainbow," and *Oz* could be "lesbian things," too.[51] Jimmy James–as–Judy was about to leave the stage without singing "Over the Rainbow" when lesbian audience members chanted for him to sing it. Relenting, s/he sat down and proceeded to sing the song to a butch woman who had rushed up to the stage to kiss "Judy" and tell her that she loved her. By the end of the number it was clear the gay drag performer–as–diva and the crowd had found a common ground in *Oz's* most famous song, turning it from the "Gay National Anthem" into something like a "Queer National Anthem." One big reason I've written all this lesbian stuff about *The Wizard of Oz*, I guess, is to recapture some of the feelings of queer connectedness that I experienced sitting in Diamondz while a drag queen and his dyke fans came together for a while as "Friends of Dorothy."

NOTES

1. *The Wizard of Oz* (1939, MGM: Victor Fleming).
2. John Fricke, Jay Scarfone, and William Stillman, *The Wizard of Oz: The 50th Anniversary Pictorial History* (New York: Warner Books, 1989), 26–30, 39–44.
3. Terry Castle, *The Apparitional Lesbian: Female Homosexuality and Modern Culture* (New York: Columbia University Press, 1993), 2–3.
4. Among the many examples of texts that allude to or use the idea of flying as

(dream-fantasy) coding for women's non-normative, "excessive" sexual desires, whether straight or queer, are Kate Millet's *Flying*, Erica Jong's *Fear of Flying*, and Dorothy Arzner's *Christopher Strong*. So witches don't ride those broomsticks just to get from one place to another!

5. Wayne M. Bryant, in *Bisexual Characters in Film: From Anaïs to Zee* (New York and London: Harrington, 1972), suggests there are bisexual elements in the film. When Dorothy can't decide which branch of the Yellow Brick Road to take, as they look the same, the Scarecrow finally says "Of course, people do go both ways." (1) Given the centrality of the Scarecrow in attempts to heterosexualize the narrative, one might queer the narrative by understanding the Scarecrow as (re)presenting a bisexual option in Dorothy's fantasy. Garland's rumored bisexuality might further foreground this reading for some viewers. As I see it, Dorothy finally does select one path—one that leads her into confrontations with the dyke Wicked Witch.

   Among the lengthier straight and queer critical pieces on the film are Salman Rushdie, *The Wizard of Oz* (London: BFI Publishing, 1992); John Fricke, Jay Scarfone, and William Stillman, *The Wizard of Oz: The 50th Anniversary Pictorial History* (New York: Warner Books, 1989); Aljean Harmetz, *The Making of The Wizard of Oz*, new. ed. (New York: Delta/Dell, 1989); Danny Peary, "The Wizard of Oz," in *Cult Movies* (New York: Dell, 1981), 390–93; Janet Juhnke, "A Kansan's View," in *The Classic American Novel and the Movies*, ed. Gerald Peary and Roger Shatzkin (New York: Frederick Ungar, 1977), 165–75; Harvey Greenberg, "*The Wizard of Oz*: Little Girl Lost—And Found," in *The Movies on Your Mind* (New York: Saturday Review Press/E.P. Dutton, 1979), 13–32; Michael Bracewell, "The Never-Ending Story," *Times Magazine* (London), January 29, 1994, 18–19; Bonnie Friedman, "Relinquishing Oz: Every Girl's Anti-Adventure Story," *Michigan Quarterly Review* 35:1 (Winter 1996): 9–28; Richard Smith, "Daring to Dream," *Gay Times* 211 (April 1996): 60–61; Daniel Dervin, "Oz; or, Over the Rainbow and Under the Twister: the Primal Scene as Movie; the Movie as Primal Scene," in *Through a Freudian Lens Deeply: A Psychoanalysis of Cinema* (Hilldale, N.J., and London: Analytic Press, 1985), 56–65; Linda Rohrer Paige, "Wearing the Red Shoes: Dorothy and the Power of the Female Imagination in *The Wizard of Oz*," *Journal of Popular Film and Television* 23:4 (Winter 1996): 146–53; Inez Hedges, *Breaking the Frame: Film and the Experience of Limits* (Bloomington and Indianapolis: Indiana University Press, 1991), 109–21; and Paul Nathanson, *Over the Rainbow: The Wizard of Oz as Secular Myth in America* (Albany: State University Press of New York, 1991). Of course there are hundreds (thousands?) of shorter reviews of and commentaries on the film, dating back to the announcement of its production in 1938.

6. The introduction to the anthology *Out in Culture: Gay, Lesbian and Queer Essays on Popular Culture*, which I coedited with Corey K. Creekmur (Durham, N.C.: Duke University Press, 1995), includes a brief discussion of certain gay camp readings of the film. In "Fasten Your Seat Belts: The Ten Gayest Straight Movies—Ever," *Genre* 28 (May 1995): 71, Steve Greenberg quotes college instructor Daniel Mangin: "Gays seem to identify with this [film] early in their

lives. Some gays say they've always identified with Dorothy's pals because their body language and manner of speaking seem so gay."

To this and other remarks by gay journalists and scholars, can be added understandings of the film that center around its production history, particularly around the contributions of gay men like production advisor George Cukor and coscenarist Edgar Allan Woolf, who MGM story editor Sam Marx remembered as "a wild, red-headed homosexual" who contributed "whatever levity and foolishness there was in *The Wizard of Oz*" (Harmetz, *The Making of*, 46).

7. For a more detailed analysis of the representation of homosexuality and adolescence in film and popular culture, see Ben Gove, "Framing Gay Youth," *Screen* 37:2 (Summer 1996), 174–92.

8. The phrase "compulsorily heterosexual" is, of course, adapted from Adrienne Rich's landmark essay "Compulsory Heterosexuality and Lesbian Existence," which has been reprinted many times since its initial appearance in *Signs: Journal of Women in Culture and Society* 5, 4 (1980): 631–60. Most recently, this essay has appeared, with an "Afterword" from 1986, in *The Lesbian and Gay Studies Reader*, ed. Henry Abelove, Michele Aina Barale, and David M. Halperin (New York and London: Routledge, 1993), 227–54.

While placed within heterosexualizing contexts, two pieces on *The Wizard of Oz* contain comments that, taken together, might be read as alluding to certain lesbian understandings of Dorothy. The first is by Salman Rushdie to the effect that "The scrubbed, ever so slightly lumpy *unsexiness* of Garland's playing is what makes the movie work" (*Wizard*, 27). At the other extreme, a review in *Times Magazine* (London) states, "One doubts this film would have resonated so much or aged so well if any actress other than Judy Garland had played Dorothy.... [That] a corseted, nubile 17-year-old was asked to play a 12-year-old adds a muted but persistent undertone of sexuality to an already disturbing film" (June 8, 1994): 41 (no author, BFI microjacket cuttings file). Not surprisingly, when taken together these remarks echo conventional notions of lesbianism as a state of being either nonsexual or oversexed.

9. Ibid., 25, 30.

10. Greenberg, 22. Greenberg's understanding of the men in the film as lacking in some way is echoed by many commentators. For example, Bonnie Friedman finds that, "The men of Oz are all missing one key organ.... One suspects that, in Dorothy's mind, the men on Aunt Em's farm all lack an organ, too" ("Relinquishing Oz: Every Girl's Anti-Adventure Story," *Michigan Quarterly Review* 35:1 [Winter 1996]: 25–26). It would seem to be a very short step from comments like these to understanding Dorothy as a dyke-in-the-making. But it seems that this one small step is, indeed, a giant leap for most people to make.

11. Rich, "Compulsory Heterosexuality."

12. Rushdie, 43.

13. Ibid., 42.

14. Ibid.

15. In a short story appended to his critical study of *Oz*, entitled "The Auction of the Ruby Slippers" (58–65), Rushdie places the slippers in a heterosexual context

as the male narrator recalls making love to his cousin Gail, who liked to yell "Home boy! Home baby, you've come home" the moment he penetrated her (61). After they split up, the narrator wants to buy the ruby slippers for Gail, in the hope that she will remember their sexual activities and come back "home" to him. While heterosexualized, the ruby slippers are still to a great extent associated with women's sexual desires in this story. The story does suggest that lesbianism and gayness are also associated with the slippers as it describes how one female "memorabilia junkie" and her (non-sex-identified) lover are electrocuted when they place their lips to the glass box in which the slippers are being displayed at an auction, thereby setting off an alarm system which "pumps a hundred thousand volts of electricity into the silicon-implanted lips of the glass kisser" (shades of the Wicked Witch of the West). "[W]e wonder... at the mysteries of love," the narrator goes on to comment, "whilst reaching once again for our perfumed handkerchiefs" (58–59).

16. Bonnie Friedman, "Relinquishing Oz: Every Girl's Anti-Adventure Story," *Michigan Quarterly Review* 35:1 (Winter 1996): 27.

17. Ibid., 10.

18. Ibid., 9.

19. Rushdie, 42.

20. Harmetz, 43–44.

21. Fricke, Scarfone, and Stillman, 24.

22. Harmetz, 122.

23. Fricke, Scarfone, and Stillman, 62.

24. Ibid., 72–76.

25. For an excellent discussion of cultural associations between lesbianism and the monstrous, see Rhona J. Berenstein, "'I'm not the sort of person men marry': Monsters, Queers, and Hitchcock's *Rebecca*," *CineAction!* 29 (August 1992), 82–96; rpt. in Creekmur and Doty, *Out in Culture*, 239–61.

26. Both Danae Clark's "Commodity Lesbianism," *Camera Obscura* 25/26 (January/May 1991): 181–201; rpt. in Abelove, Barale, and Halperin, *The Lesbian and Gay Studies Reader*, 186–201, and Creekmur and Doty, *Out in Culture*, 484–500, and Christine Holmlund's "When Is a Lesbian Not a Lesbian?: The Lesbian Continuum and the Mainstream Femme Film," *Camera Obscura* 25/26 (January/May 1991): 145–78, discuss the complexities and complications of popular culture coding that seeks to simultaneously represent the straight feminine and the lesbian femme. I use the term "femme-ininity" in this essay to express this coding and decoding dilemma. When I use the term "femme," I am indicating specifically lesbian and gay contexts and readings.

27. Among the many books and articles that discuss the connections between lesbianism and witchcraft are Vern L. Bullough, "Heresy, Witchcraft, and Sexuality," in *Sexual Practices and the Medieval Church*, ed. Vern L. Bullough and James Brundage (Buffalo, N.Y.: Prometheus Books, 1982): 206–17; Judy Grahn, *Another Mother Tongue*, rev. ed. (Boston: Beacon Press, 1990): 80–82, 93–98, 218, 242–43; Arthur Evans, *Witchcraft and the Gay Counterculture* (Boston: Fag Rag Books, 1978); Anne Llewellyn Barstow, *Witchcraze: A New History of the Euro-*

pean Witch Hunts (London and New York: Pandora, 1995): 72, 139–41, 216–17. I'll let two popular culture examples stand in for many, many others that use the lesbian = witch paradigm. Mrs. Worthington's Daughters, an English theatre company, presented "Any Marks Or Deviations," by Charles Hughes-D'Aeth, on a national tour between May and June 1997. The play was advertised as "[a] chilingly witty ghost story harking back to a time when the love of two women could only mean the dealings of witchcraft." In *The Haunting* (1963, MGM: Robert Wise) a doctor calls the two central female characters (one an out lesbian, one a closet case) "witches."

28. For most of her fantasy, Dorothy is positioned—or, rather, positions herself—in between the butch and the femme figures. This butch, femme, and femmy butch (or butchy femme) triad is repeated in a number of popular culture texts, such as the Nancy Drew mystery series, which features butch dark-haired cousin George, femme-inine blonde cousin Bess, and in-between redhead Nancy. The major women characters in the film *All About Eve* (1950, 20th-Century-Fox: Joseph L. Mankiewicz) also fall into these roles: blonde Karen (femme); ambitious, short-haired Eve (butch), and femmy butch/butchy femme Margo. Not surprisingly, the "star" of these kinds of texts always seems to be the character positioned between butch and femme. In *The Wizard of Oz* it seems to me as though Dorothy is moving toward becoming a femme, if her Emerald City beauty makeover is any indication.

29. Janet Juhnke, "A Kansan's View," in *The Classic American Novel and the Movies*, ed. Gerald Peary and Roger Shatzkin (New York: Frederick Ungar, 1977), 175; quoted in Peary, *Cult Films*, 392. In an August 28, 1939, review in the *Minneapolis Star-Journal* by nine-year-old Mary Diane Seibel, she says that "Everybody but Dorothy and Toto thought it was a dream. I don't know what to think" (quoted in Fricke, Scarfone, Stillman, *50th Anniversary*, 186).

30. *Before Stonewall* (1984: Greta Schiller and Robert Rosenberg); Allan Bérubé, *Coming Out under Fire: The History of Gay Men and Women in World War II* (New York: Plume, 1990).

31. Rushdie's description of Emerald City is worth repeating as it suggests something of the queerness of the place: "[M]embers of the citizenry are dressed like Grand Hotel bellhops and glitzy nuns, and they say, or rather sing, things, like 'Jolly good fun!'" (*Wizard*, 51). It is also worth remembering that Emerald City is where Dorothy and her male companions receive their beauty makeovers, which leave the Cowardly Lion looking like Dorothy with a curly coiffeur and a bow in his hair. And while we're pointing out the signs that mark Emerald City as queer, let's not forget "green" as in "green carnation," a favorite gay-coded accessory of urban dandies from the end of the nineteenth century into the early decades of the twentieth. For more on the green carnation in gay culture, see Neil Bartlett, *Who Was That Man?: A Present for Mr. Oscar Wilde* (London: Serpent's Tail, 1988), 39–59.

32. While certainly prominent in Dorothy's fantasy, the Scarecrow, the Tin Man, and the Cowardly Lion function as figures Dorothy has "go along for the ride" with her. She seems to have translated the three ostensibly straight farmhands who

work for her aunt and uncle into gay companions mostly to help make her fantasy more queer friendly. The support of these gay men (as well as femme Glinda) allow Dorothy to persist on the path to lesbianism even in the face of the "interruptions" she has the Wicked Witch devise for her. Considering what appears to be Dorothy's problems with more "obvious" signs and forms of lesbianism, it makes sense she would have gay men and femme-inine women represent benevolent queerness in her fantasy.

33. Noel Lagley, Florence Ryerson, and Edgar Allan Woolf, *The Wizard of Oz* (Monterey Park, Ca.: O.S.P. Publishing, 1994): 12. All further quoted references to dialogue and action in this essay are taken from this version of the script, which is a transcription of the final release version of the film. This script also contains appendices of material cut from the final release version of the film.

34. There is actually some confusion about just which Wicked Witch is the one who flies past Dorothy's window. Dorothy and the Munchkins' duet here suggests it is the Wicked Witch of the East as "The house began to pitch / The kitchen took a slitch / It landed on the Wicked Witch in the middle of a ditch." However, the Witch who flies past Dorothy in the cyclone is played by Margaret Hamilton, who is the Wicked Witch of the West in the rest of the film. Perhaps the two witches are meant to be twin sisters, or the confusion of the two is meant to suggest that Dorothy still conventionally sees all witches (particularly of the butch variety) as being alike. In any case, the points made later in this section about sexualizing the butch witch as well as those addressing the transformation of spinster Gulch into butch Wicked Witch remain valid no matter which Wicked Witch is looking to "satisfy [her] itch" with Dorothy. See also note 35.

35. The associative connection between Miss Gulch's last name and "West"—as in Western locales like "Dead Man's Gulch"—adds one more point to the case for Gulch turning into the Wicked Witch of the West here, and not into the one from the East. See also note 34.

36. Harmetz, 40.

37. Rushdie offers "[t]he heretical thought" that "maybe the Witch of the East *wasn't so bad as all that*—she certainly kept the streets clean, the houses painted and in good repair . . . she [also] seems to have ruled without the aid of soldiers, policemen or other regiments of repression. Why, then, is she so hated?" (*Wizard*, 42). So from all that we can gather from Dorothy's fantasy, this particular butch witch may not have been such a monster after all. Perhaps Dorothy understands this at some level, for while she has Glinda and the Munchkins rehearse conventional cultural ideas about "ugly" butch witches by having them tell her how horrible the Witch of the East has been, Dorothy also protests to them that she killed the witch only "by accident."

38. Besides being a fetish item within Dorothy's fantasy narrative, the ruby slippers have become a more general cultural fetish. Outside of the Salman Rushdie short story, "At the Auction of the Ruby Slippers," mentioned in note 15, there are many fiction and nonfiction references, stories, and articles about *Oz*'s ruby slippers. Various pairs of the slippers created for the production have been auctioned over the years, and they have always set records for the most money ever paid

for a piece of movie memorabilia. Two popular postcards reproduce the shots in the film of the ruby slippers on Dorothy's feet with (1) Glinda's star-tipped wand next to them and (2) the Wicked Witch's green hands receiving a shock as she tries to take them off. There is even a book about the slippers, *The Ruby Slippers of Oz* (Los Angeles: Tale Weaver Publishing, 1989), which centers around the attempts of writer Rhys Thomas to discover just how many pairs of slippers existed and exactly how they related to the making of *The Wizard of Oz*.

For the record, Thomas found that "[f]our pairs of ruby slippers are known to have survived the fifty years since the making of *The Wizard of Oz* at MGM in Culver City" (219). Thomas labels these four pairs "Dorothy's Shoes" (won in a contest in 1940 by Roberta Jeffries Bauman and auctioned in June 1988 for $165,000), "The People's Shoes" (now on display at the Smithsonian Institution's National Museum of American History, these are probably the pair purchased by an anonymous buyer at the MGM auction in 1970 for $15,000), "The Traveling Shoes" (owned by collector Michael Shaw), and "The Witch's Shoes" (formerly owned by MGM employee Kent Warner, purchased at an auction in August 1988 for $165,000 by Philip Samuels, they are now on display at his art gallery in St. Louis) (218–24).

A more queer-specific cultural appearance of this fetish can be found in its recent translation into glittering rhinestone-studded pin versions of the red AIDS-remembrance ribbons. Shocking Grey, a gay and lesbian mail-order outfit, has advertised these pins ("the new gay and lesbian icon") in their catalog with an accompanying photo of an interracial lesbian couple, one of whom wears the ruby pin.

39. Rushdie, 43. One suggestion scriptwriters Florence Ryerson and Edgar Allan Woolf had for revising Noel Langley's script was to have Dorothy actually take the slippers ("Dorothy has always wanted red slippers") from a temporarily stunned, but not dead, Wicked Witch of the East (Harmetz, *Making of*, 48). This action would have made Dorothy much more active in expressing and attaining her desires than she is in the final film, where her fantasy consistently places her in the position of being "done to," or "accidentally" doing things to others. As noted elsewhere in this chapter, this position might be indicative of Dorothy's fears and hesitancies about more directly expressing her "forbidden" dyke desires even in her own fantasy.

40. Rushdie, 43.

41. Greenberg, 15–25. Friedman's "Relinquishing Oz" more directly discusses Em as Dorothy's "heart's desire," but largely within a heterosexualized "home versus the world" analysis of Dorothy's choices in life (21).

42. Fricke, Scarfone, and Stillman, 30. While Freed continued to insist that *Oz* scriptwriters carefully maintain one important emotional center of the film around the relationship between Dorothy and Aunt Em, he also realized that, at the same time, "the Wicked Witch must be made more of an antagonist" for Dorothy (30).

43. In the sequel *Return to Oz* (1985, Disney: Walter Murch), it is Aunt Em who wants to take Dorothy to a doctor for "electric healing" after she "returns" from

Oz. "Electric healing," is, of course, just another word for electroshock therapy, which was a favored treatment to help "cure" homosexuality. "It's been six months since the tornado, and she hasn't been herself since," Aunt Em tells a skeptical Uncle Henry. The electric healing machine is presented by a seemingly benevolent patriarchal doctor as a "he" who will help Dorothy forget her "fantasies" about Oz. Looking at Mr. Machine, however, Dorothy sees a blonde girl about her own age staring out at her. After this vision, the doctor intones "Now we have the means to control those excess currents." Later, this blonde girl will rescue Dorothy from her electroshock treatment, and the pair will escape the asylum in which Dorothy was left by Aunt Em to be cured.

44. Greenberg, 25.
45. Friedman, 12.
46. Rushdie, 57.
47. Derek Jarman, "*The Wizard of Oz*," *Observer Magazine* (London) (April 1, 1981): n.p., in the British Film Institute library microjacket collection of clippings. Jarman also cites the film overall as a major influence on his own films.
48. Homocult, *Queer with Class: The First Book of Homocult* (Manchester, England: MS ED [The Talking Lesbian] PROMOTIONS, 1992): n.p.
49. *Snow White and the Seven Dwarfs* (1937, Disney Studios: Walt Disney); *101 Dalmatians* (1960, Disney Studios: Wolfgang Reitherman, Hamilton Luske, and Clyde Geronimi); *The Little Mermaid* (1989, Disney Studios: John Musker and Ron Clements).
50. Michael Bronski, "Gay Men and Movies: Reel to Real," *Gay Life: Leisure, Love, and Living for the Contemporary Gay Male,* ed. Eric E. Rofes (Garden City, N.Y.: Doubleday, 1986), 226–35.
51. Some lesbian enthusiasms for Judy Garland might have their source in the rumors of her affairs with women, which have been variously labeled "lesbian" and "bisexual." One episode of "The Rosie O'Donnell Show" (October 1997) had a *The Wizard of Oz* motif, with the rumored-to-be-lesbian talk show host dressed as Dorothy and queer diva Bette Midler as the Wicked Witch. They sang the Cowardly Lion's "sissy" song as their big duet. Another possible queer or lesbian popular culture *Oz* connection has been pointed out by Bruce A. Austin, who noticed that Columbia, in the film version of *The Rocky Horror Picture Show* (1975, 20th Century-Fox: Jim Sharman), "wears Dorothy-like *Wizard of Oz* ruby slippers" (cited in J. Hoberman and Jonathan Rosenbaum, *Midnight Movies* [New York: Harper and Row, 1983], 182). As for "Over the Rainbow," recent evidence suggesting that this once almost exclusively gay cultural reference is now understood as also relating to lesbian, and more generally queer, culture(s) include the rainbow symbol (which is widely used and marketed in various forms—flags, pins, bumper stickers, etc.), and a four-part television documentary titled *Over the Rainbow* (1994, Testing the Limits/Channel Four UK), which traces lesbian, gay, and queer cultures and politics from the 1950s to the present.

Queerness, Comedy, and The Women

How do queers—lesbians, gays, bisexuals, and other non-straight people—make sense of, and take pleasure in, a mass culture that we have been told time and again is made by and for straight people (especially men)? While our queer pleasures in film, television, music, videos, and other forms are many and varied, they are often rooted in the tensions between understanding ourselves as members of a *sub*culture that subversively or secretly reinterprets products not made with us in mind and seeing our readings and pleasures as standing alongside of (rather than as being alternatives to) those of straight people. This complicated positioning—simultaneously feeling within, outside, and alongside (mass, straight) culture—is evident in the relationship of queers to comedy production and interpretation.

When queers and comedy come together, most people think of camp and "bitchy" wit (gays) and sociopolitical humor (lesbians). Simultaneously comic forms and reading strategies, camp and the sociopolitical continue to be mainstays of queer humor, particularly as gay and lesbian producers and audiences have been sharing and combining these two forms/strategies more and more since the mid-1970s. This essay will deal with camp in more detail in a later section. Actually, it will also discuss queer sociopolitical approaches to comedy later, but this material will not always be clearly labeled as such. Indeed some of the material that follows on camp is analyzed from sociopolitical positions. So what is a queer sociopolitical angle on comedy? In lesbian cultures, it has historically been linked to feminist concerns about critiquing the patriarchy's limited and oppressive notions regarding gender. Lesbian humor has expanded these gender concerns to include comic examinations of straight culture's misconceptions about homosexuality. But lesbian sociopolitical comedy production and reading practices are also concerned with commenting upon dyke cultural experiences (butch-femme roles; coming out to parents; fashion, dietary, and dating trends, etc.). Influenced by feminist and lesbian comedy over the past twenty years or so, many gays and bisexual men have adopted a more overt sociopolitical edge in their humor. This is perhaps most evident in uses of camp—which has been considered either apolitical or a form of *implicitly* political gay humor—within progressive and radical queer politics (ACT-UP, Queer Nation) since the mid-1980s.

Besides camp and the sociopolitical (or combined with them), comic texts and performers have been queerly understood through many other academic and nonacademic reading strategies: star cults, auteurism, gossip and other forms of extratextuality, and various types of emotional-erotic connections between characters, actors, and audiences. Within queer cultures, fandoms develop around certain performers whose star image is appreciated for containing qualities important to individual queers and particular queer communities. Major queer star cults have formed around comedy (and musical-comedy) performers such as Doris Day, Judy Garland, Lily Tomlin, Bette Midler, Sandra Bernhard, Cary Grant, Lucille Ball, Carmen Miranda, Pee-wee Herman (Paul Reubens), Roseanne, Reno, Lypsinka, Charles Busch, Divine, and Mary Tyler Moore. Often, queer comedy readings will bring in star cult material related to performers not generally considered comic actors: Greta Garbo (*Ninotchka*, *Two-Faced Woman*) and Katharine Hepburn (*The Philadelphia Story*, *Pat and Mike*, *Adam's Rib*), for example.[1] Of course, whether considering comic or dramatic actors, many queer star cults include erotic fantasies about performers.

In relation to film comedy, directors can challenge stars as important figures through which to read comic texts—particularly among queer scholars. While classic "cult of the director" auteurism has been reviled or revised within the academy, seeing film texts as the expression of a director's "world view" is still a popular way to interpret films. This is particularly the case when the director is known, or rumored to be, queer (or homosexual, gay, lesbian, bisexual): George Cukor, Dorothy Arzner, James Whale, Gus Van Sant, Ulrike Ottinger, Emile Ardolino, Edmund Goulding, and others. With knowledge of a director's queerness, some readers will construct readings that interpret certain visual and aural codes in their films with reference to specifically queer cultural contexts.

Although, as suggested earlier, queer readers don't really need to know about a director's sexual status to read their films from within queer cultural contexts, information about this status comes up readily as part of the general round of gossip and other extratextual information that circulates within queer communities about texts and personalities. Queer communities have always had their versions of *Entertainment Tonight* and the *National Enquirer* within an oral tradition that conveys news, opinions, and rumors of interest to gays, lesbians, and bisexuals. Until the 1950s gossip, letters, and personal diaries were the ways in which most queer mass culture history and opinion was recorded and transmitted, as this material was considered too trivial, shocking, or dangerous to commit to the public print and electronic media. Since the 1950s a handful of gay, lesbian, bisexual, and queer journals, magazines, 'zines, radio programs, and cable access and public television shows have begun the process of publicly recording queer information and opinion about mass culture. Now even some "mainstream" magazines have gotten into the act, with articles on lesbian fashion, queer cinema, and AIDS and the media. In any case, between gossip and gleaning information in print and on the air, queer cultures circulate a wide range of "background material" people can use as part of how they queerly understand mass culture texts and performers.

Of course, certain comic texts and performers present themselves as being *about* queerness (*Victor/Victoria, Some Like It Hot, Sylvia Scarlett, I Was a Male War Bride,* Kate Clinton, Reno, Marga Gomez, Paul Reubens/Pee-wee Herman, late-90s Ellen De Generes, Kids in the Hall, Lea De Laria, Bob Smith, Suzanne Westenhoefer, Funny Gay Men).[2] But the queerness of comedy consists of far more than humorous representations of queerness. Let's face it, as a genre comedy is fundamentally queer since it encourages rule-breaking, risk-taking, inversions, and perversions in the face of straight patriarchal norms. Although you could argue that most comic gender and sexuality rule-breaking is ultimately contained or recuperated by traditional narrative closure (as it attempts to restore the straight status quo), or through the genre's "it's just a joke" escape hatch, the fact remains that queerness is the source of many comic pleasures for audiences of all sexual identities.

While comedy can be queer in a number of ways, not all of these are specific to producing or reading comedy *as* comic. Queer reading strategies involving the sociopolitical, star cult, gossip/extratextuality, auteurism, identification, and erotics are employed across mass culture texts and personalities. On the other hand, camp, a distinctively queer strategy for reading comedy as comic, is also used to humorously read not-intended-to-be-comic performers and texts like Bette Davis or *Valley of the Dolls.*[3] What follows in this essay is an attempt to cover a number of queer approaches to comedy, including camp, by using *The Women* as an illustrative text. Why *The Women*? Because it is both a typical traditional comic narrative film, as well as an unusual one in certain respects (its all-woman cast, its gay director, its lengthy Technicolor fashion show insert). In addition, *The Women* has been the subject of a wide range of print and conversational readings in queer cultures as a cult film.[4]

Queer readings of *The Women*, as with any cult film, are often set within the context of (sub)cultural gossip, publicity, and other extratextual information. For example, part of the way many queer audiences understand the "bitchy" comedy of *The Women* has to do with knowing something about the long-standing professional animosity between stars Joan Crawford and Norma Shearer; or the fact that director George Cukor was gay; or that the director and many of the stars were *Gone With the Wind* rejects;[5] or about how the press at the time attempted to exploit much of this information in order to promote an on-the-set feud between Crawford and Shearer, while at the same time characterizing Cukor as the alternately dispirited and harassed mediator for a jealously temperamental cast of 135 women.[6]

CAMP READINGS

Gossip, publicity, and other extratextual information are important to queer comic readings of films not only because they can furnish a broader under-standing, but because considering extratextual material often helps create the conditions for camp readings. Extratextuality can foster a certain camp dis-tance and irony toward narrative and characters by encouraging a passionate involvement in "behind-the-scenes" news about the production and the actors. Camp: almost everyone has heard of it, many have tried to define it, but few have succeeded in capturing on the printed page what camp is.[7] At most, I think, you can descriptively approach and encircle camp. Camp is sometimes a reading strategy ("in the eye of the beholder") and sometimes an approach used in constructing texts or performances (and sometimes it's both). Camp's central interests are taste/style/aesthetics, sexuality, and gender—or, rather, sexuality as related to gender role-playing (via style codes). Camp's mode is excess and exaggeration. Camp's tone is a mixture of irony, affection, seriousness, playfulness, and angry laughter. Camp's politics can be reactionary, liberal, or radical, depending on the example you are considering and your ideological agenda as a reader. But one thing about camp is cer-tain—at least for me: Camp is queer. There is nothing straight about camp.

While camp is queer, however, not all queers are camp or do camp. On the other hand, straight-identifying people can use camp strategies in pro-ducing or reading cultural texts. But try as they might to neuter or to het-erosexualize it, camp remains a queer thing, even when it is employed to homophobic ends. After all, it's not as if queers haven't done self-oppressive homophobic (and misogynistic) camping themselves. So to go camping in culture is to place yourself within queer discourses that comically consider a wide range of issues through their connections to ideologies of taste/style/aesthetics, gender, and sexuality. As noted earlier, while camp's ironic humor always foregrounds straight cultural assumptions and its (per)version of reality—and therefore seeks to denaturalize the work of dominant (patriarchal, heterocentrist) ideologies—its political agenda is not always progressive. Camp's position and that of the camp reader, however, is in some way non-, anti-, or contra-straight: it is queer.

The camp in *The Women* begins with its notorious credit sequence, which, as one critic points out, compares the world of women to a "vast bestiary" through dissolves linking animals to each actor-character.[8] Women are not just like animals here, they arise from various animals. This overly literal representation of patriarchy's metaphoric connection of women and nature is audaciously funny and ridiculous to many queer viewers—it is campy. But the political end of this camp depends upon the reader. It is misogynist if you decide the intent of the sequence is to ridicule straight women rather than to ridicule the cultural paradigms that compare them to animals. Even apart from any camp reading, however, comedy genre considerations make it difficult to decide the intent of an excessive section like *The Women's* credit sequence. After all, isn't the point of much comedy to exploit excess and exaggeration? So most critical statements about comic "intentions" actually express particular ideological interpretations of a text's comic message(s). Certainly, one general camp reading of *The Women* has been built around laughing at the idiotic extremes straight women will go to in their attempts to catch and keep straight men. This reading would not be particularly concerned with how the (off-screen) patriarchy surrounding these women might force them to such extremes.

Another general camp reading of the film does consider this sociopolitical context, however. Taking its cue from the film's juxtaposition of the credit sequence with the beauty salon sequence that follows, this reading works from within a dialectic that encourages a less misogynistic reading of the film's excesses. Considered together, the opening sequences expose a central cultural paradox about gender that queers any straight reading of the film. For while the credit sequence tells us that women are (like) animals—that they are natural forces—the salon scenes insist women are artificial, that they are carefully constructed for certain gender and class roles. The idea that culture demands a "naturalized artificiality" or an "artificial naturalness" of women has been campily established through the film's opening moments as the ideological "Catch-22" which informs certain camp readers' responses to the film's subsequent comic revelations about women.

But the misogynistic and feminist camp readings of *The Women* suggested above don't exhaust the range of camp readings queers perform on the film. Besides those camp readings that understand characters either as representing something essential about straight women or as representing the cultural construction of straight women, there are also a variety of cross-gender camp readings that have been the source of great pleasure and great ideological tension for gay men. These cross-gender readings are carried out in two forms that are opposite sides of the same cultural coin: (1) seeing the women characters (and/or the actors) on the screen as "really" being gay men, and (2) seeing gay men as being *like* the female characters or performers. But feminist questions about appropriating women's images and queer questions about capitulating to straight paradigms that pejoratively define homosexuality as always being about gender "inversion" can arise when gay men either read women stars and characters as if they were somehow also representing gay men, or read themselves as somehow being represented by female stars and characters.

As you might expect by this point, there are no simple analyses of the pleasures and politics of cross-gender identification for gays—or for lesbians and other queers. For example, gays who identify with (or who identify other gays as) Sylvia/Rosalind Russell, Crystal/Joan Crawford, or Mary/Norma Shearer in *The Women* might be identifying with certain shared, positive qualities in these characters and stars (wit, determination, stylishness, etc.), or they might see themselves and other gays as being in, or being culturally forced into, the places of these bitchy or masochistic characters and stars. The complicated humor involved when gays conduct camp readings of *The Women* within this latter cultural position finds its perfect expression when showgirl Miriam Aarons (Paulette Goddard) reminds Shearer's Mary Haines, "Heck, a woman's compromised the day she's born!" Since patriarchal, heterocentrist culture sees gay men as women wannabes and women-substitutes, this line, spoken as a half-bitter, half-resigned wisecrack, needs little translation to make it register with gay spectators culturally trained as cross-gender readers.

So within any of the general camp reading strategies of *The Women* outlined above, the politics of camp as it is connected to the text or the reader can become contested ground, often negotiated scene-by-scene and character-by-character, as readers move between different camp positions, sometimes cued by textual codes, sometimes by their cultural background. In terms of characters and camp politics, the most complicated and problematic figure in *The Women* is Sylvia Fowler, particularly as performed by Rosalind Russell. Russell recalls in her memoirs how while testing for the part she played Sylvia in three distinct styles: "drawing-room comedy," "realistically," and "flat out, in a very exaggerated style."[9] To her amazement, Cukor insisted Russell play the "very, very exaggerated version" of Sylvia throughout the film, in contrast with the playing of the rest of the cast.[10] The director also told Russell he wanted Sylvia to be outrageous, even within the context of a farce, because he wanted audiences to like her, despite any malicious things the narrative had her do.[11] For Pauline Kael the resulting performance is an "all-out burlesque of women as jealous bitches," that is, a caricature of a stereo-type.[12] Critic Carlos Clarens finds Russell's Sylvia is "somewhat like a female impersonator trying to crash the powder-room."[13]

The readings of Sylvia suggested by Kael, Clarens, Cukor's directions to Russell, and Russell's initial response to these directions, also hint at the var-ied ideological positions camp allows for. Russell is astonished by (and indicates elsewhere in her autobiography that she was initially resistant to) Cukor's insistence that Sylvia be played as what she considered a grotesque, while Kael hails the performance/character as a brilliant use of camp in the service of deconstructive masquerade. Cukor wanted Sylvia to be a larger-than-life bitchy woman that audiences (particularly queer audiences?) could laugh at, but he was also concerned that Sylvia be someone audiences liked *because* of her unrelenting outrageousness. Finally, Clarens indicates that, for gay audiences at least, the campy laughter in this case is less directed at (straight) women than at gays, as Sylvia is being read as a woman-as-gay-man, or, perhaps more precisely, a drag queen among straight women. Even considering just the two gay responses to Sylvia as a camp figure (Clarens's and Cukor's), the ideological bottom line remains uncertain. For while in Sylvia's case the camp caricature and laughter might work to satirize cultural cliches (the aggressively envious woman, the dishing drag queen), it also has the potential to disempower through misogyny and gay self-hate.

CUKOR AND AUTEURISM

Director George Cukor's cross-gendered auteurist reputation as a "woman's director" forms the background for understanding his complicated response to the camp elements in Sylvia and throughout the rest of the film.[14] Designer Edith Head once invoked a "third sex" paradigm to describe Cukor when she observed in an interview, "If you were going to star in a film, who would you want to direct you—a man or a woman? I think I'd choose George Cukor myself."[15] Most writing about Cukor, however, has less aligned him with both or neither gender(s) than identified him with women, particularly strong women actors. In terms of queer cultures and auteurism, I find it difficult to believe that it is sheer coincidence that Cukor is both gay and the director of many films and stars central to queer cults: *Dinner at Eight, Sylvia Scarlett, Camille, The Women, The Philadelphia Story, Born Yesterday, A Star Is Born*, Joan Crawford, Judy Garland, Rosalind Russell, Katharine Hepburn, Jean Harlow, and Greta Garbo.[16]

But the ways in which cross-gendered critical labels have been used by critics (even sympathetic ones) in order to dismiss Cukor as a serious auteur have strong and disturbing parallels to the process by which women and queers are labeled, categorized, and dismissed within mainstream culture. Thus Cukor is discussed as "just" a woman's director; theatrical; concerned with costuming, decor, and aesthetic detail; committed to style, glamour, and chic; and a director of dialogue. One strategy by which Cukor recently has been (re)claimed as a gay auteur takes these traditionally cross-gendered characteristics, as well as his uses of camp, as signs of a positive difference in the director's work.[17] But this is not to say that all queer auteurist readings of Cukor and his films will consider these qualities as positive ones. Indeed, there is much in Cukor interviews and biographies (particularly Patrick McGilligan's *George Cukor: A Double Life*) to suggest the director was often ambivalent about both camping and his identification with women actors or characters.[18]

While acknowledging the possibility for auteurist readings of Cukor and his films which examine their expression of misogynistic and/or gay (self-) oppressive themes, I will briefly indicate certain points within a more affirmative construction of Cukor-as-gay-auteur, focusing in particular on camp and cross-gender identification with reference to *The Women*. For one thing, Cukor's affinity with the women actors in the film appears to have created such rapport between cast and director that the group improvised on the set, something rare in Hollywood at the time, and came up with such inspirations as the multipaneled mirror image of Sylvia in Mary's dressing room, and the Countess DeLave's cry "la publicité" as she bemoans her public embarrassment at a nightclub.[19]

In collaboration with scriptwriters Anita Loos and Jane Murfin, one way Cukor's cross-gender identification appears to have expressed itself "theatrically" in *The Women* is in the decision to preface the narrative proper with an extended version of the original play's scene two exposé of a beauty and health salon–as–Frankenstein laboratory. As suggested earlier, this serves to foreground from the start the idea that social identities are culturally constructed, and that the characters, consciously or not, are role-playing gender, sexuality, and class parts throughout the narrative. This woman-as-manmade motif is later picked up in the lengthy fashion show sequence, which initially depicts haute couture incongruously within stylized reconstructions of "everyday situations," but which finally associates both high fashion and the daily world of bourgeois women with/as the products of a mad scientist's expressionistic laboratory, as models with electrodes on their gloves parade before giant retorts and circular glass tubing.

Encouraging the audience's awareness of women actors with strong star images playing characters for whom role-playing is important is perhaps the central (and often campily *mise-en-abyme*) thematic in Cukor's work: *Girls about Town, What Price Hollywood?, Our Betters, Dinner at Eight, Sylvia*

Butch women and camp costumes: Peggy (Joan Fontaine), Sylvia (Rosalind Russell), Nancy (Florence Nash), and Edith (Phyllis Povah).

Scarlett, Camille, Zaza, The Women, Susan and God, The Philadelphia Story, A Woman's Face, Two-Faced Woman, Her Cardboard Lover, Keeper of the Flame, Adam's Rib, A Life of Her Own, Born Yesterday, The Actress, It Should Happen to You, A Star Is Born, Les Girls, Heller in Pink Tights, Let's Make Love, The Chapman Report, and *My Fair Lady.*[20] Cukor often signals an implied antiessentialist position on identity—in particular women's gender identity—by the use of an antinaturalist visual aesthetic that is often trivialized by critics who call the director a "stylist."

For *The Women,* Cukor seems to have developed many of the film's antinaturalistic visual touches from the long and garish Technicolor fashion show he claims he was forced to incorporate into the otherwise black-and-white film. In interviews, the director says he found it impossible to introduce any "nuance" into the segment, faced as he was with the prospect of garish color processing and Adrian's "tacky" creations.[21] From the evidence onscreen, however, it appears Cukor and his collaborators became perversely inspired by Adrian and Technicolor, pushing the kitschy color and couture into the realm of camp satire by emphasizing surreal details or adding bizarre touches to the staging: monkeys in a cage wearing the same creations as the women feeding them peanuts; tracking into a closeup of a decapitated hand that serves as the clasp for a beach jacket; the previously mentioned "mad scientist's lab" finale.

Cukor's campy use of Hollywood's kitschy style in the fashion show sequence extends out into the rest of the film's mise-en-scène. Objects like Sylvia's bejeweled "Seeing Eye" dress and a series of feminized phalluses (ornamental decorative hands, perfume bottles) suggest a campy commentary on studio "realism." Things that typically function as unobtrusive background elements within conventional film codes of "realism"/ verisimilitude (visual and aural codes that seek to naturalize narratives and their ideological agendas), here become unexpectedly and disconcertingly foregrounded. The visual outrageousness of these objects, we come to realize, is really only a slight exaggeration of the type of glamorized realism MGM set designer Cedric Gibbons and costume designer Adrian display throughout the film. Camp production and readings always have this potential for conducting critiques from within, as camp takes up the styles, the technologies, and the narratives of dominant culture, and denaturalizes them through irony and excess. By doing this, camp establishes queer discursive spaces that can be used to reveal how (mass) culture's patriarchal, heterocentrist agendas are hidden in plain sight on the surfaces of its "realistic" representation.

LESBIAN READINGS, QUEER PLEASURES

But something else is "hidden in plain sight" on the surfaces of *The Women*'s comic narrative: lesbian positions that find in the tensions and the camaraderie between the all-women cast a rich space for cultural criticism, identification, and erotics. As was long true of the cultural work of gays and other queers, until recently the social history of lesbian film and mass culture spectatorship largely took the form of anecdotes, letters, diaries, gossip, and daily conversations—with most of this oral history remaining within lesbian communities. Caroline Sheldon's "Lesbians and Film: Some Thoughts" (first published in 1977) and the "Lesbians and Film" special section in *Jump Cut*'s March 1981 issue marked important steps in making this lesbian cultural work visible.[22] In the *Jump Cut* special section, the introductory essay by Edith Becker, Michelle Citron, Julia Lesage, and B. Ruby Rich, and "Hollywood Transformed," a series of interviews conducted by Judy (later Claire) Whitaker are particularly valuable sources for material about lesbian readers and mainstream films like *The Women*.[23] Both pieces consider how identification (both cross-gender and same gender), erotic desire, and "subtexting" are used by lesbian readers to derive varied pleasures from stars, characters, and narratives. Although not mentioned in these works, camp has also been a means by which some lesbian readers have understood the products of dominant culture. In discussing the development of her queer identity, Sue-Ellen Case remarks that besides cross-gender identification, "a multitude of other experiences and discourses continued to enhance my queer thinking. Most prominent among them was the subcultural discourse of camp which I learned primarily from old dykes and gay male friends I knew in San Francisco."[24]

As the subject of camp readings and *The Women* has already been covered earlier, and the topic of cross-gender identification will come up in the next section, I will confine my remarks here to same-gender identification, desire, and (sub)texting in lesbian readings of *The Women*. Certainly any film in which, for once, straight men are the ones literally out of the picture is a promising text for lesbian pleasures. More than two hours of frames filled with the sights and sounds of women energetically sparring with and supporting each other generate enough emotional intensity to make the idea of "compulsory heterosexuality" with invisible men seem pallid and uninteresting by comparison.[25] Besides, as Kayucila Brooke and Jane Cottis suggest in their video *Dry Kisses Only*, even the confrontations and arguments between women in mainstream films like *The Women* might be understood by lesbian viewers as being more indicative of the ways in which women have been forced by patriarchy into the role of rivals rather than of any fundamental hatred and jealously between women.[26] A 1996 revival of the Clare Boothe Luce play in New York City, performed under the title of *Mean Rich White Ladies*, acknowledged this possibility, as "[w]hen the famous catfight in Reno breaks out among the various divorce-seeking wives, the screeches and shovings were provided by the soundtrack from the movie, while the cast took time out to dance with each other."[27]

Within these kinds of lesbian cultural reading practices, Syliva once again becomes a key figure in *The Women*. While at times her excesses might appear to serve patriarchal heterosexuality (in her divisive role as gossiping "bitch"), she also provides a model of fast-talking assertiveness and independence that the other characters follow at one time or another. Sylvia also connects the upper-class characters with Crystal Allen, a working woman, in a sisterhood of aggressive "bitchery." The Sylvia-Crystal-Mary triangle is especially important within lesbian and other queer readings as it reveals that much of Sylvia's bitchery is actually motivated by sexual jealousy over her cousin Mary. Heterocentrism encourages us to read Sylvia's machinations as part of a plot to destroy Mary's marriage to Stephen Haines, supposedly because Sylvia can't stand to see someone in a happy marriage when her own marriage isn't fulfilling. But everything Sylvia does in the film can be read as easily—and as justifiably—as attempts to break up Mary's marriage (and later her bonds with other women) in order to have Mary all to herself.[28]

Indeed, in a scene at a Reno "divorce ranch" Mary reminds Sylvia that she doesn't love her husband just before Sylvia has a "catfight" with her supposed rival for Howard, Miriam. So heterosexual competitiveness doesn't quite explain the intensity of Sylvia's attack on Miriam, which includes a moment when Sylvia licks her lips as a prelude to biting Miriam's thigh. The film suggests there is something, and someone, else motivating Sylvia as she yells at Mary after the fight, "You're on her [Miriam's] side. . . . You'll be sorry when you need a girlfriend!" Soon after, in an attempt to make Mary jealous, Sylvia becomes Crystal's new best girlfriend. To make matters more erotically complicated and provocative here, we might recall that Sylvia's first encounter with Crystal occurs when she decides to take a look at Stephen's mistress. With this excuse, Sylvia (along with her friend Edith Potter) places herself in Stephen's position as she prowls a store, avidly gazing at likely candidates in the perfume department to determine who is the most attractive. Within the confines of a traditional narrative, this cross-gendered positioning supposedly "allows" Sylvia to direct an erotic gaze at other women.

This is certainly how Deborah Fried reads things. Discussing the department store sequence, Fried concludes:

> Since they [Sylvia/Russell and Edith/Phyllis Povah] have never seen Crystal, in order to find her they must inspect every likely candidate through the eyes of a temptable man. . . . Our first shot of Crawford [Crystal], then, is from Russell and Povah's point-of-view, but they have consigned their point-of-view to the man, or temporarily borrowed it from him. This is not to say, of course, that the shot of Crawford from their point of view implies that they find her desirous or alluring as a man would—they make it plain that they find her a contemptible mansnatcher—but they must mark her out as the proper object of their contempt by first seeing her as she must look in the eyes of a desiring man.[29]

WOMEN LOOKING AT WOMEN

The narrative strategy Fried describes above is one of many in the film that attempts to frame and contain moments of women looking at other women through references to the straight male gaze—or, rather, by counting on audiences to function within straight cultural paradigms that tell them women only look at other women as heterosexually "feminine" role models or as heterosexual rivals. But while these strategies allow for (and encourage) such straight readings of these moments, how does anyone know for certain that all the characters who are looking at other women are straight, or that they are looking at women only for straight reasons? Maybe these moments represent lesbian or bisexual cross-gender gazing: that is, they are moments

Women looking as straight men, or women looking queerly? Edith, Sylvia, and Crystal (Joan Crawford).

when women are covering themselves by using the excuse of looking at women from a male position in order to fulfill their own pleasures and desires. To take, once again, the example of the department store sequence Fried discusses, while Edith's point-of-view in the scene might be explained within Fried's terms, I think Sylvia's is not so easily contained by saying it is being borrowed from a straight man's position. For one thing, by this point the narrative has established that Sylvia is jealous of Mary's happy marriage, so would she really "find [Crystal] a contemptible mansnatcher"? Certainly her public pose would convey shock and dismay, so it might appear that her gazing at Crystal and the other women was motivated by contempt. Even if Edith and Sylvia's gazing was motivated by dislike, however, their gaze would be different from the one "of a desiring man" that Fried feels they are "temporarily borrowing " here. For one thing, their dislike of Crystal could have something to do with the class tensions between rich women and working class women displayed here and elsewhere in the film.

As I have indicated earlier, if anything, I think Sylvia is using this rather incoherent and contradictory spectatorial position (contemptuously surveying the women in the store from the position of a desiring straight male) as a pretense to mask her own queer (lesbian or bisexual) desires—and perhaps Edith is doing the same thing, as her first line in the scene is "Gorgeous torso, dear! Maybe that's little Crystal!" Besides, assuming cross-gender positions is one queer gazing strategy that has a long history in lesbian and gay cultures. It may become an ideologically problematic practice at times (as is made clear in Fried's article), but it happens. So characters in *The Women*, as well as women in the audience, may be looking at Crystal and the other women in the film from a position understood as being *like* that "of a desiring [straight] man," but not looking exactly *as* that straight man looks.

But not all narrative moments of women gazing at other women's bodies in *The Women* can be fully explained as being filtered through straight female or even cross-gendered female spectator positions. The fashion show begins with a woman exhorting other women to "study the flow of the line as it responds to the ever-changing flow of the female form divine." And Sylvia isn't in any sort of straight or cross-gendered queer position when she first arrives at the Reno divorce ranch and looks Miriam up and down, as this is before she knows anything about Miriam's involvement with Howard or her friendship with Mary. Couldn't characters like Sylvia be closeted lesbians or bisexuals?[30] The signs are there for queer readers. If having sex with men, being married, and having children aren't indisputable signs of heterosexuality in life, why must they be so in films?

Then there is the figure of Nancy Blake, author, feminist ("another lecture on the modern woman"), and big game hunter who favors tailored suits, and who enjoys goading Sylvia about her clothes, her marriage, and her jealousy over Mary: "Her happiness gets you down, doesn't it Sylvia? . . . Because she's content. Content to be what she is . . . a woman." Branding Sylvia a "female," that is, someone playing at being a "real" (read: heterosexual) woman, Nancy dubs herself "that which nature abhors, an old maid, a frozen asset"—"old maid" being a common euphemism at the time for a lesbian.[31] As with the "mannish lesbian" professional women in many 1930s and 1940s Dorothy Arzner films, Nancy represents a position which is at the same time masculine-coded yet woman-identified, suggesting you don't have to take Stephen's (or any man's) place to cast an erotic gaze at Mary (or any woman).[32] At one point, for example, Nancy responds to Sylvia's closeted, back-handed compliment regarding a picture of Mary in the paper—"Trust Mary to be photographed from her best angle"—by remarking, "Best angle, my foot, it doesn't half do her justice."

In this context, it is clear that "my foot" really refers to her eye, that is, to Nancy's dyke look, which is also present among spectators who aren't looking at the women in the film as heterosexual models for how to be appropriately "feminine" or as potential rivals for men. In addition to erotic gazing, lesbians and other queerly positioned women in the audience might look at the women in a film like *The Women* as models of strength, wit, or femme-ininity. As with gay and queerly positioned male spectators, this type of identification often centers on stars as well as characters. Besides the Sheldon and *Jump Cut* articles mentioned above, Andrea Weiss's "A Queer Feeling when I Look at You: Hollywood Stars and Lesbian Spectatorship in the 1930s" discusses the importance of star cults to lesbian cultural readings of films.[33] Performers such as Greta Garbo, Marlene Dietrich, Katharine Hepburn, Bette Davis, and more recently Julie Andrews, Sigorney Weaver, Kathleen Turner, and Jodie Foster, often structure lesbian readings of narratives as star texts through processes of identification and desire that are not always fully distinct from one another.

As in gay star cults, strength, a sense of ironic humor, or the ability to be caustically witty are among the qualities most prized in lesbian star cults. As one of Whitaker's interviewees declares,

> I loved *All About Eve*, particularly because I had a crush on Bette Davis, a wonderful model. She's a strong bitchy woman who knows what she wants and gets it and yet stayed human and sensitive. I was particularly interested to see her pitted against another woman and to see a whole bunch of other great tough women, like Thelma Ritter, in the film.[34]

This tribute also fits *The Women*, in which Joan Crawford, Rosalind Russell, Paulette Goddard, and Norma Shearer play strong, witty women. Determination and a sharp wit (if not always a bitchy wit) were central to Crawford's and Russell's star images apart from this film. Their lesbian followings have been built upon these qualities, as well as upon a certain butchness that emerges dramatically in Russell's "boss lady" films of the 1940s and in Crawford's *Mildred Pierce* and *Johnny Guitar*.[35] Shearer and *The Women* co-star Joan Fontaine also have dyke followings, but for being model femmes—generally soft-spoken, yet gradually revealing a core of strength in the face of adversity (see especially *Marie Antoinette* and *The Barretts of Wimpole Street* for Shearer, and *Rebecca* and *Frenchman's Creek* for Fontaine).[36]

MOTHERS AND BITCHES

In *The Women* Shearer's character's intense relationships with her daughter, "little Mary," and with her own mother provide another opportunity for lesbian identification and erotics that are culturally rooted in the maternal.[37] Introduced in matching tailored riding outfits, Mary and her daughter engage in some horseplay themselves, with "little" Mary filming her mother "on the

"You know, that's the one good thing about divorce—you get to sleep with your mother": Little Mary (Virginia Weidler) and Mary (Norma Shearer).

bias" with a home movie camera before trying to mount her for a "horseback ride." Soon afterward, dressed in a robe and with her husband's pipe in her mouth, Mary has a windowseat cuddle with her daughter during which the latter asks jealously, "Do you love him [her father] more than me?" "Well, that's a different kind of love," Mary replies. These mother-daughter erotics culminate later in the film when "little Mary" gets into her mother's bed one night: "You know, that's the one good thing about divorce—you get to sleep with your mother." In this context, it makes sense that Mary decides to confront Crystal only after she's been told that Crystal has been trying to gain her daughter's affection. For her part, Mary also seeks love and comfort from her mother when faced with Stephen's infidelity. "It's rather nice to have you need mother again," Mary's mother exclaims at the end of a scene in which Mary has spent a good deal of the time with her head in her mother's lap.

This two-generation matriarchy is rather short-lived, however, as a bedroom scene with Mary, "little Mary," and Mary's mother segues into the Casino Roof powder room sequence during which Mary devises a plan to win her husband back. This sequence not only concludes the film, but it marks the final showdown between straight and queer—producers, readers, and (sub)text(s)—over the meaning of the comedy in *The Women*. Taken straight, the bitchy wit, repartee, and arch role-playing (of actors and characters) in this sequence is being used to restore Mary's marriage by putting Crystal back in her working class place. But while this is being done, Sylvia's supposedly unacceptable "drag queen" bitchery is also being redeemed as a source of empowerment for "nice" straight women like Mary. While the irony of all this bitchy camping seems lost on the characters, it isn't on many queer readers. Even though she is locked in a closet (!) by the other women at one point, Sylvia's dyke/drag queen is ultimately vindicated as their imitation of her becomes the sincerest form of flattery.

But the film doesn't end here. As Mary begins to rush out for a conventional heterosexual happy-ending clinch, a newly "out of the closet" Sylvia (sporting a rag mop wig) tries one more time to keep Mary from Stephen by reminding her of her "pride." This is something Mary herself had made a compelling case for earlier in the face of her mother's advice to ignore Stephen's affair. At one point the narrative suggests Sylvia "is right" when she advises women, particularly married women, to "hang on to" their own money as their "only protection." Now, at the end of the film, Sylvia tries to say the same thing about a woman's spiritual independence from men and marriage that she has said about their economic independence. But Mary, caught up in the machinations of a capitalist, patriarchial narrative, can't recognize Sylvia's echoing of her own sentiments.

However, while bitchy dykey drag queen Sylvia is unable to stop Mary from returning to a conventional heterosexual marriage, Cukor and his collaborators are able to comment on this "happy ending." As with the opening of the film, a dialectic is set up that creates the circumstances for a campy irony to queer the finale. While following the structure of the original play, Cukor and company use strikingly different styles of performance, sound, and mise-en-scène in order to contrast the vivid, high-key, and fast-paced look and sound of the action in the powder room with the ultrasentimental, glamorous final shot, in which Mary, supported by an angelic choir, leaves Sylvia in the doorway. Gliding toward the camera with an ecstatic look on her face, Mary finally flings open her arms and rushes offscreen, as church bells ring, to abandon herself to a man who really isn't there.

Deborah Fried says of this scene, "The fadeout just before the man shows up to meet his wife's triumphant welcome . . . is playfully censored. It's an odd coyness, as if the embrace of husband and wife were not a proper subject for the movies."[38] From a queer perspective a heterosexual (re)union is not the "proper subject" for this particular movie, as it would threaten the viewer's all-women pleasures of the preceding two hours or so. Heterosexuality, particularly using a heterosexual clinch to close the narrative, is, however, the proper subject for most traditional films—indeed it is *the* subject. So the exclusion of an embrace and kiss from even the final shot of *The Women* seems much more than an "odd coyness" on the part of Cukor, Loos, and Murfin. They make heterosexuality, for once, the invisible, connotated (if not fully unspeakable) subject of a Hollywood movie, and humorously underline this point through camp style. Heterosexuality as *amour fou* has rarely been depicted so wittily—or so queerly—in a Hollywood comedy as it is in the final moments of *The Women*.

NOTES

1. *Ninotchka* (1939, MGM: Ernst Lubitsch); *Two-Faced Woman* (1941, MGM: George Cukor); *The Philadelphia Story* (1940, MGM: George Cukor); *Pat and Mike* (1952, MGM: George Cukor); *Adam's Rib* (1949, MGM: George Cukor).
2. *Victor/Victoria* (1982, MGM: Blake Edwards); *Sylvia Scarlett* (1936, RKO: George Cukor); *Some Like It Hot* (1959, United Artists, Billy Wilder); *I Was a Male War Bride* (1948, 20th Century-Fox: Howard Hawks).
3. *Valley of the Dolls* (1967, 20th Century-Fox: Mark Robson).
4. *The Women* (1939, MGM: George Cukor). Screenplay by Anita Loos and Jane Murfin. Based on the play by Clare Boothe Luce. This film has been remade twice, once by gay director Rainer Werner Fassbinder as *Frauen in New York* (1977, Norddeutschen Rundfunk [Ndr] Television). Fassbinder's version is more obviously concerned with the women's class privilege than is the Cukor version. Fassbinder often uses his camp effects to encourage Marxist readings that are critical of the characters not because they are women, but because they are complacent members of an un-self-reflexive class. But the 1939 version is not without its moments of class consciousness. For example, after Edith and Sylvia stop an exercise session with their gossiping, their frustrated trainer leaves, making a wisecrack at their expense as she goes. "Honestly, the class feeling you run into nowadays," a clueless Edith comments.

    Men appear onscreen in the 1956 musical version, *The Opposite Sex* (MGM: David Miller), which has the effect of dissipating most of the tensions and the bonding between the women. The only really well developed and deeply felt woman-woman relationship is between ex-singer Kay Hillyard (the Mary Haines character) and playwright Amanda Penrose, who is, tellingly, a composite of Mary's mother and the dyke-spinster author Nancy Blake.

    On another matter, I label *The Women* a "cult film" because its status within segments of the queer community fits the definition of cult films as films that have developed an enthusiastic band of repeat viewers who know most scenes and dialogue by heart, and for whom the text has special meaning(s). As Danny Peary notes in *Cult Movies* (New York: Dell, 1981): "Cultists believe they are among the blessed few who have discovered something in particular films that the average moviegoer and critic have missed—that something that makes the pictures extraordinary" (xiii). The following, very selective, list will give you some sense of the range of queer (gay, lesbian, bisexual, etc.) cult films: *Desert Hearts* (1986, Samuel Goldwyn Co.: Donna Deitch); *The Wizard of Oz* (1939, MGM: Victor Fleming); *Jeanne Dielman, 23 Quai de Commerce, 1080 Bruxelles* (1975, Paradise Films-Unite-Trois/Diffusion Mondiale Artco-Films: Chantal Ackerman); *Aliens* (1986, 20th Century-Fox: James Cameron); *All About Eve* (1950, 20th Century-Fox: Joseph L. Mankewicz); *Gentlemen Prefer Blondes* (1953, 20th Century-Fox: Howard Hawks); *Some Like It Hot* (1959, United Artists: Billy Wilder); *Whatever Happened to Baby Jane?* (1962, Warner Brothers: Robert Aldrich); *Calamity Jane* (1953, Warner Brothers: David Butler); *Thelma and Louise* (1991, MGM: Ridley Scott); *Scorpio Rising* (1963: Kenneth Anger); *Female Trouble* (1974: John Waters); *Mädchen in Uniform* (1931, Deutsche Film-Gemeinschaft: Leontine Sagan); *Sylvia Scarlett* (1935, RKO: George Cukor); and *Christopher Strong* (1933, RKO: Dorothy Arzner).

5. *Gone With the Wind* (1939, MGM/Selznick International: Victor Fleming). Joan Crawford, Norma Shearer, and Paulette Goddard had been considered for the role of Scarlett O'Hara in *Gone With the Wind*. Goddard had actually been signed for the part before producer David O. Selznick met Vivien Leigh, who would ultimately play Scarlett. In addition, *The Women* cast member Joan Fontaine had been asked to test for the part of Melanie Hamilton. Rumor has it that she wanted the lead role and would not consider playing Melanie, telling Selznick to try sister Olivia de Havilland instead (who eventually played Melanie). Cukor was the original director of *Gone With the Wind*, and a number of scenes he directed remain in the final version. His dismissal from the film has been the subject of much gossip and speculation. Some sources claim co-star Clark Gable didn't like being directed by a "faggot" who paid more attention to the women in the cast than to him. For accounts of Cukor's involvement with *Gone With the Wind*, see Patrick McGilligan, *George Cukor: A Double Life* (New York: St. Martin's Press, 1991); Richard Harwell, "Introduction," *GWTW: The Screenplay* (New York: Collier, 1980), 7–44; Roland Flamini, *Scarlett, Rhett, and a Cast of Thousands: The Filming of Gone With the Wind* (New York: MacMillan, 1975); Ronald Haver, *David O. Selznick's Hollywood* (New York: Alfred A. Knopf, 1980); Gavin Lambert, *GWTW: The Making of Gone With the Wind* (Boston: Little, Brown & Co., 1973); and Rudy Behlmer, ed., *Memo from David O. Selznick* (New York: Viking, 1972).

6. Typical of the publicity surrounding *The Women* at the time of its release is a *New York Times* piece, "Mr. Cukor: A Man Among 'The Women,'" which reports the rumors of a Crawford-Shearer feud and calls Cukor the only man in Hollywood who "dared tackle the job of bossing 135 women at one time"—a task that included keeping "all guerrilla warfare outside the studio gates." *New York Times*, October 1, 1939; rpt. in *New York Times Encyclopedia of Film*, vol. 3 (1937–40), eds. Gene Brown and Harry M. Geduld (New York: Times Books, 1984), n.p.

7. The following works include many approaches to defining and discussing camp: Esther Newton, *Mother Camp: Female Impersonators in America* (Chicago and London: University of Chicago Press, 1972/1979); Andrew Ross, "The Uses of Camp," in *No Respect: Intellectuals and Popular Culture* (New York and London: Routledge, 1989), 135–70; Philip Core, *Camp: The Lie That Tells the Truth* (New York: Delilah Books, 1984); Oscar Montero, "Lipstick Vogue: The Politics of Drag," *Radical America* 22, 1 (January–February 1988): 35–42; Carole-Anne Tyler, "Boys Will Be Girls: The Politics of Gay Drag," in *Inside/Out: Lesbian Theories, Gay Theories*, ed. Diana Fuss (New York and London: Routledge, 1991), 32–70; Jack Babuscio, "Camp and the Gay Sensibility," *Gays and Film*, ed. Richard Dyer (New York: New York Zoetrope,: 1984), 40–57; Andrew Britton, "For Interpretation: Notes Against Camp," *Gay Left* 7 (1978–79); Sue-Ellen Case, "Toward A Butch-Femme Aesthetic," *Discourse* 11, 1 (Fall–Winter 1988–89): 55-71, rpt. in *Making a Spectacle: Feminist Essays on Contemporary Women's Theatre*, ed. Lynda Hart (Ann Arbor: University of Michigan Press, 1989); Sue-Ellen Case, "Tracking the Vampire," *differences* 3, 2 (1991): 1–20; Al LaValley, "The Great Escape," *American Film* 10, 6 (April 1985): 29–34, 70–71; Seymour Kleinberg, *Alienated Affections: Being Gay in America* (New York: St. Martin's Press, 1980), 38–69, 118–56; Christine Riddiough, "Culture and Politics," in *Pink Triangles: Radical Perspectives on Gay Liberation*, ed. Pam Mitchell (Boston: Alyson, 1980), 14–33; Derek Cohen and Richard Dyer, "The Politics of Gay Culture," in *Homosexuality: Power and Politics*, ed. Gay Left Collective (London and New York: Allison and Busby, 1980), 172–86; Susan Sontag, "Notes on Camp," in *Against Interpretation* (New York: Farrar, Straus, Giroux, 1966), 275–92; Mark Booth, *Camp* (New York: Quartet, 1983); Judith Butler, *Gender Trouble: Feminism and the Subversion of Identity* (New York and London: Routledge, 1990), 128–49; Vito Russo, "Camp," in *Gay Men: The Sociology of Male Homosexuality*, ed. Martin P. Levine (New York: Harper and Row, 1979), 205–10; Robin Wood, "The Dyer's Hand: Stars and Gays," *Film Comment* 16, 1 (January–February 1980): 70–72; Jeffrey Hilbert, "The Politics of Drag," *The Advocate* 575 (April 23, 1991): 42–47; Lisa Duggan, "The Anguished Cry of an 80s Fem: 'I Want to be a Drag Queen,'" *OUT/LOOK* 1, 1 (Spring 1988): 62–65; Pamela Robertson, "'The Kinda Comedy That Imitates Me': Mae West's Idenitification with the Feminist Camp," *Cinema Journal* 32, 2 (Winter 1993): 57–72; Michael Musto, "Old Camp, New Camp, *Out* 5 (April/May 1993): 32–39; Moe Meyer, ed., *The Politics and Poetics of Camp* (London and New York: Routledge, 1994); David Bergman, ed., *Camp Grounds: Style and Homosexuality* (Amherst: University of Massachusets Press, 1993).
8. Carlos Clarens, *George Cukor* (London: Secker and Warburg/BFI, 1976), 64.
9. Rosalind Russell and Chris Chase, *Life Is a Banquet* (New York: Random House, 1977), 80.
10. Ibid., 80.
11. Ibid., 80.
12. Pauline Kael, *5001 Nights at the Movies: A Guide from A to Z* (New York: Holt, Rinehart and Wilson, 1984), 660.

13. Clarens, 63.
14. Robert Lindsey, reporting on a December 1976–January 1977 retrospective of Cukor's films at the Regency Theater in New York, felt that it was "appropriate" that the retrospective open with *The Women*, but reminded readers that while Cukor was "best known in Hollywood as a 'woman's director'" the term "has nothing to do with being a ladies' man." "A Festival to Honor George Cukor," *New York Times*, 24 December 1976; rpt. in *The New York Times Encyclopedia of Film*, vol. 11 (1975–1976), eds. Gene Brown and Harry M. Geduld (New York: Times Books, 1984), n.p.
15. Virginia Wright Wexman and Patricia Erens, "Clothes-Wise: Edith Head," *Take One* 5, 4 (October 1976): 13.
16. *Dinner at Eight* (1933, MGM); *Camille* (1937, MGM); *The Philadelphia Story* (1940, MGM); *Born Yesterday* (1950, Columbia); *A Star Is Born* (1954, Warners).
17. Current reevaluations of Cukor's films in the context of gay culture include Richard Lippe, "Authorship and Cukor: A Reappraisal," *CineAction!* 21–22 (Summer–Fall 1990): 21–34; and the "Whose Text Is It Anyway?: Queer Cultures, Queer *Auteurs*, Queer Authorship" chapter in my book *Making Things Perfectly Queer* (cited earlier). Patrick McGilligan's *George Cukor: A Double Life* (cited earlier) also contains critical material connecting gay culture, Cukor's "homosexuality" (he disliked the term "gay"), and his films.
18. Lindsey's *New York Times* article quotes Cukor's response to being called a "woman's director":

> "Woman's director!" Mr. Cukor said the other day in Los Angeles, a trace of annoyance in his voice. "Well, I'm very pleased to be considered a master of anything, but remember, for every Jill there was a Jack. People like to pigeonhole you—it's a short-cut, I guess, but once they do, you're stuck with it." (n.p.)

19. George Cukor, interviewed by Charles Higham and Joel Greenberg for *The Celluloid Muse: Hollywood Directors Speak* (New York: Signet, 1969), 60–78, mentions improvisations on the set of *The Women*; while Russell and Chase's *Life Is a Banquet* recalls spontaneous changes in staging and the last-minute addition of bits of business for characters in a chapter on the film (80–85).
20. *Girls About Town* (1931, Paramount); *What Price Hollywood?* (1932, RKO); *Our Betters* (1932, RKO); *Zaza* (1939, Paramount); *Susan and God* (1940, MGM); *A Woman's Face* (1941, MGM); *Two-Faced Woman* (1941, MGM); *Her Cardboard Lover* (1942, MGM); *Keeper of the Flame* (1943, MGM); *Adam's Rib* (1949, MGM); *A Life of Her Own* (1950, MGM); *The Actress* (1953, MGM); *It Should Happen to You* (1954, Columbia); *Les Girls* (1957, MGM); *Heller in Pink Tights* (1960, Paramount); *Let's Make Love* (1960, 20th Century-Fox); *The Chapman Report* (1962, 20th Century-Fox/Darryl F. Zanuck); *My Fair Lady* (1964, Warners).

Debra Fried's excellent feminist analysis of *The Women*—"The Men in *The Women*"—takes up the theme of women role-playing (self-consciously or not) in the film. But recognizing Cukor's gayness and its possible relation to women's role-playing in this film becomes particularly crucial at moments during Fried's analysis when she appears to conflate him with the straight male characters who are offscreen. Discussing scenes where characters record themselves with a home movie camera, for example, Fried notes,

> A movie character handling a movie camera is readily interpreted as in some sense a surrogate for the movie director.... But when this character is a woman taking a picture to certify an event for a man who never shows up in the film ... the identification between the onscreen filmmaker and the offscreen one becomes vexed.... The woman with the camera reminds us of the man with the camera recording this specious image of woman as image maker.... [I]n the woman's hands the movie camera becomes a device be which she may stage her own image for the unseen male viewer. (*Women and Literature*, vol. 4, *Women and Film*, ed. Janet Todd [New York: Holmes and Meier, 1988], 51)

While I agree that the women in the film are to some extent constructing their home movie images for straight male viewers, both home movie sequences also reveal that the women (and the cross-gender identifying gay director behind the other camera) resist fully catering to straight male pleasures. Little Mary films her mother's horse race victory "on the bias," even though Mary implies her father won't like it done that way. During the screening of the Bermuda home movies filmed by Mary and her mother, the offscreen commentary of Mary, her mother, and little Mary reveals that they are enjoying the home movies in their own ways ("You look pretty pretty, mother," little Mary remarks over a shot of her mother lying on the beach). Little Mary asks about showing the film to her father only after the "women only" showing is over.

21. Adrian had already designed the clothes for a Technicolor-insert fashion show in the otherwise black-and-white, Howard Hawks–directed film *Fig Leaves* (1926, Fox). While most accounts, including Cukor's own in a number of interviews, suggest the director collaborated on the fashion show even though he didn't want it in the film, McGilligan's biography claims that the sequence was "filmed by someone else." McGilligan doesn't cite a specific source for this information, although he does say in his notes that he reviewed "individual production files of Cukor's films" for MGM "during the span of his contract years," that would include *The Women* (363). If Cukor did not film the fashion show, the camp effects I discuss in this chapter are less in the eye of the gay auteur than in that of the queer spectator (or perhaps other queers working on sets and costuming for *The Women*). Whether attributable to directorial intent, the work of other queers on the production team (even Adrian, perhaps?), general studio style, or the queer spectator, however, the camp and its potentially satiric effects remain.

22. Caroline Sheldon, "Lesbians and Film: Some Thoughts," in *Gays and Film*, ed. Richard Dyer, rev. ed. (New York: Zoetrope, 1984), 5–26.

23. Edith Becker, Michelle Citron, Julia Lesage, and B. Ruby Rich, "Lesbians and Film: Introduction," *Jump Cut* 24/25 (1981): 17–21; rpt. in *Jump Cut: Hollywood, Politics and Counter-Cinema*, ed. Peter Steven (New York: Prager, 1985), 296–314; Judy (Claire) Whitaker, "Hollywood Transformed," *Jump Cut* 24/25 (1981): 33–35, rpt. in *Jump Cut: Hollywood, Politics and Counter-Cinema*, 106–18.

24. Sue-Ellen Case, "Tracking The Vampire," *differences* 3, 2 (summer 1991): 1.

25. The term "compulsory heterosexuality" comes from Adrienne Rich's essay "Compulsory Heterosexuality and Lesbian Existence," *Signs* 5 (1980): 631–60; rpt. in *Powers of Desire: The Politics of Sexuality*, ed. Christine Stansell and Sharon Thompson (New York: Monthly Review Press, 1983), 177–203.

26. Video cited: *Dry Kisses Only* (1989, Kaucyila Brooke and Jane Cottis). This video combines mock-academic discussions, "lesbian on the street" interviews, and cleverly edited clips from films such as *The Great Lie* (1941, Warners: Edmund Goulding); *Johnny Guitar* (1954, Republic: Nicholas Ray); *All About Eve* (1950, 20th Century-Fox: Joseph L. Mankiewicz); *Mädchen in Uniform* (1931, Deutsche Film-Gemeinschaft: Leontine Sagan); and *The Hunger* (1983, MGM: Tony Scott) to reveal the variety and complexity of lesbian culture's work with/in mass culture.

27. L.C. Cole, "The Unattractive Life," *New York Native* 696 (August 1996): 35.

28. One behind-the-scenes anecdote in Emanuel Levy's *George Cukor, Master of Elegance* (New York: William Morrow, 1994) is particularly interesting in connection with Sylvia and Mary's relationship, as it points out how the queer dynamics of this relationship, and of the film as a whole, might have been jokingly acknowledged by the two members of the cast playing Sylvia and Mary (as well as Ernst Lubitsch, the director originally assigned to the film):

> At a party during the shoot, Cukor was dancing with Russell. Ernst Lubitsch danced by and winked at her. "Trying to get a close-up in the picture?" he quipped. "If you want to *stay* in the picture, you'd better dance with Miss Shearer" [who was the widow of recently deceased studio boss Irving Thalberg]. Word got back to Shearer of Lubitsch's wisecrack, and a few minutes later, to everyone's amazement, Shearer grabbed Russell's arm and danced her around the floor. (124–25)

29. Fried, 60–61.

30. Sylvia has a telling queer wisecrack when she announces to Nancy Blake and Peggy Day, "I'm on to my Howard. I wouldn't trust him on Alcatraz—the mouse!" This quip simultaneously suggests that her husband is gay or bisexual (she wouldn't trust him sexually in an all-male prison/he's a "mouse," which is a slang term for a young woman); that Sylvia is lesbian or bisexual (if her statement is read as a displacement of her own closeted desire); and that their marriage may be a so-called lavender cover-up for both of them. Queer readings of the entire narrative could also recognize the film as a "(closet) lesbian" or a "bisexual" narrative. In the first case, since the affectional charge of the narrative is rooted in the interactions between women, and since these same-sex intensities are the audience's central source of pleasure in the narrative, a film like *The Women* might be said to have a "lesbian" narrative, whether the characters are coded or read as lesbian or not. Of course, this use of "lesbian" to describe a narrative's emotional and erotic temper is based upon a particular understanding of the qualities and characteristics that go into defining what is "lesbian." By other definitions, film narratives like *The Women* would remain "straight," or perhaps be only "hypothetically" lesbian (to borrow Chris

Straayer's term from "*Voyage en Douce, Entre Nous*: The Hypothetical Lesbian Heroine," *Jump Cut* 35 [1990]: 50–57).

A narrative might be understood as "bisexual" when both opposite-gender and same-gender emotional and erotic intensities are consistently made important to the working out of a narrative. Rather than see "heterosexual" narrative elements as necessarily placed in opposition to, or in tension with, "homosexual" narrative elements, this bisexual approach to narrative would consider these elements together as simultaneously viable narrative possibilities for characters, as well as simultaneously viable sources for an audience's pleasure. To a great extent, *The Women's* narrative contains the elements of bisexual construction described above. See the chapter on *Gentlemen Prefer Blondes* in this book for further discussion of bisexual narratives and readings.

31. Even though coded as a butch lesbian, Nancy is presented sympathetically by the narrative because she declares herself not sexually active ("a frozen asset"), hangs around mostly with straight people, and helps Mary carry out her plans to reunite with her husband by pushing the potentially disruptive queer into a symbolic closet during the powder room sequence. In all this, Nancy is one of a long line of homosexual supporting characters whose asexuality and willingness to bring or keep heterosexual couples together mark them as "good." See Greg Kinnear's character in *As Good As It Gets* (1997, Columbia-TriStar: James L. Brooks) for a more recent example of this character type.

32. For discussions of Dorothy Arzner and the "mannish lesbian" figures in her films, see Judith Mayne, "Female Authorship Reconsidered," in *The Woman at the Keyhole: Feminism and Women's Cinema* (Bloomington and Indianapolis: Indiana University Press, 1990), 89–123; Judith Mayne, "Lesbian Looks: Dorothy Arzner and Female Authorship," in *How Do I Look?: Queer Film and Video*, ed. Bad Object-Choices (Seattle: Bay Press, 1991), 103–43; and Sarah Halprin, "Writing in the Margins," *Jump Cut* 29 (1984).

33. Andrea Weiss, "A Queer Feeling when I Look at You: Hollywood Stars and Lesbian Spectatorship in the 1930s," in *Stardom: Industry of Desire*, ed. Christine Gledhill (London and New York: Routledge, 1991), 283–99.

34. Whitaker, 33.

35. *Mildred Pierce* (1945, Warners: Michael Curtiz); *Johnny Guitar* (1954, Republic: Nicholas Ray).

36. *Marie Antoinette* (1938, MGM: W.S. VanDyke III); *The Barretts of Wimpole Street* (1934, MGM: Sidney Franklin); *Rebecca* (1940, Selznick International: Alfred Hitchcock); *Frenchman's Creek* (1944, Paramount: Mitchell Leisen).

37. Mother-daughter bonding has been celebrated in lesbian culture long before sociocultural and psychoanalytic analyses of it, of course. In the face of anthropological and psychoanalytic accounts in the past two decades, however, at least two understandings of the lesbian erotics of the maternal have developed: (1) These erotics suggest that lesbian sexuality is "regressive" and a case of arrested development; and (2) These erotics suggest the need to radically rethink current sociocultural and psychoanalytic paradigms which (re)inscribe a phallic and

patriarchal order. Feminist and lesbian work in many areas has begun to consider this second line of thought and its implications for everyone, not only lesbians. For example, in film studies Gaylyn Studlar's *In the Realm of Pleasure: Von Sternberg, Dietrich, and the Masochistic Aesthetic* (Urbana and Chicago: University of Illinois Press, 1988) uses Gilles Deleuze's work in order to reconsider audience pleasure and desire from within maternal paradigms. For an interesting application of the mother-daughter mythos to lesbian work, see Rosemary Curb, "Core of the Apple: Mother-Daughter Fusion and Separation in Three Recent Lesbian Plays," *Lesbian Texts and Contexts: Radical Revisions*, ed. Karla Jay and Joanne Glasgow (New York and London: New York University Press, 1990), 355–76. Noted in Curb's bibilography are some important references for this topic, including Adrienne Rich, "Compulsory Heterosexuality and Lesbian Existence," *Signs* 5 (1980): 631–60; Adrienne Rich, *Of Woman Born: Motherhood as Experience and Institution* (New York: Bantam, 1976); Nancy Chodorow, *The Reproduction of Mothering: Psychoanalysis and the Sociology of Gender* (Berkeley: University of California Press, 1978); Carol Gilligan, *In a Different Voice: Psychological Theory and Women's Development* (Cambridge, Mass.: Harvard University Press, 1982); Coppelia Kahn, "The Hand that Rocks the Cradle: Recent Gender Theories and Their Implications," *The (M)other Tongue: Essays in Feminist Psychoanalytic Theory*, ed. Shirley Nelson Garner et al. (Ithaca, N.Y.: Cornell University Press, 1985), 72–88; and Azizah al Hibri, "Reproduction, Mothering, and the Origins of Patriarchy," *Mothering: Essays in Feminist Theory*, ed. Joyce Trebilcot (Totowa, N.J.: Rowman and Allenhand, 1983), 81–93.

38. Fried, 47.

The Queer Aesthete, the Diva, *and* The Red Shoes

George Du Maurier's 1894 novel *Trilby* is one of the earliest manifestations of what would become a popular Western cultural paradigm in the late nineteenth and twentieth centuries: the gay (or otherwise queer) high culture impresario or aficionado who expresses his passions and desires in public through women's bodies and voices.[1] Rooted in the dangerously fascinating Byronic (anti)hero of the British Romantic period, this figure found his home in the age of Oscar Wilde, which was a time when most popular scientific, medical, and public notions about what was beginning to be called male "homosexuality" centered around the upper class dandy and gender inversion.

Moving into the twentieth century, homosexual men of every class, newly labeled and legislated against, found themselves considered—and, as a result, often considered themselves—as being like women, or, more accurately, as being connected to the traditionally "feminine." But whereas straight women could be expressive in public—albeit usually within severely limited, compromised, and carefully monitored circumstances—homosexual men dared not speak their names openly, and resorted to expressing themselves within their own hidden (sub)culture or by using secret codes of language and style to indicate their homosexuality in public spaces. There was another way for homosexual men to express themselves within dominant culture, however: in some relation to straight women, or rather in relation to notions of the feminine attached to women, the gender homosexual men's "inversion" and "perversion" allied them to.

It is within just such a cultural context that *Trilby* presents the now archetypal figure of Svengali, a musical genius who mesmerizes both men and women into becoming accomplished performers. Tellingly, Svengali has the men perform duets with him on instruments, while he trains the women to become divas—conducting and hypnotically compelling them during concerts from the orchestra pit or a theatre box. In a move to contain Svengali's queer fascination, however, *Trilby*'s narrative is structured so that the homosocial world of (English) male artists living "la vie bohème" in Paris is established first. Svengali's entrance very early in the book, however, undermines all attempts by the novel's third person narrator, the lead male protagonist Little Billee, and Little Billee's two friends to keep control of the narrative. Indeed, the music Svengali makes when he plays the piano—sometimes accompanied by his companion Gecko—has an unmanning effect on the three artist friends (and the narrator):

> Then he fell to playing Chopin's impromptu in A flat, so beautifully that Little Billee's heart went nigh to bursting with suppressed emotion and delight.... Then Svengali and Gecko made music together, divinely... till the Laird and Taffy were almost as wild in their enthusiasm as Little Billee. (10–11)

Almost immediately after Svengali homosexualizes the very tenuously established homosocial space of the artist friends, Trilby enters. In keeping with this now queered narrative space, the narrator comments that she has "a portentous voice of great volume, that might almost have belonged to any sex," that "[s]he would have made a singularly handsome boy," and that "one felt instinctively that it was a real pity she wasn't a boy, she would have made such a jolly one" (11–12). This boyish quality will subsequently attract Little Billee and Svengali to Trilby—the former, initially, to her androgynous looks, and the latter to her deep voice. As it turns out, Little Billee will also become interested in Trilby's voice, as we discover "he had for the singing woman an absolute worship." The narrator continues: "He was especially thrall to the contralto—the deep low voice..." (40). While Svengali is set up as the gay (or homosexual) impresario in relation to women like Trilby, Little Billee is placed in the culturally queer space of diva worshipper. From the beginning, Little Billee is much less convincing as Trilby's romantic interest than as the sensitive and easily moved-to-tears aesthete who is the complement to Svengali's musical performer and impresario in the culturally feminized and homosexualized world of the arts.

Feminized though it is, the art world in *Trilby* allows little agency for women. Caught between the artistic vision of a homosexual man and the domestic vision of a (nominally) heterosexual man, Trilby can only respond and react to men's desires. For all her boyish high spirits, the narrative restricts Trilby's career choices to artist's model, rich man's wife, or dominated diva. What is more, Trilby becomes a diva whose brilliant singing voice is not really her own, but a product of Svengali's hypnotic will, which itself is the result of a burning desire to have the world recognize him as the master of the "lost" art of "il bel canto," which he says he found "in a dream" (20, 194). Finally, the narrator describes Trilby's performances as being a direct expression of her mentor's artistic passions:

> It was as if she said: "See! what does the composer count for?... The 'Nussbaum' is neither better nor worse than 'Mon ami Pierrot' when I am the singer, for I am *Svengali*; and you shall hear nothing, see nothing, think of nothing, but *Svengali, Svengali, Svengali*!" (193)

Why doesn't Svengali himself sing in public? First, the lost art of "il bel canto" that he is desperate to express is most famously associated with women singers. Then there are ethnic, class, and sexuality issues to consider, all of which are connected to each other in the narrator's initial description of Svengali:

> [He was] a tall, bony individual of any age between thirty and forty-five, of Jewish aspect, well-featured but sinister. He was very shabby and dirty.... His thick, heavy, languid, lustreless black hair fell down behind his ears on to his shoulders, in that musician-like way that is so offensive to the normal Englishman.... [He] spoke fluent French with a German accent...and his voice was very thin and mean and harsh, and often broke into a disagreeable falsetto. (9–10)

While a few pages earlier, the narrator proclaims that the possibility of a "very remote Jewish ancestor" in Little Billee's background "is of such priceless value in diluted homeopathic doses," he also makes it clear that, in the late nineteenth century English culture of the author, Jewishness "is not meant to be taken pure" (6). In the quotation above, Svengali's "pure" Jewishness is "sinister" and associated with the underclass, foreignness, and queerness (as gender inversion/homosexuality)—much like Dickens's Fagin in *Oliver Twist* and any number of characters in Western texts.[2]

After failing to make "a dirty, drabby little dolly-mop of a [French] Jewess" (39) the new queen of bel canto, Svengali turns his attentions to the more culturally attractive (to the novel's target readers) figure of Trilby O'Ferrall, a Scotch-English milk seller living in Paris. That Trilby has no artistic ambitions of her own fuels Svengali's desire to use her as a vehicle for expressing his bel canto passions in order to gain public recognition. His marriage to Trilby is conducted off page. That he has shown little romantic interest in her (or any woman) before this leads us to understand Svengali's marriage largely as a means for him to offer Trilby to the public as Madame (or La) Svengali—that is, as his feminine extension. It takes Svengali's death from a combination of heart disease and a knife wound inflicted by one of his former protégés to release the narrative and the other characters from his queer thrall and allow for their (re)heterosexualization.

After *Trilby*, most fictional gay impresarios and other aesthetes would retain some elements of Svengali's combination of fascinating monstrousness, foreignness, and "gender inversion." But they would rarely be members of the underclass again. The late-nineteenth-century example of Oscar Wilde would forever after link the gay aesthete with the upper-class dandy. Wilde's status as the most (in)famous homosexual in the Western world would also reinforce the connections between male homosexuality and the arts—for both homosexuals and heterosexuals. If they were not already, such upper-class "feminine" areas as fashion and interior decoration, and such high culture forms as opera, theatre, and ballet became bastions of coded, translated, or otherwise indirect homosexual expressiveness in the public sphere. During the first half of the twentieth century, these arenas became more and more widely, and usually pejoratively, understood by dominant culture as homosexual (or somehow queer) as well as feminine—indeed with gender inversion being the most common understanding of homosexuality, "feminine" *was* "homosexual" where men were concerned.

Almost every man who associated himself with the artistic pursuits mentioned above placed himself within what were considered homosexual or more vaguely queer spaces whether he identified as homosexual/gay/queer or not. In the twentieth century, one could add the "art film" to the list of cultural forms "queered" for men. Flourishing since the teens in Europe, these films were initially transcriptions of "famous players in famous plays" (and novels) and were usually produced to confer some measure of class and prestige upon a commercial mass culture industry. It is no coincidence that, besides transcribing plays and literary classics, many art films concerned themselves with other high culture forms: ballet, opera, classical music, and painting. Of course, fashion (as costume, hair, and makeup design) and interior decoration (as art design and set decoration) were very important to almost all of those high culture forms that made their way into art films.

As may be clear at this point, I am not using the term "art film" in the more recent American and British sense that labels only certain foreign films—generally by auteur directors—as "art films." Indeed, most of these films would not fall under my use of the term. I employ "art film" in the older sense of prestige productions with some connection to high culture forms, or with some pretensions to high culture status through their subject or style. These are generally films produced within studio systems, but ones that fall outside the prevailing standards of popular (that is, working and middle-class) tastes. These films are calculated risks taken by studios, producers, and directors—bids for critical acclaim, awards, business from the limited class of "discerning" moviegoers, and some crossover business from regular moviegoers who might temporarily be convinced to place themselves in queerer viewing spaces for their (high) cultural enrichment. By the definition I am using, I would consider as art films such works as *Sunrise, Fantasia, A Song to Remember* (and most 1940s and 1950s biopics about classical composers), *Lust for Life* (and most biopics about the lives of painters), *Specter of the Rose, Invitation to the Dance, Don Giovanni* (and other British and American attempts to transcribe opera), and a number of films by Michael Powell and Emeric Pressburger, including *Black Narcissus, The Tales of Hoffmann, The Red Shoes,* and *Oh . . . Rosalinda!!*[3]

While films like these are frequently reviled as middlebrow kitsch for what appear to be their failed attempts to combine high culture subjects with popular cinema forms and styles (or, occasionally, vice versa, as with *Sunrise*), I see the tensions in these films as also a function of attempts to mask or neutralize the feminine queer (or queerly feminine) charge of high culture subjects through certain heterosexualizing film and cultural conventions. We should recall, though, that tensions similar to these already exist in such high culture forms as opera, ballet, and theatre. Consider the musical and visual "excesses" of many opera productions in relation to their very conventional gender and sexual narratives. Putting high culture forms like these on screen—particularly into mainstream films—just complicates the discussion of how femininity, masculinity, straightness, and queerness circulate in relation to these studio art films.

One of the films that most strikingly illustrates the frequent queerness of the studio art film—both on screen and behind the scenes—is *The Red Shoes.* Not only is the narrative centrally concerned with the world of classical ballet, but the film appears to have been planned self-consciously as an art film by Britain's most famous writing, producing, and directing partners, Michael Powell and Emeric Pressburger.[4] Once under the sign of the art film, both those making the film and the film narrative itself became associated with queerness—more particularly with male homosexuality. Discussing the concept of "gay sensibility," Seymour Kleinberg remarks, "In our times, two dominant areas of this expression in art and commerce have been in ballet and movies"—and *The Red Shoes* combined them both.[5] Powell recalls how producer Alexander Korda never understood the success of *The Red Shoes,* as he felt that men associated with the ballet "were a lot of poofs,"[6] while the film's director of photography, Jack Cardiff, thought ballet was "sissies prancing about." Even so, he became a self-confessed "balletomane" while working on the film.[7]

Adding to the the aura of queerness surrounding the making of *The Red Shoes* are certain production events that strikingly parallel the film's narrative, as Powell and Pressburger became determined to make a film star of

ballet dancer Moira Shearer, just as gay impresario Boris Lermontov is consumed by the idea of making Victoria (Vicky) Page a star through his staging of a ballet based upon Hans Christian Andersen's "The Red Shoes,"
which itself is the story of a young woman who is tempted by a queer shoemaker into wearing shoes that will not let her stop dancing. To carry the
"male aesthetes expressing themselves through a diva" parallels surrounding
The Red Shoes a step further: Andersen, himself homosexual, has been
described as a "would-be dancer and actor who channeled many of his own
frustrated desires" into stories like the one about a young woman who
dances around the world in red shoes.[8]

The Red Shoes takes its place in Powell's two autobiographies and in the
Pressburger biography by grandson Kevin Macdonald as the film that, in retrospect, marked the height of the Powell-Pressburger team collaboration, as
it became the film that did the most to keep their names twinned in cinema
history.[9] It was a creative partnership of which Powell said in the 1980s, "The
press were intrigued and puzzled by the collaboration. . . . Nobody understood it at the time, and nobody understands it now."[10] Wayne Koestenbaum's
book, *Double Talk: The Erotics of Male Literary Collaboration*, offers an angle
from which we might understand Powell and Pressburger's work as the collaboration of queer, if not exactly gay, artists:

> I would say that collaboration between men in the 19th and early 20th cen-
> turies was a complicated and anxiously homosocial act, and that all the
> writers in this study, regardless of their sexual preference, collaborated in
> order to separate homoeroticism from the sanctioned male bonding that
> upholds patriarchy.[11]

While he acknowledges that there is the *attempt* to separate the homosocial from the homosexual in these collaborations, Koestenbaum goes on to
say that artistic collaborations by heterosexual men always finally work
"within a framework dominated by homosexual desire, whether draped in
the discrete [sic] charm of the 'homosocial continuum,' or left impolitely
naked."[12] Since anxieties about the lines between the homosocial and the
homosexual have persisted up until the present, Powell and Pressburger's
partnership might still be discussed within Koestenbaum's notions of the
erotics of male artistic collaboration.

The autobiographies, biography, and letters of Powell and Pressburger
are filled with intriguing tidbits that, added together, make a good case for
there being a very blurred homosocial-erotic line between the two men during their friendship and creative partnership. Powell refers to his first meeting with Pressburger, to work on *The Spy in Black*, as something akin to love

at first sight.[13] Part of what Pressburger's grandson, Kevin Macdonald, calls the "uncannily close relationship [that] began to develop between the two men"[14] seems to have been initiated over the body of someone Powell describes as "one of the most romantic and magnetic men alive"—the star of *The Spy in Black*, gay actor Conrad Veidt.[15] Recalling their first meeting with Veidt, Powell says: "Conrad Veidt was seated alone at a table by the window drinking coffee. . . . Emeric and I exchanged a glance. This magnificent animal was reserved for us. Then we looked at each other."[16] Queerly creative ménage à trois, anyone? "It's like a marriage without sex," Powell said about his creative relationship with Pressburger, "[L]ucky the collaborator who finds his rightful partner."[17]

If Powell and Pressburger's pairing was a marriage without actual physical sex, it was a union that did express itself erotically and romantically in many other ways, on and off screen. Powell's correspondence to Pressburger is filled with touching and funny salutational endearments: "My angel Imre," "Dearest One of Both," "My Dear First Class Male!" "Old Austrian Cock," and two particularly interesting ones in the context of this essay—"Dear Old Fruit" and "Dearest Red Shoemaker."[18] In one note to Pressburger, Powell comments on their late-1970s business affairs and plans: "I think things are shaping [up] better for us. What a romance!"[19] After Powell, Pressburger, and their films had been rediscovered in the 1980s, they were asked how they had managed to remain together for so long: "[T]he two men looked at one another for a moment, each awaiting a reply from the other, before Powell quite unselfconsciously replied: 'The answer is love. You can't have a collaboration without love. We had complete love and confidence in each other.' "[20] "For twenty years we had been as close as a man and wife,"[21] Powell remarked in one autobiography about their partnership, "I knew Emeric better than his wife, better than his daughter, better than all his girlfriends, better than his current mistress, but not, I hope, better than his two Scottish grandsons."[22]

This last women-excluding "between men" remark should remind us that, since we are speaking of studio filmmaking here, discussions of the production contexts of the Powell-Pressburger films as queerly charged might be extended beyond the writing-producing-directing team to include their other regular Archers Production collaborators: Alfred Junge, Brian Easdale, Jack Cardiff, Hein Heckroth, Anton Walbrook, Christopher Challis, F.A. Young, Reginald Mills, Arthur Lawson, Sydney Streeter, and others. Indeed, far from invoking classic patriarchal auteurist or studio mogul rhetoric, Powell and Pressburger usually spoke of their filmmaking as a close collaboration among a team of men. In his autobiography, Powell recalls a scene cut out of *The Red Shoes* that "illustrat[ed] the way Emeric and I [and, one might add, the Archers team] worked together." During this scene Lermontov and

The diva, Victoria Page (Moira Shearer), and her queer collaborators, including impresario Boris Lermontov (Anton Walbrook).

his collaborators toss around ideas for "The Red Shoes Ballet," something Powell and Pressburger found themselves doing off camera with their collaborators. According to Powell, when the time came to film the scene, "[t]here was no longer anything to talk about or explain, because we were going to show the film audience what we had created." By Powell's final "we," the Archers film team has overlapped and even replaced the "we" of the Lermontov Ballet company as the group of creative male artists producing what Powell calls "the fruit of all this collaboration and love."[23] Elsewhere in his autobiographies, Powell does recall a sequence involving male artistic collaboration that did remain in the film: "[T]he scene when Marius [Goring, who plays Julian Craster] comes to the villa and plays the new Red Shoes music to Lermontov, Ljubov, Ratov and Livy.... There are lots of clever scenes in *The Red Shoes*, but this is the heart of the picture."[24] As Kevin Macdonald put it, "*The Red Shoes* was probably the pinnacle of the collaborative principle of movie-making.... It is ridiculous to speak of *The Red Shoes* as a Powell-Pressburger film. It is a production of the Archers."[25]

However much the Lermontov Ballet and the Archers Production company liked to see themselves as a men's club of collaborative artists, the truth is they vitally depended upon women—or at least one woman per project.

Indeed, these teams often focused their collective creative energies upon a straight female character and the performer playing her. Where Lermontov trusts the talents of neophyte ballerina Victoria Page to preserve the reputation of his company, Powell and Pressburger (and the rest of the Archers) counted upon film neophyte Moira Shearer to carry their most ambitious and expensive art film to date. Where Lermontov (and his creative team) become fixated upon red shoes (there is even a shot of Lermontov selecting just the right pair for Page from a row of ballet slippers), Powell, Pressburger, and most of the Archers became transfixed by Shearer's red hair—not surprising considering the film's investment in Technicolor. Powell's autobiography *A Life in Movies* is almost embarrassing in its rhapsody: the "most glorious hair of Titian red that I have ever seen on a woman," "red-headed beauty," "red-headed mackerel," "that glorious, tall, red-headed dancer," her "cloud of red hair as natural and beautiful as any animals, flamed and glittered like an autumn bonfire."[26] "The main thing that all publicity, exploitation, advertising and selling should concentrate on is The Girl. The Red-Head who wears the Red Shoes," Powell wrote in a letter to Pressburger discussing promotional ideas for the film's American release.[27]

From all accounts, once a number of the Archers had seen red-haired Shearer no one else would do for the *The Red Shoes*. But they were hard-pressed to convince her to take time off from the Sadler's Wells Ballet, where she was just beginning to make a name for herself, to star in a Powell-Pressburger-Archers film. Her artistic sights were set upon being a prima ballerina; the Archers were fixed upon making another successful art film after *Black Narcissus*. In short, they needed her more than she needed them—and they all seemed to recognize this situation, although not without some resentment on Powell's part. In his autobiographies, Powell praises Shearer as a great talent, and even includes her in his usually all-male list of collaborators when he discusses the film, but his frustrations at her resistance to making *The Red Shoes*, and his feeling that she saw the Archers team as being far less sensitive and artistic than her ballet company, finds its outlet in some rather crude straight patriarchal rhetoric:

> I never let love interfere with business, or I would have made love to her. It would have improved her performance.... We were very much alike.... It was a curious relationship. I sometimes wonder whether she had a heart to break.[28]

Shearer's involvement with *The Red Shoes* appears to have made Powell feel somewhat threatened as one of the major (queerly positioned) auteurs of a ballet art film. Indeed, at one point in the quotation above, he casts Shearer as Lermontov and himself as the diva by reworking one of the lines in the film with a gender switch: "He has no heart to break, that man." By her resistence to filmmaking—even to being in a classy Powell-Pressburger-Archers production—Shearer made the importance of her contribution to the otherwise "boys only" collaboration stand out. Perhaps recognizing that the Archers might be producing *The Red Shoes*, but that Shearer was actually wearing them, Powell was left to reassert himself, where and when he could, by shifting the terms of the discussion from artistic creation (the red shoes/*The Red Shoes*) to personal matters (the red hair). By doing this, Powell the heterosexual man might have felt he could put Shearer in her gender place for Powell the queerly positioned artist. The director's complicated relationship with ballet diva Shearer in connection with *The Red Shoes* is classic. In his queer position as ballet film director-producer, Powell identifies with ballet dancer Shearer ("[w]e were very much alike"), but he also seems somewhat resentful and threatened by the ways in which Shearer's attitude about the production emphasize his (and the Archers team's) artistic dependence upon her and her red shoes/red hair.

Given this creative situation between diva and "impresario," it comes as no surprise to discover that a number of Archers productions include an onscreen male character who attempts to control or regulate the central female character(s) and the development of their heterosexual relationships. Often this character is not only coded as homosexual or otherwise queer, but is played by an actor who is homosexual. Think of Theo Kretschmar-Schuldorff/Anton Walbrook in *The Life and Death of Colonel Blimp*, Thomas Colpepper, JP/Eric Portman in *A Canterbury Tale*, Mr. Dean/David Farrar in *Black Narcissus*, Boris Lermontov/Anton Walbrook in *The Red Shoes*, Edward Marston/Cyril Cusack in *Gone to Earth*, Hoffmann's rivals/Robert Helpmann in *The Tales of Hoffmann*, and Dr. Falke/Anton Walbrook in *Oh…Rosalinda!!*[29] Quite a few critics have understood characters like these as Powell's alter egos—even though one might point out that they were largely written by Pressburger, and, therefore, could also be considered Pressburger's screen representatives in some way.[30] Indeed, Powell and Pressburger were not averse to pointing out connections between themselves and many of these characters, as well as the actors who played them.

To be more specific, the queer aura of many Archers collaborative productions—and of the Powell-Pressburger partnership—is often linked to gay Anton Walbrook, the performer most closely and frequently associated with their films—just as gay actor Conrad Veidt had been for pre-Archers Pressburger and/or Powell films: *The Spy in Black*, *Contraband*, and *The Thief of Bagdad*.[31] Walbrook's homosexuality, the queerness of many of the characters he played, and the elements of foreignness and an aristocratic bearing associated with his image came together at least twice to create a figure who

seemed to represent the Powell-Pressburger team in their queer position at
the head of a multinational group of men collaborating to produce art films
under the Archers' banner. In *Oh . . . Rosalinda!!* Walbrook plays an upper-
class doctor who, as part of a revenge plot, seeks to manipulate the heterosexual lives and loves of a number of people in postwar Vienna. An updating
of the operetta *Die Fledermaus*, the action revolves around an elaborate masquerade party stage-managed by the Walbrook character ("the Bat") in order
to entrap and embarrass many of his guests. Crucial to his direction of
events is the Bat's ability to encourage two women to come to the party disguised, so that they can fool the men who know them. This scheme enables
the Bat to wreak havoc on their straight relationships, at least temporarily.
While their characters are not singers, the two women here, for all intents
and purposes, register upon audiences as operetta divas—and the Bat
becomes another gay man who uses their various talents to express his
desires (here for control and revenge) indirectly. In discussing Walbrook's Bat,
Powell conflates the character with the actor playing him:

> As the champagne flowed on the screen, I thought of Anton and the strange
> art of acting. Larry [Olivier] said that real acting, the big stuff, is walking
> a tightrope between the two sexes: sooner or later you fall off one side, or
> the other. . . . No actor that I have known had such control as Anton
> had—until he played the Bat. Then, the Bat controlled him. . . . The Bat was
> different. In order to play Dr. Falke, Adolf Wohlbruck had to return to his
> sources. . . . I knew that this was Anton's only failure, because he had to play
> himself.[32]

If Powell hints at the gayness of Walbrook and his director-impresario
type character in *Oh . . . Rosalinda!!* by resorting to suggestive references to
gender inversion, he lays all the cards on the table in discussing the actor and
his role as Boris Lermontov in *The Red Shoes*: "When it came to *The Red Shoes*
and that devil, Boris Lermontov, there was no question in our minds as to who
should play him, and give a performance filled with passion, integrity, and,
yes, with homosexuality. . . ."[33] Written with Walbrook in mind, Pressburger
contended that in Lermontov there is "something of [homosexual ballet
impresario Serge] Diaghilev, something of Alex Korda, something of Michael,
and quite a bit of me."[34] In considering the connections between Lermontov,
Powell, and Pressburger, it might be wise to reemphasize here that the queerness I am discussing in relation to Powell-Pressburger and their (male)
Archers collaborators has more to do with the circumstances surrounding
their creative work than with their conscious gender and sexuality identifi-
cations. As John Russell Taylor puts it, more generally, in terms of Powell:

[There] is ample evidence of Powell's identification with his artist-super-men. He has, for instance, compared the film-maker's role so often to that of the Diaghilev type of impresario, channelling and co-ordinating the headstrong talents of many other artists to one unified end, that it is barely conceivable there could be no sort of identification in his own mind between himself and the impresario Lermontov in *The Red Shoes*. It seems, too, that some of the more abrasive and highly-coloured of his favourite actors, Eric Portman and Anton Walbrook in particular, regularly stand in for the director as *meneur du jeu* and therefore represent Powell the artist, if not necessarily Powell the man, within his work.[35]

All evidence onscreen and behind the scenes to the contrary, however, many people insist upon heterosexualizing the Diaghilev-like Lermontov and his relationship with Page. Besides general cultural heterocentrism, this might be traced, in part, to frequent discussions of the film as a "heterosexual reworking of the Diaghilev/Nijinski/Romola triangle," with Lermontov, Craster, and Page, respectively, taking on these roles.[36] But far from setting up Lermontov and Page as lovers, the critical tendency to make Page the Nijinski figure should emphasize the theme of the gay impresario's vital investment in the diva as his erotically expressive stand-in. Karen Backstein suggests that "at a point in which Powell [and, one might add, Pressburger] could not openly explore a gay relationship, [he] collapses female physicality and homosexual identity."[37] The narrative of *The Red Shoes* works itself out to force Page/Nijinski to choose between Lermontov–high art–queerness and Julian Craster–domesticity–straightness—although you would never know this from most of the contemporary reviews of *The Red Shoes*, nor from almost all of the subsequent popular and academic pieces on the film. For most viewers and commentators, Page's choice between a ballet career and a domestic life is also a choice between two straight men. In other words, many people understand Lermontov as romantically desiring Page for himself, and because of this supposedly suppressed passion, he is jealous of Craster's romantic relationship with her. Comments like, "Intertwined with Lermontov's stern supervision of Victoria's career is an underlying love and sexual attraction," are representative of this kind of heterocentric reading.[38]

To be fair, even Page initially misreads Lermontov's intentions when he invites her to his villa for what she thinks is a date. Dressing in a lavish ball-gown, Page ascends the stairs to the villa only to find Lermontov (sporting a red neckerchief) surrounded by his male collaborators—and they are all discussing her suitability for their new production. In the novelization of the film written by Powell and Pressburger, the narrator makes it clear that Lermontov "loved [Page] not as a woman, but as an equal."[39] Later in the book, Lermontov sets up Page's choice not as being between himself and Craster,

The diva torn between husband Julien Craster (Marius Goring) / straight domesticity and Lermontov / queer artistry.

but as being between "*The Red Shoes* against Julian Craster."[40] Besides moments like this, which indicate Lermontov's lack of romantic interest in Page, the film suggests the queer difference in Lermontov's jealousy over Page when, during the climactic argument in Page's dressing room, Craster accuses Lermontov of "waiting day after day for a chance to get her back." When Lermontov asks Craster if he knows why he has waited, Craster replies, "Because you're jealous of her." "Yes, I am," Lermontov shouts back, "but in a way that you will never understand."

So Lermontov is not jealous of Page in the heterosexual way Craster and many viewers think he is. Then how is he jealous of her? Lermontov does not elaborate, but the evidence of the rest of the film leads to two interrelated propositions: (1) He is jealous of her artistic abilities because he needs to use them for his own creative expression, and (2) He is jealous of her career because he wants to see her fulfill her promise as a great dancer—so that (1) can occur, it should be pointed out. To these counts of "red shoes envy" might be added Lermontov's jealousy of Page's red shoes as fetishistic reminders of her easy sexual access to men—particularly to Lermontov's most important "Red Shoes Ballet" collaborator, composer Julian Craster.

Like Svengali before him, Lermontov "makes music" with this male collaborator, while using the bodies of his divas for the artistic expression of his sublimated sexual desires. Recall, along these lines, that the story of "The Red Shoes Ballet" has the protagonist, in her red shoes, promiscuously move between many men.

In *The Red Shoes* this situation sets up a relationship between the gay impresario and the woman artist that is, to say the least, fraught. From very early on, the film wants us to understand Lermontov and Page as being alike and connected in their intense devotion to ballet. Lermontov asks Page, "Why do you dance?" To which she replies, "Why do you live?" But even this exchange hints at the difficult positions culture has them take in relation to each other and to artistic expression, for, as it turns out, Lermontov lives to have dancers like Page perform ballets he develops and stages with his collaborators. Page lives to dance, but feels she must put herself under the disciplinary tutelage of Lermontov and company to push her art to its highest level. As one critic puts it, Lermontov is "[a]n artist without talent of his own, he seeks personal satisfaction by finding others with budding talent and nurturing them to greatness: 'I want to create something big out of something little,' he confides to Vicky. 'To make a great dancer out of you.'"[41] Later, Lermontov adds, "You shall dance, and the world will follow. Shhh! Not a word. I will do the talking, you will do the dancing." Just as Powell, Pressburger, and company were not particularly interested in Shearer's aesthetic opinions (she was "infuriated by the Archers' lack of ballet knowledge"),[42] Lermontov reveals time and again in the film that he is artistically interested only in Page's body as an instrument or a vehicle and not in her mind. Page wants to be "a great dancer," but the cost will be her subjugation to Lermontov's will and his artistic vision, and, secondarily, to those of the men who make up the creative staff of the Lermontov Ballet. The novelization makes the complicated artistic relationship between the straight woman and her queer collaborators explicit when Lermontov tells Page,

> All that Grisha, Sergei, and Craster can contribute has to filter through you. That's your contribution.... The process of creation ... is intoxicating. In a sense you will feel like someone "under the influence." Your personality will split. Suddenly there will be two of you. One is dancing, the other watching.... The first person is created by us, by Sergei, Grisha, Julian, me; the second is your very own.[43]

Part of what Page is asked to give up in order to enter Lermontov's charmed circle is being a practicing heterosexual. While she is still in the corps de ballet, she hears Lermontov's railing against the company's diva, who has announced her engagement:

> I am not interested in Boronskaja's form anymore, nor in the form of any other prima ballerina who is imbecile enough to get married. . . . She's out, finished. You cannot have it both ways. The dancer who relies upon the doubtful comforts of human love will never be a great dancer—never!

When Grischa Ljubov, the choreographer, comments, "That's all very fine, Boris, very pure and fine, but you can't alter human nature," Lermontov responds, "No, I think you can do better than that—you can ignore it." The terms in which Lermontov discusses love/sex are interesting. "Human love" seems to be equated here with heterosexual relationships/marriage, the implication being that women dancers should turn to the "inhuman" or "non-human" love of Lermontov and his ballet company in order to become great.

This suggestion that what Lermontov offers Page is, somehow, the antithesis of "human love," connects with some common cultural notions about the spaces of high art: these spaces are homosexual or queer and, therefore, perverse and suspect (both Page and Powell refer to Lermontov as being monstrous, as do a number of critics);[44] and these spaces are somehow "beyond" or "above" such messy things as sexuality. Both ideas are attempts to place high art, and those who create it, in non-straight territory, with the second notion really being just a way for people to avoid dealing with the first, as it allows homophobic and heterocentrist viewers to take comfort in the idea that someone like Lermontov (or Powell, or Pressburger) is asexually consumed with desexualized notions of high art and aesthetics. So understanding high art and artists as being beyond sexuality is, finally, just another case of the "I know it's/(s)he's gay, or somehow queer, but would rather not think about it" position that homophobia encourages in people whether they are responding to characters or to real personalities.

But cultural pressures being what they were—and are—many gay, lesbian, bisexual, and queer artists also have come to understand their creative work as being beyond or above issues of sexuality. It appears Lermontov is such a person from the evidence of his comment about ignoring "human nature"—in this context meaning any type of sexuality, as opposed to "human love," which is contextualized to refer to heterosexuality and marriage. For Lermontov, "ignoring human nature" seems to mean suppressing the direct expression of his (homo)sexuality while also attempting to control the expression of the (hetero)sexuality of his prima ballerinas. What is more, Lermontov's desire to have Page (and before her, Irena Boronskaja) forego heterosexual love is linked in the film to his artistic aspirations. So by a tortuous route of suppression and substitution he is able to have his divas stand in for him. Supposedly purged of their heterosexual desires, they can become the vehicles for expressing the gay impresario's disavowed desires, through codes of the "feminine," within the queer spaces of ballet.

We might pause here to wonder about the homosexual men on stage in ballets, including the Lermontov Ballet's lead male dancer, Ivan Boleslawsky. Why can't they be the vehicles of gay, or otherwise queer, expressiveness? The most obvious response, of course, is that open gay/queer expression was not possible in high art venues—and still is not, to a great extent. Thus, while almost all male ballet dancers are considered queer by most of the public, they perform within heterosexualizing narrative contexts.[45] Granted, even given these contexts, queerness enters into many people's understanding of the ballet as they see the male dancers as (to quote Jack Cardiff again) "sissies prancing about," or, more benignly, as gay men being artistically expressive. There is some space for gayness to be expressed in public by ballet performers, then, but this kind of expressiveness seems to be less about direct and open expression, and more about homosexuality being signalled or read in spite of the heterosexual narrative and cultural frames of reference both the male dancers and the audience are asked to work within.

For someone like Lermontov, who has decided to "ignore human nature" in relation to his art, and therefore place himself within the acceptable dominant cultural category of "asexual artist," using gay dancers to express himself would most likely open up a troublesome Pandora's box. As suggested earlier, men like Lermontov could not be seen—and often did not want to see themselves—as creating "obvious" homosexual art. Although they work behind the scenes with homosexual and otherwise queerly positioned men, and might even find certain ways to express their gay desires through gay performers, high art producers like Lermontov choose—or feel forced to choose—to be expressive in less direct ways by using feminine codes connected to women performers—with the Diaghilev-Nijinski team as perhaps the most notable real life exception in the ballet world.

A preliminary draft of the film's script contained a short exchange that encapsulates the very different relationships gay impresarios-aesthetes like Lermontov have with divas and with gay performers. Prima ballerina Boronskaja is late again, and Boleslawsky confronts Lermontov:

Boleslawsky: Well, if I dared to be as late as that . . .
Lermontov: You would, of course, be discharged immediately. But you, my dear boy, are *not* Boronskaja. Furthermore, you've got too much make-up on. Go to your room and do something about it.[46]

Lermontov is willing to make concessions for the diva, but he feels compelled to put some distance between himself and his company's leading male dancer. However, Lermontov's admonitions to the dancer are symptomatic of his confused, self-oppressive position. For while Lermontov takes pains to point out that the gay performer will always fall short for the impresario because he is not the diva, he also warns the dancer that his appearance is too effeminate for him to go on stage. It seems that for Lermontov, having a gay male diva performing in one of his ballets would be like coming out himself, as he has sublimated his homosexuality into the creating and staging of female diva–focused ballets.

So where does this leave the straight woman diva? In earlier versions of the script, Page was given a close woman friend, who was also a member of Lermontov's troupe. With this friend came opportunities for Page to be more expressive about her artistic ambitions, as well as to be more vocal about her frustrations with Lermontov's treatment of her. By the final script, however, the friend-colleague is gone.[47] In the finished film, we find that Page, caught between the all-male creative collaborators of Lermontov's ballet company and the conventional domestic demands of her husband Craster, is left with only her moments onstage to call her own, and only partially. The film emphasizes Page's artistic dilemma through some startling subjective camerawork during the two extended ballet sequences. In the first of these sequences Page dances "Swan Lake" for a small ballet company run by a woman. Soon after her entrance, the sequence is presented to mirror Page's experience while dancing. A series of zip pans over the audience alternate with shots of her ecstatic face to convey how intensely she feels these moments of artistic creation. When she sees Lermontov in the audience, however, her face registers panic, and there is a rough changeover between the records Page is dancing to. Her brief moment of laying sole claim to her art is over.

The second sequence of Page dancing onstage is more extended, and it is more disturbing in representing the precarious and compromised position of women performing artists. Page is dancing "The Red Shoes Ballet," which, as noted earlier, is the story of a young woman who wants to dance, and the queer shoemaker who gives her a pair of red shoes that allow her to dance—but, ultimately, to their/his (or Lermontov's and composer Julian Craster's) tune. Most of the ballet is shot "objectively," that is, from the position of the theatre or film audience watching it. As the ballet's narrative reaches the point where the protagonist realizes the red shoes are controlling her, the filming style becomes more subjective, inviting the viewer to understand and to empathize with both the ballet protagonist's and Page's conflicting feelings about putting on those red shoes. At one point, the queer shoemaker changes into Lermontov, and then into Craster, before Page's horrified eyes. Page then dances with a man made of newspaper before the shoemaker returns to lead her on. Soon afterward, Page hallucinates that Craster leaves the orchestra pit (where he is conducting) and walks out over the footlights to be her partner. When he lifts her, she changes into a flower, a cloud, then a bird. After these shots, the style of filming the ballet returns to the "objective."

During what should be the moment of her greatest artistic expression and satisfaction, Page is haunted and hemmed in by the two key men in "The Red Shoes Ballet" creative team. Her connecting Lermontov and Craster to the shoemaker, and Craster to her dancing partner, trouble her creative pleasure and suggest that she is becoming aware of how she is being monitored onstage and off: by Lermontov and Craster as the queer collaborators of "her vehicle" (she is really their vehicle), and by Craster as a creative and, potentially, as a personal partner (later, she will be "lifted" by him out of her place as prima ballerina and into a position as ethereal love object and artistic muse). However, within the subjective portion of "The Red Shoes Ballet," we are presented with those shots of Page in a newsprint dress as she elegantly and skillfully dances with that newspaper man. Here we are made aware that Page's art can stand on its own, apart from her male dance partners and those behind-the-scenes male collaborators, who become mere paper men when the diva dances. However, her newsprint dress also suggests she is the three-dimensional, flesh-and-blood *doppelgänger* of the newspaper man, who is associatively linked to Lermontov, Craster, and Boleslawsky, her gay dance partner. Between them, the two onstage dance sequences present Page as both "little more than the projection of... [gay and queerly positioned] men's desires" and as someone who feels, even if momentarily, the "power and pleasure" of putting on her red ballet slippers (which also allow her to see these men as projections of *her* fears and desires).[48]

Koestenbaum notes that within much of male artistic collaboration "[h]omoeroticism and misogyny palpably intersect," as "collaborators [make] use of the 'feminine' in appropriative ways...improperly diffusing homoerotic desire in female go-betweens."[49] In light of Koestenbaum's ideas, it is interesting to recall that at the same time Lermontov forms his important new collaboration with Craster, he is also beginning his gay impresario-diva relationship with Page. Initially, Page does act as the "go-between," being passed among Lermontov, Craster, Ljubov, and Boleslawsky as they attempt to get her ready to dance "The Red Shoes Ballet." The role of the diva as a (not fully successful) heterosexualizing counter in what otherwise might seem too intensely and clearly queer male collaborations is most strikingly presented in *The Red Shoes* during the scene in which Lermontov tells Craster the story of the ballet. As he summarizes the tale, Lermontov moves away from Craster to stand next to, and then to fondle, a marble statue of the "dismembered" foot of a ballerina on point. Considering Lermontov by himself, it is possible to understand the statue as representing his intense identification with the

Just before he fondles his feminine phallic foot statue, Lermontov explains the story of "The Red Shoes" to Craster.

diva. In the artistic collaboration between men, however, the diva becomes a fetishized artistic object. Even more outrageously telling, the diva, in this particular scene, becomes an aestheticized "feminine" phallus in the possession of the gay impresario, to be displayed by and for himself and his collaborators as they discuss their productions.

Given these circumstances, it is fitting that the protagonist of the ballet, danced by Page, should be given the red shoes by a queer shoemaker (read: Lermontov, Craster, and the other members of the creative team).[50] While the red shoes initially allow the nameless woman character to dance gracefully, winning the romantic attentions of a young man (read: Craster away from Lermontov), she soon finds that she cannot take the shoes off (read: Lermontov's pressures upon her to stay in the queer world of ballet at the expense of heterosexual relationships). Compelled to dance wherever the shoes take her, she is prevented from continuing her heterosexual romance—as well as from returning home—because the slippers constantly dance her away from her lover and her mother (that is, away from heterosexuality and homosocial bonding). What the shoes do is dance her into sexual adventures, including promiscuous "back alley" encounters with "rough trade" men and lesbian-suggestive situations with prostitutes: that is, the red shoes dance her into gender and sexual "excesses," which she seems to enjoy initially. In this way the queerly created red shoes/"Red Shoes Ballet" offers straight women the opportunity to express their sexual and artistic desires: to be exhibitionistic rather than fully objectified. In the end, however, these shoes are presented as seemingly queerly controlled ones that dance the character—and Page as it turns out—to her death. In the novelization, Page comments while dancing the title ballet (in a stream-of-consciousness passage): "I'm the greatest dancer in the world!... It isn't true! It's the red shoes that dance and I follow! It's the spell of the Shoemaker that makes me dance."[31]

Once again, in high art—the ballet, the art film narrative—queerly positioned men appropriate a woman's body. However, as mentioned earlier, this practice is encouraged by certain interconnected misogynistic and homophobic patriarchal attitudes, which require gay men to give over the direct expression of their sexuality in order to achieve career success, while also demanding that women in the public sphere somehow be monitored or controlled by men (either gay or straight). But The Red Shoes' narrative also seems to suggest that male queerness in one form or another is to blame for Page's death: first the Lermontov-Craster-et al. collaboration on "The Red Shoes Ballet," and later Lermontov's possessive desire to have Page do his artistic bidding at the expense of her heterosexual relationship. Since it was created under the queer sponsorship of the Lermontov Ballet company, it makes sense that Craster's split from Lermontov leaves "The Red Shoes Ballet" in the maestro's possession and marks the beginning of Craster's solo "straight" career as a composer, which, unsurprisingly, coincides with the beginning of his domestic life with Page as his wife and artistic muse. Because of conventional cultural prejudices about these things, most viewers and critics feel that Page's death is largely Lermontov's fault, as the film finally emphasizes how he, rather than Craster, has forced her to choose between the queerly coded spaces of high art and a straight domestic life. Recall how in the final sequence the film crosscuts between the poignant moment when Craster takes the red shoes off a dying Page—at her request—and Lermontov's unsettling, guilt-ridden curtain speech announcing that Page will not dance "The Red Shoes Ballet." The death of the gay impresario's artistic stand-in forces him onto the stage and into the public eye, where he is exposed for many viewers as a pathetic (queer) monster.

On the other hand, Lermontov may be understood, and even be empathized with, as a tormented figure culturally encouraged to suppress, displace, and camouflage his gay desires, and who tries to find some means to express these desires within one of the few public spaces straight culture has left open for him, the high art of ballet. Besides, even if Lermontov tries to control Page on- and offstage in an attempt to express himself queerly through her "feminine" artistry, he is also concerned that Page fulfill her potential as a great dancer, which is more than can be said for Craster, who is more concerned that Page stay close to him while he becomes a great composer, allowing her to take only what second-rate dance engagements she can find in the vicinity of their apartment. To some extent, Lermontov and his male collaborators provide a space within which women's creative talents can be expressed and their career goals achieved. One critic summarizes the complex and contradictory responses *The Red Shoes* elicits in connection to its gay impresario and his relationship to the diva as follows:

> Boris comes across as the bad guy because he insists Vicky sacrifice Julian for dance. . . . But what Boris wants for Vicky is what is best for her, what she truly wants for herself. . . . The selfish Julian is the piece's villain—Boris would never have removed the shoes from Vicky's feet at the end.[52]

No, Lermontov would not have removed the red shoes, but let us not forget that it is Page who asks Craster to "take off the red shoes" as she lies dying, just as in the ballet the protagonist asks a clergyman to take off the shoes, and, in the original story, the young woman begs a woodsman to chop off her feet (he then makes her artificial feet and teaches her how to walk again). All these versions suggest that the straight women protagonists finally recognize their queerly influenced transgressive ways as bad. The key moment in this recognition is the woman asking a straight man to relieve her of the symbol of her transgression. That is, to "castrate" her by removing the powerful, queerly feminine phallus.

In the film narrative and in the ballet, the red shoes are reclaimed by the homosexual men who really own them, and both the ballet and the narrative go on with a spotlight where Page, as the ballet's protagonist, should be dancing. In one way, then, it all seems horribly clear now: the "feminine" power of the red shoes was just on loan to the women artists, and Page and the ballet's protagonist are stand-ins to express something else—after all, the show can go on without them. But publicly exposing the mechanisms behind the production of queer aesthete-and-diva art also forces Lermontov to "come out" in a way, which leads him to a near nervous breakdown on stage—while actor Walbrook was himself accused of being too "over the top" in his performance of this moment by certain critics and some of the Archers production team.[53] Martin Scorsese finds that Lermontov's "hysteria" during his final speech before a red curtain makes him like a "puppet": "Barking out a eulogy for his creation, he has become a character in one of his ballets—Dr. Coppelius."[54] The ballet and the film end simultaneously with the queer shoemaker offering the red slippers to the camera/audience.

In more than one context, Powell has said that *The Red Shoes* encouraged audiences to "die for art," after a period of being told to die for patriotic ideological reasons (in World War II, most recently).[55] While Powell may have thought the film was celebratory about this idea of defending and sacrificing oneself for the queer spaces of art, rather than dying for the patriarchy, *The Red Shoes* seems to end on a note of warning for certain audience members. Most immediately, the finale seems to reinforce the suggestion that straight women like Page are the ones being asked to sacrifice themselves, in one way or another, on the altar of queer high art—and Lermontov does refer to the ballet as his "religion," while seeing himself as one of this religion's celibate high priests. However, men like Lermontov, Powell, and Pressburger who are offstage, out in the theatre audience, or behind the camera are also being proffered the red shoes by the ambiguously sad-sinister shoemaker. As their mirror image, the shoemaker appears to be asking gay and queerly positioned aesthetes who have some expressive investment in straight women to reconsider their position. Lermontov and company will most likely discover and build up another prima ballerina in another original ballet. From the spectacle of Lermontov's near breakdown in public, however, it is difficult to believe that he has not been chastened somehow.

All of *The Red Shoes'* (melo)dramatic warnings to straight women and queer men about their relationships with each other, particularly where artistic creation and collaboration is concerned, should not keep us from remembering that these relationships usually are carried out within straight patriarchal cultural contexts. Consider this thought: Craster is the only major character whom the film suggests does not have a problem or a dilemma as an artist or in his personal life. It is only people like Page and Lermontov who have problems. Once Craster has broken away from Lermontov—and left him with the now-tainted "Red Shoes Ballet" score—he successfully moves on to both a solo composing career and a marriage. Craster is able to express grand heterosexual passions in his opera, "Dido and Aeneas," and to expect that Page will remain by his side during its composition. Within this privileged position, he feels he can pass judgment on the ambitions of his talented wife, on her "jealous" former impresario, and on their artistic relationship.

Craster—and most of the film audience—conveniently forget that the culture that allows straight, white, middle-class heterosexual men so much expressive freedom, as well as the luxury of not having to choose between a personal and a professional life, is the very culture that encourages or forces Page and Lermontov to carry out a love-hate relationship with each other. While he might not mean for us to take "love" as "homosexuality" here, David Thomson, with reference to *The Red Shoes*, concisely sets down what living and working within homophobic and misogynistic cultures means for many gay artists and straight divas: "[T]he impresario urges her to perform at the cost of her life and the love he cannot even admit."[36] For me, the final lesson of *The Red Shoes* is that, for the gay aesthete and diva team, artistic creation within dominant culture can exact two interrelated costs. Since it often costs the aesthete the open expression of "the love that he cannot even admit," he frequently turns to the diva to speak for him through codes of the "feminine."

Using the diva to express the homosexually feminine, however, often leads the gay aesthete to forget there is a straight woman artist with desires of her own. If it doesn't often cost the diva her physical life, this situation can cost her something in terms of her creative life. Yes, she is the one who is actually performing, but with a largely queer male creative context frequently surrounding her, and with straight patriarchy surrounding that, she must often wonder "whose art is it anyway?" Page's final, desperate, beautifully executed ballet leap to her death might be her way of asking Lermontov, Craster, the Archers, and the rest of us divas and aesthetes in the audience to carefully consider this loaded question.

NOTES

1. George Du Maurier, *Trilby* (London: Penguin, 1994). All quotations in the text are from this edition.
2. Edgar Rosenberg's *From Shylock to Svengali: Jewish Stereotypes in English Fiction* (Stanford, Ca.: Stanford University Press, 1960) discusses how a number of Jewish characters in English literature from 1600 to the late nineteenth century were linked to sorcery and sexual "degeneracy." In his chapter on Svengali, Rosenberg reads the sexual threat Svengali poses as being connected to miscegenation: the "mating of the inferior racial type with the higher" (256). While I agree that Du Maurier encourages some miscegenation anxieties in relation to Trilby and Svengali, the novel also suggests that Svengali's sexual "degeneracy" is not limited to heterosexual forms.
3. *Sunrise* (1927, Fox: F.W. Murnau), *Fantasia* (1940, Disney: Ben Sharpstein), *A Song to Remember* (1945, Columbia: Charles Vidor), *Lust for Life* (1956, MGM: Vincente Minnelli), *Specter of the Rose* (1946, Republic: Ben Hecht), *Invitation to the Dance* (1954, MGM: Gene Kelly), *Don Giovanni* (1979, Gaumont-Opera-Camera One: Joseph Losey), *Black Narcissus* (1946, GFD/The Archers: Michael Powell and Emeric Pressburger), *The Tales of Hoffmann* (1951, British Lion/London/The Archers: Michael Powell and Emeric Pressburger), *The Red Shoes* (1948, GFD/The Archers: Michael Powell and Emeric Pressburger), *Oh . . . Rosalinda!!* (1955, ABP/The Archers: Michael Powell and Emeric Pressburger).
4. See, for example, Pressburger's comments in relation to *The Red Shoes* in Kevin Macdonald's *Emeric Pressburger: The Life and Death of a Screenwriter* (London: Faber and Faber, 1994): "I was always fascinated by the idea of actually creating and showing a genuine piece of art on the screen" (279).

5. Seymour Kleinberg, *Alienated Affections: Being Gay in America* (New York: St. Martin's Press, 1980), 39.
6. Michael Powell, *Million-Dollar Movie* (London: Walter Heinemann, 1992), 83.
7. Jack Cardiff, commentary track, *The Red Shoes* laserdisc, Criterion Collection, Voyager Company, 1995.
8. Ian Christie, *Arrows of Desire: The Films of Michael Powell and Emeric Pressburger* (London and Boston: Faber and Faber, 1994), 64. For an interesting take on the opera diva and her gay fans ("opera queens"), see Wayne Koestenbaum's *The Queen's Throat: Opera, Homosexuality and the Mystery of Desire* (New York: Vintage, 1993).
9. Besides Macdonald's *Emeric Pressburger* and Powell's *Million-Dollar Movie*, there is Powell's first volume of autobiography: Michael Powell, *A Life in Movies: An Autobiography* (New York: Alfred A. Knopf, 1987).
10. Powell, *A Life in Movies*, 649.
11. Wayne Koestenbaum, *Double Talk: The Erotics of Male Literary Collaboration* (New York: Routledge, 1989), 3.
12. Ibid., 5.
13. Powell, *A Life in Movies*, 304–6; Powell, *Million-Dollar Movie*, 153–54.
14. Macdonald, 155.
15. Powell, *A Life in Movies*, 306.
16. Ibid., 304.
17. Powell, *Million-Dollar Movie*, 153.
18. These salutations are taken from various letters and notes in the Emeric Pressburger Collection, British Film Institute Library, special collections.
19. Note from Powell to Pressburger, March 30, 1979, Emeric Pressburger Collection.
20. Mark Brennan, "Powell and Pressburger at the NFT," *Films and Filming* 373 (October 1985): 27.
21. From certain remarks and letters, it seems clear that Powell saw himself as the often difficult and ill-tempered "husband," and Pressburger as the long-suffering "wife." For example, writing to Pressburger to apologize for his delays while working on the novelization of *The Red Shoes*, Powell says, "I was very inconsiderate, you poor housewife! I'm sorry." "Housewife" is also a reference to Pressburger's penchant for cooking, something Powell enjoyed the results of many times. Later, in reference to the same novelization, Powell remarks, "Dearest Imre—I have discovered rather belatedly that I love you: your faults as well as your virtues. In any case your virtues outweigh your faults. Unlike mine, alas!" (Letters from Powell to Pressburger, July 1977 and January 21, 1978, Emeric Pressburger Collection).
22. Powell, *Million-Dollar Movie*, 420–21.
23. Powell, *A Life in Movies*, 616–17.
24. Ibid., 657.
25. Macdonald, 284.
26. Powell, *A Life in Movies*, 619, 625, 634–35, 659.
27. Letter from Powell to Pressburger, n.d. [1947?], Emeric Pressburger Collection.
28. Powell, *A Life in Movies*, 656.

29. *The Life and Death of Colonel Blimp* (1943, The Archers: Michael Powell and Emeric Pressburger), *A Canterbury Tale* (1944, The Archers: Michael Powell and Emeric Pressburger), *Gone to Earth* (1950, London Films/The Archers/ Vanguard Productions: Michael Powell and Emeric Pressburger).
30. See, for example, John Russell Taylor, "Michael Powell: Myths and Superman," *Sight and Sound* 47, 4 (Autumn 1978): 226–29, and David Thomson, "The Films of Michael Powell: A Romantic Sensibility," *American Film* 6, 2 (November 1980): 48–52.
31. *The Spy in Black* (1939, Harefield/Korda: Michael Powell), *Contraband* (1940, British National: Michael Powell), *The Thief of Bagdad* (1940, Korda Films: Michael Powell, Ludwig Berger, Tim Whelan).
32. Powell, *Million-Dollar Movie*, 280–81.
33. Ibid., 279.
34. Macdonald, *Emeric Pressburger*, 286.
35. Taylor, 228.
36. Andrew Newman, "Film Choice: *The Red Shoes*," *Observer Magazine*, June 14, 1981: n.p. (in the cuttings files of the British Film Institute Film Library). See also Christie, *Arrows of Desire*, 67; Beth Genne, "The Red Shoes: Choices Between Life and Art," *Thousand Eyes Magazine* 7 (February 1976): 8–9; and Karen Backstein, "A Second Look: *The Red Shoes*," *Cineaste* 2, 4 (1994): 42–43.
37. Backstein, 42. A more openly gay acknowledgment of the collapsing of "female physicality and homosexual identity" is found in *The Birdcage* (1996, MGM/UA: Mike Nichols), when drag diva Starina (played by gay actor Nathan Lane) refuses to go on by saying, "Victoria Page will not perform 'The Red Shoes' tonight, or any other night." Here Starina places herself/himself simultaneously in the position of the diva and the gay impresario. A similar use of Lermontov's line by a gay character, this time in a play and a film written by a gay man, happens in Terence McNally's *Love! Valour! Compassion!* (play, 1995; film, 1997, Fine Line; both directed by Joe Mantello).
38. Patricia Erens, "A Childhood at the Cinema: Latency Fantasies, the Family Romance, and Juvenile Spectatorship," *Wide Angle* 16, 4 (October 1994): 33. Peter Fraser, in "The Musical Mode: Putting on *The Red Shoes*," *Cimema Journal* 26, 3 (Spring 1987): 44–54, similarly understands the film's narrative as structured around "[t]he tragic, forbidden romance of Lermontov and Vicki" (49), as does Scott Salwolke in *The Films of Michael Powell and the Archers* (Lanham, Md., and London: Scarecrow, 1997), in which he mentions Lermontov's "growing passion for [Page] as a woman" (163).
39. Michael Powell and Emeric Pressburger, *The Red Shoes* (New York: St. Martin's Press, 1978), 195.
40. Ibid., *The Red Shoes*, 275.
41. Danny Peary, *Alternate Oscars* (New York: Delta, 1993), 97.
42. Macdonald, 293.
43. Powell and Pressburger, 139.
44. See, for example, Powell, *Million-Dollar Movie*, 280; Danny Peary, *Cult Movies* (New York: Dell, 1981), 287.

45. According to Richard Dyer, "heterosexuality in classical ballet is so . . . ethereally idealized that it becomes rather unreal. . . . In a camp appreciation, this means enjoying the spectacle of heterosexuality parading as glittering illusion" (quoted in Backstein, "A Second Look," 42). For a similar discussion of gay men and ballet's heterosexual aspects see Kleinberg, 59–64, where he says things like, "The ballet then, represented an idealized image of a romantic relationship that gay men did not find alienating because it had no correspondence in reality. . . . [It was] a celebration of feminine grace that ignored conventional masculine posing and could be interpreted as a justification for accepting one's own effeminate yearnings" (63).

46. Emeric Pressburger and Keith Winter, "The Red Shoes," draft script, n.d., #S946, British Film Institute Library.

47. Emeric Pressburger and Keith Winter, "The Red Shoes," draft scripts, n.d., #S946 and #S4204, British Film Institute Library. An example of Page's lashing back at Lermontov and company to her girlfriend: "Oh, it's so damned unfair! Haven't I behaved like an early Christian martyr ever since I got here? . . . Have I ever complained when they have been marching me up and down that stage like an old race-horse? Or made a single protest about any one of the idiotic things they make me do?" (n.p., script #S946).

48. Ian Christie, commentary track, *The Red Shoes* laserdisc.

49. Koestenbaum, 6–7.

50. Danny Peary, in *Cult Movies*, objects to the staging of "The Red Shoes Ballet" because he sees it as being more in the style of Powell-Pressburger-the Archers than in the style of "ballet purist" Lermontov and his company (288). This is a very astute point, and it might be taken as more evidence of how Lermontov and his ballet company can be read as the onscreen representatives of Powell, Pressburger, and the Archers in this art film.

51. Powell and Pressburger, 186.

52. Peary, *Alternate Oscars*, 97.

53. Powell, *A Life in Movies*, 640.

54. Martin Scorsese, commentary track, *The Red Shoes* laserdisc.

55. See, for example, Powell, *A Life in Movies*, 653.

56. David Thomson, "The Pilgrim's Progress," *The Movie* 27 (1980): 532.

Everyone's Here for Love: Bisexuality and Gentlemen Prefer Blondes

Of course, as a case study, "Gentlemen Prefer Blondes" defies categorisation. Hilarious, perverse, it pulls and tugs in every which way.

Geoffrey Macnab[1]

How to define bisexuality? Some people, working within conventional binaries, understand it as a movement between, or a combination of, heterosexuality and homosexuality and the straight and lesbian or gay identities that are usually attached to these desires and practices. Others find their bisexuality works itself out as a desire for both the same sex and the opposite sex in tandem with a social or political identification with either gayness, lesbianism, or straightness. Still others see it as having desires for both the same sex and the opposite sex within bisexual identities that don't reference straight or lesbian or gay ones, but may reference less binarily defined queer or non-straight identities.

Of course, each of these understandings of bisexuality has its cultural implications—they don't mean the same things sociopolitically. As with competing understandings of "gay" and "lesbian," where you position yourself definitionally will determine if, where, and to what degree you recognize something about a text as "bisexual," as well as what you might say ideologically about this bisexuality.[2] This even functions at the level of overt representation—where the sexual and romantic activities of characters are shown or these characters are explicitly labeled. For example, the title character in the film *Chasing Amy* is understood as a cool bisexual by some viewers and as a dubious lesbian who has affairs with men by others.[3]

Given all this, I realize that making claims for the bisexuality of a main-stream text like *Gentlemen Prefer Blondes* is always done within the context of definitional and ideological debates that are themselves complicated by the fact that heterocentrism makes the queer erotics of mainstream films invisible or "subtextual" for most people in the first place.[4] One caveat about what follows: I don't need an explicit representation of romantic or sexual activity to understand something as erotic. Since the points I will be making through the case of *Gentlemen Prefer Blondes* are about mainstream films, most of which are bound by institutional and cultural censorship, you can't really expect to find much same-sex romantic and sexual explicitness, in any case. But this doesn't mean that there can't be a queer charge to the proceedings.

However, with a woman-centered film like *Gentlemen Prefer Blondes* (or *The Wild Party*, *Stage Door*, and *Thelma and Louise*), where you place yourself within the debates and struggles over defining and demarcating female friendship and/vs. sexual attraction—Are they fully separate? Is there an erotic component in certain friendships, even if it's not sexually acted upon?—will also determine how open you are to the bisexual reading of *Gentlemen Prefer Blondes* that follows.[5] For political and personal reasons, I haven't changed my earlier position: same-sex erotic charges can arise in life and in narratives around any intense relationship. Nothing has to be acknowledged or acted upon for there to be something erotic going on up there on the screen—or, taking things from another perspective, for viewers to have an erotic response to, or reading of, what is on the screen.

When you think about it, it makes sense that mainstream films produced within a capitalist system keep the range of erotic responses available for audiences as open as possible. Both Andrew Britton, writing about Katharine Hepburn, and Andrea Weiss, writing about Greta Garbo and Marlene Dietrich, note that (in Weiss's words), "Hollywood studios went to great lengths to keep the star's images open to erotic contemplation by both men and women."[6] In her excellent article on bisexual spectatorship, Maria Pramaggiore makes the case that contemporary Hollywood and independent films often "'cheat' their representations of homosexualities for mass audience appeal," in order to "make inroads into gay and lesbian markets while not offending 'traditional' audiences."[7] The result, for Pramaggiore, is often an opening up of the text to the "ambiguities, doubleness and 'both/and' of bisexual desire."[8] Classic mainstream films also often "cheat" their representations of heterosexuality in a manner that, whether self-consciously done or not, creates the conditions for bisexual readings of various kinds.

Most basically, narratives like *Gentlemen Prefer Blondes* give roughly equal emphasis to both same-sex and opposite-sex relationships, perhaps focusing somewhat more upon the importance of same-sex intensities, which has the effect of challenging straight-favoring cultural biases. Gerald

Mast finds that *Gentlemen Prefer Blondes'* greater narrative focus on the women's relationship is emphasized by its visual style:

> Hawks also conveys the essential spiritual similarity of the two women with his camera, which balances them perfectly in every frame they share; they occupy symmetrical halves of the frame, sitting still or stealthily moving...in perfect framed unison. The perfect compositional symmetry implies an absolute spiritual symmetry. True enough, the perfect balancing of the two stars in Hawks's frames may well have originated in their contracts...[but] [h]e succeeds not just in balancing their contracts, but in equating the two women's spirits with his balanced frames.[9]

Gentlemen Prefer Blondes' narrative positions Dorothy and Lorelei's relationship as central from the precredit number, "Two Little Girls from Little Rock," to the final reprise of "Two Little Girls" that has the camera dolly up to the about-to-be-married pair of women gazing fondly into each other's eyes. None of that conventional straight narrative "together until some man comes along" crap as with the follow-up film, *Gentlemen Marry Brunettes.*[10] In its very construction, *Gentlemen Prefer Blondes* keeps the narrative events representing the women's emotional commitment to each other running parallel to, and intertwined with, those representing their relationships with men.

In a lengthy endnote to the introduction of *Making Things Perfectly Queer: Interpreting Mass Culture,* I first considered how the narrative construction of *Gentlemen Prefer Blondes* might be understood as bisexual in some way.[11] Lucie Arbuthnot and Gail Seneca's feminist reading provided me with an important insight with their notions of "text" and "pre-text." Arbuthnot and Seneca felt that the film's "narrative of [heterosexual] romantic adventure" serves as "a mere pre-text" for the more important narrative of women-bonding.[12] But where Arbuthnot and Seneca found that the opposite-sex narrative was "continually disrupted and undermined" by the same-sex narrative, I understand both narratives as coexisting in the text—so that both are presented as desirable in their different ways. This goes along with the experiences of a number of bisexual women as reported by Sue George:

> Some women wanted different things from men and women: for example, they might fall in love with women and want sex from men; or find men exciting and women nurturing; or women passionate and men protective. Or vice versa.[13]

The film's consistent "both/and" approach to narrative erotics wasn't the case with Anita Loos's 1925 novel.[14] The book begins with scenes of Lorelei and men. Dorothy is only mentioned once or twice in passing. In another classically straight move, the narrative of *Gentlemen Prefer Blondes* takes the form of a diary Lorelei is writing for a man to read. While Dorothy does become Lorelei's chaperone when she goes to Europe, their trip is punctuated by arguments, backbiting, and wisecracks Dorothy makes at an unwitting Lorelei's expense. So when Lorelei says, "I really think that there is nothing so wonderful as two girls when they stand up for each other and help each other a lot,"[15] we are supposed to understand this as another instance of Lorelei's dimwittedness.

The wedding that closes the story dramatically reveals the difference between the novel's straightness and the film's bisexuality. In the novel, Lorelei marries Henry Spofford (who is a little boy in the film), while Dorothy laughs and wisecracks in the background during and after the ceremony. Lorelei comments in her diary that Dorothy's behavior shows that even "matrimony" is "not sacred" to Dorothy, and that she does "not believe that Dorothy is such a true friend after all."[16]

The film's shipboard wedding finale is an entirely different matter. The sequence begins with a long shot of the two grooms and a row of men in uniform lined up on either side of an altar, behind which is painted large pseudoancient Greek images of a man and a woman facing each other. But the apparent heteroconventionality of this shot is complicated by what follows. Entering as a team in matching outfits, as they have a number of times in the film, Lorelei and Dorothy pause for a moment at the top of a flight of stairs, behind which is a drawing of two ancient Greek statues of women standing side-by-side. One of the drawn statues is headless—a warning, perhaps? After Dorothy reminds Lorelei that she can have sex with a man—"Remember, honey, on your wedding day it's OK to say 'yes' "—the pair proceed down the steps in unison, singing a slightly reworded version of the film's opening number, "Two Little Girls from Little Rock": "At last we won the big crusade / Looks like we finally made the grade...." As the women look from their diamond rings to the men, the film presents a two-shot of Dorothy and Malone before panning over to frame a two-shot of Lorelei and Gus Esmond. A four-shot frames the group as the ceremony begins. But, then, in a tracking movement celebrated by Arbuthnot and Seneca, the camera closes in on the foursome, dropping the men into off-screen space in order to frame the film's final couple, Lorelei and Dorothy, who look lovingly at each other before turning their faces forward again to continue the marriage ceremony.

In the way it is constructed and filmed, this ceremony serves as a double wedding in two senses, as it unites two male-female couples as well as bonding the female partners to men and to each other. Aside from the final shot, the bisexual charge of this double-double wedding is perhaps most strikingly represented by the two-shot, pan, two-shot presentation of the foursome before the altar, as it connects male-female and female-female couples to each other rather than separating them into two opposite sex couples, as a two-shot, cut, two-shot presentation would have. Rarely has a mainstream American film offered a finale so open to, and affirming of, bisexual erotics. But this final sequence only puts the capper on what has been a narrative filled with bisexual joie de vivre.

One might profitably compare the narrative construction of *Gentlemen Prefer Blondes* with that of *How to Marry a Millionaire*, a film made a year later and co-starring Monroe, in order to better understand the differences between a bisexually charged narrative and a straight one.[17] In the latter film, three women—Pola (Monroe), Schatzie (Lauren Bacall), and Loco (Betty Grable)—band together and pool their resources so they can find rich husbands. After a couple of expository scenes featuring the women, the narrative contains very few scenes with the women alone together, in pairs or as a trio. Instead, *How to Marry a Millionaire* concentrates upon lengthy sequences between women and men. Even when the women are in the same scene, they are generally paired off with men, or men come between them, literally or through the dialogue. To make matters worse, when the narrative does present a scene with the women alone together, it is certain to have them sniping at each other. Schatzie, in particular, disrupts any attempts at close, warm women-bonding, as she calls Pola and Loco dimwits and threatens to hit both of them at different times for what she sees as their interference with her plans to catch a rich man. "Watch the fur fly" when these women go after men, the trailer promised viewers in 1953.

In place of the double-double wedding that closes *Gentlemen Prefer Blondes*, *How to Marry a Millionaire* has the three couples seated "girl-boy" at a diner counter, initally all in the same CinemaScope frame. Schatzie's supposedly poor fiancé pulls out a wad of thousand-dollar bills to pay for their hamburger dinners. Then, over a close-up of the money, we hear thuds. Returning to the master shot, we discover that the women have fainted while offscreen, and they remain offscreen as Schatzie's fiancé leads the other two men in a beer toast to their "wives." Earlier, after Schatzie has described her terrible first marriage, Loco remarks that she's surprised Schatzie would ever want to get married again. "Of course I want to get married," Schatzie says, "Who doesn't? It's the biggest thing you can do in life."

How to Marry a Millionaire reinforces Schatzie's comment time and again in its narrative construction and visuals. Where Dorothy and Lorelei are bound to each other by love and career, the women in *How to Marry a Millionaire* are bound to each other only by the desire for money through marriage (or just getting married when the money part doesn't quite work out). True, Lorelei wants to marry a rich man, and wants Dorothy to marry one, too. But Lorelei's search for a millionaire never undercuts her relationship with Dorothy—nor does it cut into the time the narrative spends with her and Dorothy. Men and marriage are the goal in *How to Marry a Million-aire*, while *Gentlemen Prefer Blondes* is all about keeping Dorothy and Lorelei's relationship front and center even while they find men.

Hardly a sequence goes by in *Gentlemen Prefer Blondes* that doesn't concern itself with simultaneously developing both male-female and female-female bonds and affective intensities in ways that consistently encourage bisexual visual and narrative pleasures. To take a small, but typical, example: even while Lorelei is talking marriage and money with Gus and his father, the narrative creates the opportunity for her to show Mr. Esmond a nightclub table card picturing her and Dorothy in twin outfits as a means of verifying who she is. Here and elsewhere, the narrative insists that while she may want to marry Gus—and Dorothy may fall in love with Malone—Lorelei's life is also intimately bound up in her relationship with Dorothy. It's never a matter of the women choosing either men or each other, but of having both women and men available to them.

As the scene with Gus and his father suggests, even when Lorelei and Dorothy are apart from each other, whether they are alone with men or doing a solo musical number, the narrative contrives to remind viewers of the importance of same-sex connections. And vice versa: often, when the women are together on- or offstage, the narrative will interrupt the scene with a reminder that, just offscreen, men are watching or waiting for their opportunity to become part of the fun. But the difference appears to be that while, in general, the women, particularly Dorothy, take the initiative in bringing women into their scenes with men or into their solo numbers, the men must wait and be invited to enter the women's spaces. Take, for example, the parallel scenes in which Dorothy invites Lorelei into the middle of an argument with Malone ("Come in, honey, you can hear better in here"), and the one in which Lorelei asks Dorothy if she minds if Gus comes into their dressing room ("I don't mind, if you don't mind," Dorothy replies). The classical narrative convention of privileging male-female relationships is consistently being counterbalanced in *Gentlemen Prefer Blondes* by narrative elements that reinforce the equal importance of the main woman-woman relationship.

Central to reinforcing the film's balance of, and alternation between, man-woman and woman-woman relationships is a section of the film that establishes Dorothy's romantic interest in Malone. Walking into the ship's bar, Lorelei, Dorothy, and Malone sit down for a drink and a cigarette. After probing into his finances, Lorelei approves of Malone's interest in Dorothy. When he says that he'll try to "catch on to" Dorothy's sense of humor, Lorelei remarks: "That's good. Dorothy's the best and loyalest friend a girl ever had. She'll make some man a wonderful wife." The last line Lorelei says here appears to be a non sequitur if you are thinking monosexually. Typical of this bisexual film, Lorelei's encouragement of Malone's interest in Dorothy begins with the reaffirmation of her own bond with Dorothy. The women's relationship and the relationship between Dorothy and Malone need not exclude each other. Indeed, in Lorelei's statement the relationships are made parallel and interrelated—because Dorothy is such a good girlfriend, she'll make a "wonderful wife" for some man. As Lorelei begins to leave, Dorothy asks (protectively? suspiciously?), "Where are you going?" Lorelei tells her not to worry, she's "thinking about" Dorothy, even as she suggestively mentions "there's a wonderful moon out tonight" that Dorothy and Malone should take advantage of.

The next night, on the moonlit deck, Dorothy and Malone stroll for a few paces before Dorothy's eye is caught by something offscreen, frame right. Malone trails after her, and, initiated by Dorothy's gaze, they look into a porthole to catch sight of Lorelei's undulating, gold-laméd backside as she dances with Piggy. Moving away from what has been presented as an erotic spectacle for both women and men, the scene continues to bisexually emphasize strong, simultaneous male-female and female-female connections. When Malone begins to criticize Lorelei, Dorothy angrily stops him: "Now listen, Malone, nobody talks about Lorelei but me. She's quite a girl, you just don't know her." "You don't mind if I like you better," Malone replies, to which Dorothy ruefully remarks, "We settled that quarrel in a hurry." In this short exchange, the narrative both (re)establishes Dorothy's intensely protective feelings for Lorelei, while making it clear that Dorothy also desires men, as long as they don't undermine her relationship with her girlfriend.

Malone is also involved in a jokey bi-suggestive ménage-à-trois—one that picks up on Dorothy's earlier remark to Malone, "You sound interested. I think I know where we can find her [Lorelei]"—after the women realize he is a detective sent to spy on Lorelei. Attempting to retrieve an incriminating roll of film, Lorelei and Dorothy concoct a plan to search him that involves inviting Malone for some drinks in their cabin. "If we can't empty his pockets between us, we're not worthy of the name 'woman,'" Dorothy remarks. Entering the cabin just before Malone, Dorothy decides to turn the thermostat down. "Leave it on, dear," Lorelei requests. "But honey, it's hot," Dorothy complains, before realizing it's all a part of Lorelei's plan to get Malone's clothes off. By plying the sweating Malone with doctored drinks and spilling water on his pants, the women are able to strip him bit by bit, running into the bedroom together between strips to search Malone's clothes for the film. Caught at the height of the ménage by a steward, the women dress Malone in one of their pink sheer robes and send him off—they've got the bulge in his pants that they were after, and they did it as a team.

Just how invested *Gentlemen Prefer Blondes* is in keeping woman-woman and man-woman relationships running neck and neck, and side by side, is also made clear in the courtroom sequence near the end of the film. In order to buy Lorelei some time to get money from Gus to replace a missing tiara, Dorothy disguises herself as Lorelei for a court appearance. After throwing the courtroom into chaos by performing "Diamonds Are a Girl's Best Friend," Dorothy discovers Malone has come in and is about to expose her. Before he can speak, Dorothy, as Lorelei, launches into a convoluted explanation of how Dorothy would be angry with Malone if anything happened to "me," Lorelei, and that it would be too bad if Malone made Dorothy mad because "she," Dorothy, thinks she loves Malone. Given what has come before, it makes perfect sense that Dorothy should declare her love for Malone while impersonating Lorelei, and that she should make her relationship with Malone contingent upon how he responds to her relationship with Lorelei. In the world of *Gentlemen Prefer Blondes*, women, men, love, sex, and friendship are intricately, wonderfully, and bisexually intertwined and interdependent.

This bisexually charged atmosphere pervades even the women's solo numbers. Dorothy's "Ain't There Anyone Here for Love?" and Lorelei's "Diamonds Are a Girl's Best Friend," begin as man-centered in their construction and address, but quickly open themselves up for bisexual pleasures by having women intently connect with other women, while questioning the inevitability of male-female unions. The "Ain't There Anyone Here for Love?" sequence begins its bisexual coding by putting both sexy men and women over, beside, and around Dorothy. The sequence begins with a dissolve that places the image of Lorelei lounging on a deck chair over a shot of Dorothy positioned amid the swimsuit-clad American men's Olympics team and next to, and a little under, a water slide filled with women. When the athletes rush off at the sound of the coach's whistle, Dorothy is left alone to gaze and walk out after them, frame right. The next shot reveals a crowd of women looking straight ahead as the athletes bound into, and out of, the frame. Suddenly, the women's gaze is drawn to the frame left offscreen space. A coach enters and positions himself in front of the gazing women, bottom center frame. But the women continue to look frame left for a few moments even after the coach takes his place. What could they be looking at? What could have drawn their attention away from the half-naked athletes? Then we remember: Dorothy was headed in this direction the last time we saw her. After a moment, the women return their gaze to the athletes. The film doesn't provide a reverse shot of Dorothy as the women look at her, and the moment is over quickly so that it is easy to overlook. But the bisexual implications are clear as the women's gazes move from men, to a woman, and then back to men again with the greatest of ease. The coach makes a failed attempt to draw the women's gaze back to the men by entering the frame and standing in front of them—an attempt to mediate the women's desiring gaze so as to diffuse its power.

If anything, the coach's appearance and function opens up gay and male bisexual spaces in this sequence, as his look replaces the desiring look of the

The queer complexities of the gaze: Dorothy (Jane Russell), the men's Olympics team, and their male and female admirers in a production still for "Ain't There Anyone Here for Love?"

women, who are involved at the moment in gazing at another woman who has just been deserted by athletes eager to follow their coach's order to work out with each other. The "Ain't There Anyone Here for Love?" number that follows keeps gay and bisexual (in this case male and female) narrative and spectatorial spaces open. It also offers spaces for lesbian readings and pleasures, as the women turn to contemplate each other at times during the number. Initially, Dorothy strides around the athletes-cum-chorus boys, looking for a sex partner. But this group of men is more intent upon exercising together than they are in "playing" with her, so Dorothy moves over to address a group of women in the pool—perhaps they are part of the unacknowledged women's Olympics team?:

I can't play tennis.
My golf's a menace.
I just can't do the Australian crawl.
And I'm no better at volleyball.
Ain't there anyone here for love?

In other words, admitting to these women that she is not good at the type of physical activities in which the men are engaged, she asks the women if there is "anyone" among their number ready for love. While she is singing to these women, Dorothy displays herself in a sexy lounging pose for both the women in the pool and for a group of women who are gazing at her in the background of the shot. The exercising men in the shot remain unengaged with Dorothy and the other women.

However, as Dorothy has also admitted to the swimming women that she "just can't do the Australian crawl," she returns to try again with the men. After some rather contradictory lyrics about wanting a "man who can nestle" and who "don't have to be Hercules," but also liking a man with "big muscles" and "red corpuscles," Dorothy puts everything that has gone before into a bisexual context with a clever metaphor when she picks up two tennis rackets, crosses them over her chest, swings them, and sings "Doubles anyone? Court's free!" With its possibility for both mixed-sex and same-sex pairs, playing "doubles" is what this number has been about all along.

Lorelei's solo, "Diamonds Are a Girl's Best Friend" is less audacious about constructing its bisexual space. Its first crane shot isn't promising, as it sweeps over scantily clad women strapped up to create human chandeliers. Then, male-female pairs of dancers leap into the picture. To add to the hetero conventionality, Gus and an older man sitting next to him in the club are set up as the initial audience for the number. But Gus' smiles stop when Lorelei turns around and begins to take command of the stage, rejecting the male dancers who first hold out large hearts to her and then shoot themselves. Stepping over their bodies, Lorelei exhorts women, in song, to get financial security from men in the form of diamonds. Dressed in pink, as they are, Lorelei sits down among the now partnerless women, who huddle around her. Continuing to give them financial advice, Lorelei makes repeated eye contact with the women, something she doesn't do with the men, although later she does stare at the diamonds they offer her. Standing at the head of the group of women, Lorelei marches down the stairs with them to meet the men, but on her terms. They now offer her the diamonds that are the prerequisite to gaining access to her body.

While it might be argued that the gold-digging philosophy informing this number, and Lorelei's character in general, is hardly progressive, the manner of its expression in "Diamonds Are a Girl's Best Friend" (and *Gentlemen Prefer Blondes*) does keep Lorelei available to both men and women in a way that fosters bisexual spaces and spectator positions. Lorelei does have an interest in men, but it is predicated on their having money/diamonds. Does Lorelei love or sexually desire these men, or does she get turned on by their money, and the cultural power it represents? Of course, it could all be mixed together, as money, power, and sexuality often are in capitalism. What is clear

"Diamonds Are a Girl's Best Friend": Lorelei (Marilyn Monroe) counsels her sisters in pink to "get that ice, or else no dice."

is that Lorelei emotionally connects most strongly with women. She loves Dorothy, and addresses the women in "Diamonds," with an intensity that simply isn't there in her interactions with men.[18] Lorelei can put on a show of affection when a man has some diamonds to give her, but she can turn it off as quickly. So, in different ways, Lorelei is available to both men and women on the screen and in the theatre.

Also consider this: by the end of the film, the diamonds that Lorelei covets are connected to both the desires of the men who give them to her, as well as to the sisterhood of women, including Dorothy, that Lorelei feels she is looking after when she advises them to "get that ice, or else no dice!" Besides, while the title and end credit song is "Diamonds Are a Girl's Best Friend," Lorelei tells us sometime in between that "Dorothy is the best and loyalest friend a girl ever had"—and the two girlfriends do look from the male-bestowed diamond rings to each other to close the narrative. To top things off, for some viewers, the bisexual suggestiveness surrounding Lorelei might also be intensified by Monroe's rumored bisexuality.

For most viewers, however, the heart of the film's bisexual charge lies with Dorothy, as performed by Jane Russell. The butch to Monroe's femme Lorelei in certain lesbian readings of the film, Dorothy is more outgoing with her emotions and desires, whereas Lorelei seems autoerotic at times—one can imagine her doing without men or women, as long as she has herself and her diamonds. For me, the ground zero for bisexual understandings of *Gentlemen Prefer Blondes* is the musical number that Dorothy initiates when she invites the men's Olympics team and a number of young women into her and Lorelei's cabin for a bon voyage party. Even the title is deliciously obvious—"Bye, Bye, Baby." For the only time in the film, all the erotic players are in the same room: Dorothy, Malone, the men's Olympics team, a representative group of young women, Lorelei, Gus. Greeting the first male guests at the door, Dorothy tells Gus and Lorelei that they are "the relay team." Once they come in, however, it becomes clear that they are only the front men for a large crowd of women and men. That this group is one big, happy bisexual "relay team" for Dorothy becomes apparent in the musical number that follows.

Center frame and initially surrounded by men, Dorothy begins her song, glancing between the men as she sings. Soon, women enter the edges of the frame. Without missing a beat, Dorothy looks at one of the women and sings "Bye, Bye, Baby, Bye, Bye," then turns back to the men to continue, "Baby, Bye." In a bit of gender reversal, some of the women sing to a group of men "Bye, Bye, pretty baby. . . ." After some musical back and forth between the men and the women, the men return to Dorothy, as do some of the women, to bi-sex it up again:

Dorothy: I'll be gloomy,
Men: (To Dorothy) But send that rainbow to me,
Dorothy: (Looking at the same woman she addressed earlier)
Then my shadows will fly.
(Looks back at the men)
Though you'll be gone for a while,
I know that I'll be smiling,
With my baby, bye and bye and bye,
With my baby, bye and bye.

Ironically, Gus is the only "baby" who is going. Along with Malone, he seems the least bi of the lot, although the narrative does involve him later in a comic scene with a Frenchman that has them blowing kisses to each other as they stand admiring a poster of Lorelei and Dorothy. At this point in the narrative, however, Gus is presented as being caught up in conventional (hetero)sexual jealousy and possessiveness. Sensing this, Lorelei pulls Gus into a bedroom where she can sing him a private, heterosexualized version of Dorothy's song, which actually invokes the Bible (as "that book by Mr. Gideon"), in order to soothe him. Beckoning the men and women partygoers around her, Dorothy eavesdrops on Lorelei and Gus for a moment before interrupting them with a slap on the wall. This slap snaps Lorelei out of her breathy heterosexiness, and she smiles at Dorothy. Looking back and forth between Dorothy and Gus, Lorelei sings: "With my baby / Bye and bye and bye / With my baby / Bye and bye." Entering with her coterie of men and women, Dorothy stands before Lorelei and Gus for a moment before everyone jumps up to exit en masse in answer to the last call for all those going ashore.

The series of group framings that close the number serve to reinforce the "bi" in "Bye, Bye, Baby." A shot of Dorothy and two athletes begins the series. She looks off frame right. The next shot finds Lorelei kissing Gus as Dorothy enters the frame and positions herself between the pair. After pointing out the gangplank to a dazed Gus, Dorothy and Lorelei take their places, frame right, in a shot that also contains Malone and two athletes. Finally, an over-the-shoulder shot once again places Dorothy center frame, between Lorelei, at her side, and Gus, who is facing them and waving from the dock, as an unseen background chorus of men and women sing "Bye, bye, bye, bye."

Dorothy's active bisexual butchy-femmeness is also crucial to the lesbian and bisexual pleasures of her two big duets with Lorelei. Arbuthnot and Seneca make an important observation when they note that:

> A typical characteristic of [the] movie musical genre is that there are two leads, a man and a woman, who sing and dance together, and eventually become romantically involved; that they sing and dance so fluidly together is a metaphor for the perfection of their relationship. In *Gentlemen Prefer Blondes*, it is Monroe and Russell who sing—they even harmonize, adding another layer to the metaphor—and dance as a team. The men they supposedly love are never given a musical role, and therefore never convincingly share in the emotional energy between Monroe and Russell.[19]

One might add that the "fluidity" with which the leads in a musical sing and dance together represents, more than anything, their sexual desires for, and sexual compatibility with, each other. With most viewers' heterocentrist, homophobic, and biphobic training, however, this sexual metaphor usually only registers consciously when a man and a woman are up there on the screen. So, in *Gentlemen Prefer Blondes*, while male-female relationships are developed within the prosaic part of the narrative, the women's union is more excitingly expressed in song and dance. Men do get mentioned in Dorothy and Lorelei's duets "Two Little Girls from Little Rock" and "When Love Goes Wrong," but both numbers move viewer attention between the "men doing them wrong" lyrics and the enjoyment the women are getting from singing and dancing together. Actually, the women's pleasure in performing with each other (innuendo intended) finally supplants the sorrow and anger the songs express about their simultaneous relationships with men.

Beginning as a precredit number, "Two Little Girls from Little Rock" establishes the kind of clever and subtle direction of both musical (by Jack Cole) and nonmusical (by Howard Hawks) sequences that will keep *Gentlemen Prefer Blondes* bi-friendly. Perhaps opening with a musical number was the filmmakers' first smart move, as the film begins outside of conventional—and conventionally patriarchal and heterocentrist—narrative spaces. Yes, I realize that if you are a straight man, starting the film with a spectacular musical number pivoting around two women in form-fitting red sequined dresses is hardly unconventional, but there are other spectators, and there are other things going on in the number besides the fulfilling of straight male desires. As with the film as a whole, this number moves between laments about men and evidence of women being close and enjoying each other's company.

After a striking entrance together, Dorothy and Lorelei perform the first part of the number with precision parallel movements. On the line "Someone [that is, in the context of the song, some man] broke my heart in Little Rock," Lorelei moves away from Dorothy as the latter leaves the frame. Dorothy returns when Lorelei sings "I came to New York and I found out," and sings the rest of the line with her, "that men are the same way everywhere." Later, Dorothy sings "Now one of these days in my fancy clothes," then taps Lorelei on the chest before continuing "I'm going back home and punch the nose / Of the one who broke my heart." Lorelei joins Dorothy to finish the song ("The one who broke my heart / The one who broke my heart / In Little Rock / Little Rock / Little Rock"), as Dorothy smiles wryly over at her, as she has done at certain points throughout the number. Arbuthnot and Seneca also note that in this number "Russell dances with her hands on Monroe's shoulders" frequently, which, for them, is one sign of the women's "comfort with each other's bodies" that pervades the film.[20] So while the lyrics, and some of the staging, develop the idea of (failed) relationships with men, the women's performances—their glances, smiles, touches, and body language in relation to each other—are developing another, and more positively inflected, erotic space.

Bisexually structured like the "Two Little Girls" number, "When Love Goes Wrong" juxtaposes lyrical laments about male-female relationships with the energies and pleasures two women take in performing with each other. However, "When Love Goes Wrong" is even more striking about presenting its woman-woman erotics. Dressed in black and sharing a small coffee at an outdoor cafe, Lorelei and Dorothy musically mourn their breakups with Malone and Gus: "When love goes wrong, nothing goes right." After two Moroccan boys enter the shot, the women snap out of their doldrums and launch into a livelier version of the song, suggesting that "when love goes wrong" with a man, something can go very right with another woman. As the tempo picks up, Dorothy begins encouraging and directing Lorelei's sexy moves. When Lorelei shimmies, Dorothy watches her and shouts out "Do it, honey! Do it!" before hitting a high note that can only be described as orgasmic in this context. Following this, the pair dance together in unison until they sing "Love is something you just can't fight," whereupon Dorothy grabs Lorelei by the shoulders and shakes her while yelling "You just can't fight it, honey, you can't fight it!" From this point, Dorothy moves Lorelei into the cab that will take them back to their lives as on- and offstage partners: "No bows, honey, just eight bars and off." It's no wonder, then, that in both the "Two Little Girls" and the "When Love Goes Wrong" numbers, Lorelei and Dorothy can smile while singing such lyrics about male-female relationships as "It's like we said / You're better off dead / When love has lost its glow"—they still have, and have always had, each other.

Danny Peary speculates that "[t]he reason the friendship [I would say the erotics of the friendship] between Lorelei and Dorothy is so convincing is that Monroe and Russell became good friends while making the picture.... [T]hey got along from the start."[21] As Lorelei and Dorothy always have each other for comfort and support in the narrative, Monroe and Russell found that they were frequently turning to each other during the course of filming.[22] Peary relates that Russell would escort Monroe "when she was too frightened to emerge from her dressing room," and that "when Tommy Noonan complained Monroe 'kissed like a vacuum cleaner,' Russell comforted her."[23]

Under one publicity photo of Monroe as Lorelei in Louis Giannetti's *Masters of the American Cinema*, the caption reads: "Hawks didn't understand her very well. He thought her strange, neurotic, and lonely."[24] Indeed, in a discussion at the 1970 Chicago Film Festival, Hawks recalled Monroe as "just a frightened girl" who "never felt that she was good enough to do the things that she did.... [T]here were a lot of times when I was really ready to give up the ghost."[25] Whenever Hawks was ready to give up on Monroe, however, Russell would step in: "Jane Russell would say, 'Look at me—all he wants you to do is such-and-such a thing.' And Marilyn would say to her, 'Why didn't you tell me?' Very strange girl."[26] In effect, Monroe was asking Russell, rather than Hawks, to direct her, not unlike what Dorothy does for Lorelei in the "When Love Goes Wrong" number and elsewhere. But Hawks was also comfortable with Russell directing Monroe. He "admitted that the film might never have been made if Russell hadn't befriended Monroe."[27] And the final result of this man-woman-woman filming situation? Hawks always said, "We had a lot of fun doing *Gentlemen Prefer Blondes*."[28]

Might this film be a case of production circumstances imitating the narrative, or of the narrative's affective charge being influenced by production circumstances? On the set, Russell seemed to be a "woman's woman" who could also relate to Hawks as one of his "men's women," allowing her to do his job even better when it came to another woman. Offscreen, Russell is again at the center of the bisexually charged situation. It could be that the unacknowledged bisexual elements surrounding *Gentlemen Prefer Blondes* on- and offscreen have contributed to making the film one of the most controversial texts in Hawks's canon. Because whether it is dismissed as a minor work or an aberration, or hailed as Hawks's masterpiece, critics most often return to the "problems" of gender and sexuality in the film. Robin Wood quotes Hawks saying that the film "was a complete caricature, a travesty on sex. It didn't have normal [read: conventional heterosexual] sex," before critiquing the film for its grotesque and embarrassing attempts to establish heterosexual love relationships between Dorothy, Lorelei, and weak, ineffectual men.[29] Though Wood has said he would like to rethink his work on Hawks in light of his (Wood's) coming out, the strong women + weak men = unconvincing heterosexual relationships idea is a critical commonplace about the film—and an interesting one to think about in terms of bisexual readings. Of course the relationships between Dorothy and Malone and Lorelei, and Gus are "unconvincing" as conventional straight relationships: they are male-female relationships within a female bisexual paradigm. Far from being "weak" men, then, Malone and Gus might be understood as men who ultimately understand and accede to the needs and desires of their bisexual female partners. Granted, the film ends with a wedding ceremony, with its implicit ties to institutional heterosexuality, but the double-double nature of the wedding (men marrying women, women "marrying" women) makes it no "normal" ceremony.

Hawks himself was no "normal" person or filmmaker, either, from all I can gather about his life and works. Gerald Mast and Todd McCarthy, among others, have read his life and work as containing a "gay subtext" that found its expression in his intense friendships with men, particularly his brother Kenneth, and in the representation of male friendship in many of his films as (to quote Hawks on *A Girl in Every Port*) "really a love story between two men."[30] Then there are the "pretty boys" that populate Hawks's male buddy films: Montgomery Clift, Dewey Martin, Ricky Nelson, James Caan, and Jorge Rivero, to name a few. With rare exceptions, the women Hawks was attracted to—and the women actors in his "male buddy" films—are described as "male-ish females," or "men's women" who must prove themselves "worthy of entry" into Hawks's, or into the male buddies', world.[31] However, it is just as easy—and more accurate, I think—to understand all of this as evidence for a male bisexual "subtext" (although I dislike this word, as it makes the reading too easy to dismiss) in Hawks's life and adventure films, as this reading would acknowledge that Hawks's life and films seem structured around equally important love relationships between men (even if they are not always acknowledged or acted upon sexually) and between men and women.

But where does this leave us with *Gentlemen Prefer Blondes*, as it is not a male buddy adventure film, but a musical comedy? One connection between the two in terms of bisexual readings is the way that both Hawks's adventure films and his comedies trouble the opposition between the conventionally masculine and feminine "by depicting male-ish females and female-ish males."[32] While his films, finally, don't profoundly confuse or fully invert traditional notions of masculinity and femininity, the consistent appearance of "male-ish females" (Lauren Bacall, Joanne Dru, Jean Arthur, Frances Farmer, Ann Dvorak, Barbara Stanwyck, Jane Russell, to name a few) and "female-ish" males (Cary Grant, Danny Kaye, Tommy Noonan, and that list of "pretty boys" above) indicates a more than passing interest in androgyny, which is closely linked with certain bisexual practices, identities, and theories.

However, it is *Gentlemen Prefer Blondes*' status as a "buddy film" that marks its most important connections with the male adventure films in light of bisexual readings. *Gentlemen Prefer Blondes* is the only Hawks film to feature women buddies, and much of what critics have to say about the director's male buddy films applies here. These critical remarks shore up bisexual understandings of *Gentlemen Prefer Blondes* by pointing out the erotics within buddy relationships, while understanding opposite-sex relationships in Hawks's films as often being more like friendly partnerships. Gerald Mast, for example, sees Hawks's adventure films as "collapsing" "the opposition of the terms *love* and *friendship* . . . by revealing that those who love can, and should, and must be friends if their love is to mean anything at all, and those who are friends are also kind of lovers."[33] Along these lines, Louis Giannetti notes:

> Hawks described most of his movies as "a relationship between two friends"—buddies in the action films, lovers (or would-be lovers) in the comedies. He rarely intercut between the lovers: He wanted them sharing the same space, close enough to respond to each other's physical presence.[34]

As a buddy comedy, *Gentlemen Prefer Blondes* complicates, and bisexualizes, Giannetti's neat scheme, as it presents buddies Lorelei and Dorothy who are "rarely intercut between," like the (would-be) lovers in other Hawks films, as well as often presenting their lovers and would-be buddies Malone and Gus in separate shot–reverse shot editing patterns when they are with the women.

As suggested earlier, however, Hawks's male buddy films aren't without their bisexual aspects. Lee Russell constructs a "typical dialogue" from Hawks's male buddy films that "sums up" their (bisexual) position:

> Woman: You love him, don't you?
> Man: (embarrassed) Yes . . . I guess so . . .
> Woman: How can I love him like you?
> Man: Just stick around.[35]

With very little tampering, this could be the model dialogue for *Gentlemen Prefer Blondes*:

> Man: You love her, don't you?
> Woman: (unembarrassed) Yes . . . I do . . .
> Man: How can I love her like you?
> Woman: Just stick around.

Thus, whereas in the adventure films, the women need to be trained by the example of men's relationships to become "men's women" who are as worthy of a man's love as another man is, the men in *Gentlemen Prefer Blondes* must become "women's men," trained by the example of the women's relationship with each other to become an appropriate partner for one of the women. This is because the women in *Gentlemen Prefer Blondes* are not really like the "men's women" of the Hawks adventure films, they are "women's women" who bond in the feminine, and who ask the men in their lives to do likewise with them.[36] Perhaps this is why *Gentlemen Prefer Blondes* does what the male buddy films can't seem to bring themselves to do without subjecting the characters and the audience to a great deal of physical and psychic violence—that is, the film allows the easy expression of multiple, bisexed, erotic desires. It could be that the somewhat greater latitude for women in patriarchal culture to express their feelings toward each other and to be physically intimate in varying degrees (which, at its cheesiest, includes "lesbian" representation in straight male porn)[37] lets Hawks and his collaborators relax a bit, allowing bisexuality a more open and celebratory narrative space.[38]

Besides the fact that the two main characters in *Gentlemen Prefer Blondes* are women, Hawks, Russell, Monroe, et al. may have been comfortable developing the film's bisexual esprit, whether consciously or not, because much of it might be understood as a straight-identified bisexuality. Discussing male "trade" (a "heterosexual identified, homoerotically inclined" man), Chris Cagle points out that many gay, lesbian, and queer-identified bisexuals reject straight-identified bisexuals for a number of reasons, but most often because it appears that these bisexuals can enjoy the protection of straight privilege.[39] Most often, straight-identified bisexuals maintain their primary relationships with someone of the opposite sex, and have same-sex partners in less long-term circumstances or on the side.

If we look at the film with this in mind, we can see that while there are official weddings for men and women, there seems to be nothing in the narrative to set Dorothy and Lorelei's relationship within complementary women-women institutions or communities. Nothing, that is, except the narrative's insistence that their primary bond with each other establishes a "woman's world" within which the men who love them must be tested. The film even comes close to representing a woman-woman wedding by eliminating the words of the minister and closing in for that final two-shot of the women looking at their rings and then at each other. These elements alone trouble an understanding of the film as fully straight identifying. On the other hand, the woman-woman erotics in the film are more suggested than shown, more a case of calling out to viewers' desires than one of concrete representation—as opposed to the kissing and protestations of love between the men and the women. However, Dorothy is connected to a handful of explicit woman-woman erotic moments that offer strong parallels to the film's representations of male-female sexuality: she initiates a voyeuristic gaze through a porthole that focuses upon Lorelei's backside, she addresses a group of women in swimsuits by singing "Ain't There Anyone Here for Love?" and she yells out "Do it honey! Do it!" while looking at a shimmying Lorelei.

When all is said and done, then, the narrative presentation of Lorelei, Dorothy, and their men confounds any definitive reading of the film's (bi)sexual politics. It's no secret by this point, however, that I find the film's characters and events make the most sense when they are placed within a woman-centered bisexual context. Lorelei and, especially, Dorothy aren't like most straight women as they make their relationship with each other the defining center of their lives; but they also aren't like most lesbians as they allow men into their lives as romantic/sexual partners. These women invite men's erotic gazes, return them, initiate their own, and, occasionally, also invite and return women's erotic gazes. Like *The Wizard of Oz*, *Psycho*, and the other films covered in this book, *Gentlemen Prefer Blondes* has become many things to many people: in this case, progressively lesbian or straight feminist, regressively antifeminist, exhiliratingly or foolishly campy, comfortingly or problematically straight-identified bisexual, excitingly women-centered bisexual, or some combination of these positions.[40] As for me, *Gentlemen Prefer Blondes* is, along with *Sylvia Scarlett*, classic American studio filmmaking at the top of its bisexual form.[41]

NOTES

1. Geoffrey Macnab, "Blondes Have More Funds," *Time Out: London* 1347 (June 12–19, 1996): 163.
2. For more detailed discussions of bisexual definitions and identities, see Donald E. Hall and Maria Pramaggiore, ed., *RePresenting Bisexualities: Subjects and Cultures of Fluid Desire* (New York and London: New York University Press, 1996); Sue George, *Women and Bisexuality* (London: Scarlet Press, 1993); Bi Academic Intervention, ed., *The Bisexual Imaginary: Representation, Identity and Desire* (London and Washington: Cassell, 1997); Fritz Klein, *The Bisexual Option*, 2nd ed. (New York: Harrington Park Press, 1993); Marjorie Garber, *Vice Versa: Bisexuality and the Eroticism of Everyday Life* (New York: Touchstone, 1995); Martin S. Weinberg, Colin J. Williams, and Douglas W. Pryor, *Dual Attraction: Understanding Bisexuality* (New York and Oxford: Oxford University Press, 1994); Elizabeth Reba Weise, ed., *Closer to Home: Bisexuality and Feminism* (Seattle, Wash.: Seal Press, 1992); Loraine Hutchins and Lani Kaahumanu, ed., *Bi Any Other Name: Bisexual People Speak Out* (Boston: Alyson, 1991).
3. *Chasing Amy* (1997, Miramax: Kevin Smith). There is a wonderful fantasy-nightmare sequence in Rose Troche's *Go Fish* (1994, Goldwyn) that has one of the protagonists defending herself against a group of women, most of whom question her lesbian credentials after she has slept with a man.
4. *Gentlemen Prefer Blondes* (1953, 20th Century-Fox: Howard Hawks).
5. *The Wild Party* (1929, Paramount: Dorothy Arzner); *Stage Door* (1937, RKO: Gregory La Cava); *Thelma and Louise* (1991, MGM: Ridley Scott).
6. Andrea Weiss, " 'A Queer Feeling When I Look at You': Hollywood Stars and Lesbian Spectatorship in the 1930s," in *Multiple Voices in Feminist Film Criticism*, ed. Diane Carson, Linda Dittmar, and Janice R. Welsch (Minneapolis and London: University of Minnesota Press, 1994), 331; Andrew Britton, *Katharine Hepburn: The Thirties and After* (Newcastle upon Tyne, England: Tynside Cinema, 1984), 16.
7. Maria Pramaggiore, "Straddling the Screen: Bisexual Spectatorship and Contemporary Narrative Film," in *RePresenting Bisexualities: Subjects and Cultures of Fluid Desire*, ed. Donald E. Hall and Maria Pramaggiore (New York and London: New York University Press, 1996), 275.
8. Ibid., 275.
9. Gerald Mast, *Howard Hawks, Storyteller* (Oxford and New York: Oxford University Press, 1982) 62.
10. *Gentlemen Marry Brunettes* (1955, Allied Artists: Richard Sale). While this film opens promisingly enough with sister team Bonnie and Connie Jones (Jane Russell and Jeanne Crain) singing "You're Driving Me Crazy" about men (ending the song with a shouted "I just don't care!"), *Gentlemen Marry Brunettes* quickly pairs the women off with men and downplays their sisterly bond. As with *Gentlemen Prefer Blondes*, the finale takes place aboard an ocean liner, but here the women are immediately split to become part of heterosexual couples (and

filmed in separate two shots with their future husbands), while their mother (also played by Russell), goes off to the ship's bar with two old male admirers.

11. Alexander Doty, *Making Things Perfectly Queer: Interpreting Mass Culture* (Minneapolis: University of Minnesota Press, 1993), 105–6, n. 13.

12. Lucie Arbuthnot and Gail Seneca, "Pre-Text and Text in *Gentlemen Prefer Blondes*," in *Issues in Feminist Film Criticism*, ed. Patricia Erens (Bloomington and Indianapolis: Indiana University Press, 1990), 116.

13. Sue George, *Women and Bisexuality* (London: Scarlet Press, 1993), 170.

14. Anita Loos, *Gentlemen Prefer Blondes* (New York: Boni and Liveright, 1925).

15. Ibid., 103.

16. Ibid., 213.

17. *How to Marry a Millionaire* (1953, 20th Century-Fox: Jean Negulesco).

18. Compare "Diamonds Are a Girl's Best Friend" to Madonna's music video homage to the number in "Material Girl" (1985) to see the difference between texts that establish bisexual spaces and ones that offer only straight ones. Where Lorelei ignores men except when they offer her diamonds and is concerned about the women, Madonna's character has no other women in her musical number. While she ignores the men in the number to some extent, and rejects the necklace of an admirer who works behind-the-scenes, she ends the video by going off with a studio executive (played by Keith Carradine) who puts on a "just plain guy" act for her.

19. Arbuthnot and Seneca, 122.

20. Arbuthnot and Seneca, 121.

21. Danny Peary, *Cult Movies 3* (New York: Simon and Schuster, 1988), 96.

22. Monroe and Russell's friendship and teamwork in *Gentlemen Prefer Blondes* was publicly recognized when they were invited to put their prints and signatures in cement together at Grauman's Chinese Theatre after the opening of the film. Once again, they wore matching outfits.

23. Peary, 96.

24. Louis Giannetti, *Masters of the American Cinema* (Englewood Cliffs, N.J.: Prentice-Hall, 1981), 202.

25. Joseph McBride and Michael Wilmington, ed., "A Discussion with the Audience of the 1970 Chicago Film Festival," in *Focus on Howard Hawks*, ed. Joseph McBride (Englewood Cliffs, NJ: Prentice-Hall, 1972), 20.

26. Ibid., 20.

27. Peary, 96.

28. McBride and Wilmington, 20–21.

29. Robin Wood, *Howard Hawks* (Hertford, England: BFI Publishing, 1983), 171–72.

30. Mast, 380, n. 17; Todd McCarthy, *Howard Hawks: The Grey Fox of Hollywood* (New York: Grove Press, 1997); Diane Jacobs, "Split Screen" [review of McCarthy's *Howard Hawks*], *New York Times Book Review*, section 7, July 20, 1991: 10. Even with his comment that *A Girl in Every Port* is really "a love story between two men," Hawks responded with "That's a god-damn silly statement to make," when asked about the "homosexual subtext" in some of his films

[Joseph McBride, "Hawks," *Film Comment* 14:2 (March 1978): 39]. Not that he was thinking about this consciously, but it would be a "silly" statement to make if you understand these films as constructing (male) bisexual narratives.

31. Mast, 68, 85.
32. Mast, 68.
33. Mast, 69.
34. Giannetti, 194.
35. Lee Russell, "Howard Hawks," *New Left Review* 24 (March–April, 1964), rpt. in *Howard Hawks: American Artist*, ed. Jim Hillier and Peter Wollen (London: BFI Publishing, 1996), 85.
36. As Danny Peary puts it: "Even though they marry at the end of the film, Lorelei and Dorothy do not want to be welcomed into the male world" (95).
37. For a discussion of the woman-women aspects of *Gentlemen Prefer Blondes* in relation to the use of "lesbians" in straight male porn, see Maureen Turim's "Gentlmen Consume Blondes," in *Issues in Feminist Film Criticism*, ed. Patricia Erens (Bloomington and Indianapolis: Indiana University Press, 1990):

    > Lesbians exist in pornography and advertising as a trope; they are not really women given to each other erotically rather than to men, but pseudo-lesbians given over to the gaze which truly possesses them. In *Gentlemen* the narrative assures us that, despite the bonds between Dorothy and Lorelei, their relationship is not self-sufficient; it seeks males for completion, so that when (heterosexual) love goes wrong, nothing goes right (110–11).

    This straight reading seems to ignore the narrative's insistence on the primacy of the women's relationship. If anything, the film suggests that these women's unions with men will be the "add-ons" to their relationship with each other—think of all the critics and viewers who find the women's relationships with men far less compelling and believable than the women's partnership. As far as lesbian readings constructed around Dorothy and Lorelei are concerned, the Arbuthnot and Seneca article "Pre-text and Text in *Gentlemen Prefer Blondes*" (cited elsewhere) offers a persuasive, implicitly lesbian-positioned, answer to Turim's understanding of the pair as "pseudo-lesbians," as they discuss the film as "a feminist text which both denies men pleasure in some degree, and more importantly, celebrates women's pleasure in each other" (113).

38. Certain feminist psychoanalytic critics would see culture's greater understanding of women's emotional and physical closeness to each other in terms of Freud's theory of female bisexuality, which posits that women maintain their attachment to the mother (and other women) throughout their lives, and that this attachment coexists with later relationships with men (unless, of course, they are lesbian). But see also Tania Modleski's discussion of female bisexuality in *The Women Who Knew Too Much: Hitchcock and Feminist Theory* (London and New York: Methuen, 1988): 6–7. Here Modleski, citing Gertrud Koch, mentions that there are many prohibitions patriarchy tries to place upon women-women connections in attempts to police bisexuality and lesbianism.

39. Chris Cagle, "Rough Trade: Sexual Taxonomy in Postwar America," in *RePre-senting Bisexualities: Subjects and Cultures of Fluid Desire*, ed. Donald E. Hall and Maria Pramaggiore (New York: New York University Press, 1996), 235, 249.
40. Jonathan Rosenbaum, in "Golddiggers of 1953: Howard Hawks' *Gentlemen Pre-fer Blondes*," *Sight and Sound* 54:1 (Winter 1984/85), finds that the film "man-ages to accommodate some of the viewpoints and fantasies of heterosexuals *and* homosexuals of both genders" (46). This chapter has also been making a case for the film's appeal to the "viewpoints and fantasies" of bisexuals of both sexes, and, I suppose, of both gender identities, regardless of the sex they are aligned with—as well as to the "viewpoints and fantasies" of bisexuals with no particular gender alliance.
41. *Sylvia Scarlett* (1936, RKO: George Cukor). In certain ways, *Gentlemen Prefer Blondes* has it over *Sylvia Scarlett* as the latter film constructs its bisexuality largely in male terms that exclude the female central character. Sylvia enters a male world dressed as a young man and has queer experiences thrust upon her. It is as a young man that she arouses the bisexual interest of two men who are also attracted to women. Sylvia herself doesn't seem particularly interested in having experiences with women, even though they are attracted to her (whether she is dressed as a young man or a young woman), as she is interested in a bisex-ual male artist. In a sense, Sylvia, like many people in the audience, is finally asked to accept the gender queerness and bisexuality as the terms for the con-struction of couples at its conclusion: she is paired with the bisexual artist, while a second couple is made up of a bisexual female aristocrat and a bisexual male con man and performer.

"He's a transvestite!"
"Ah, not exactly."
How Queer Is My Psycho

The more I watch *Psycho*, and read what has been written about it, the less certain I am about what to make of Norman Bates psychosexually.[1] Should I read him as homosexual/gay? Or does the film seem to represent him as straight? Maybe he's bisexual? Some viewers attempt to steer clear of these questions by suggesting Norman is asexual or childlike, and, therefore, he should not be considered in sexual terms. To these people, I would say that anyone who constructs a peephole in order to watch women undressing is not asexual, and that the term "polymorphous perversity" isn't connected to children for nothing. Most critics and the public appear to be divided between understanding soft-spoken, stuttering Norman as another one of Hitchcock's "crazy—and I mean crazy—dykes and faggots," and finding him a frightening and/or pitiable straight guy ruined by his too-close relationship with his mother.[2] Even in its straight incarnations, however, Norman's sexuality is understood as perverse somehow: he is the quintessential mama's boy gone horribly bad. But this incestuous mama's boy coding is also the basis for reading Norman as homosexual. Granted the dominant cultural trope of mama's-boy-as-homosexual is a tired one, but it has maintained its pop Freudian, pop culture power.

Like Robin Wood, I would be only too happy to call Norman "straight" and cite statistics that show straight men are the perpetrators of almost all violent crime against women.[3] Besides this, straight men often maintain intense, adulatory relationships with their mothers: "I want a girl just like the girl that married dear old dad," and all that. Even the original Oedipal tale about a man killing his father and sleeping with his mother was, to put it in contemporary terms, a straight narrative. But much as I'd like to understand

Norman as straight, the film, coupled with certain hoary, yet culturally pervasive, cliches, finally makes it difficult.

Psycho is a more subtle case of what, more recently, generated arguments in relation to the Buffalo Bill figure in The Silence of the Lambs.[4] While director Jonathan Demme and scriptwriter Ted Tally denied that woman-skinner Buffalo Bill was meant to be understood as gay, critics and audiences were split in their responses. Of those who consciously considered his sexuality, some saw Bill's murdered male lover, desire to be a transsexual, nipple ring, colorful silk wrapper, made-up face, tucked penis, and dog named Precious as certain signs of gayness, while others felt these things were not necessarily codes of homosexuality, but of a gender crisis. As with Psycho, however, most viewers who did not want to label Buffalo Bill "gay," had to admit that there was something (or many things) nonheteronormative about him.

I said it during the The Silence of the Lambs debates, and I'll say it again here about Psycho's Norman Bates: why not use the term "queer" in these cases?[5] Looking back, it seems that the often divisive debates between and among gays, lesbians, and straight feminists over The Silence of the Lambs actually may have helped foster some of the early development and use of queer theory within film and popular culture studies, as the concept of "queerness" offered a way to discuss nonheteronormative gender and sexuality, and their interrelationship, in a way that avoided the "yes s/he is–no s/he isn't" binaries that can pit gay men against lesbians and straight feminists. In the case of *The Silence of the Lambs*, private and press arguments found many gay men condemning the film for perpetuating what they saw as yet another gay psycho killer stereotype (or two, if you count effete Hannibal Lecter), while some lesbians and straight feminists lauded the film's feminist hero, Clarice Starling, while ignoring or downplaying the question of Buffalo Bill's sexuality.[6]

"Queer": as in not clearly identified as homosexual, bisexual, or heterosexual, while also, in certain, usually gender, particulars, not fitting into current understandings of normative straightness. This describes Buffalo Bill, but it also describes Norman Bates if you look at what might otherwise be called the "incoherent" or "muddled" gender and sexuality coding surrounding his representation, as well as the range of psychosexual readings audiences and critics have given the character. Even *Psycho*'s famous preview trailer, in which Hitchcock takes the audience on a tour of the Bates house and motel, encourages such a range of readings as the director refuses to complete his thoughts about Norman:

> This young man, you had to feel sorry for him. After all, being dominated by an almost maniacal woman was enough to drive anyone to the extreme of... Well, let's go in [to the parlor]. (Pointing to the picture of Susannah and the Elders that hides Norman's peephole) This picture has great significance because... Let's go along to cabin number one. I want to show you something there.

Calling Norman Bates "queer" doesn't necessarily free his character from the charges of pejorative or stereotypic representation that have been brought against him (or, rather, against the makers of the film) by some critics and audiences, but it does allow us to consider his character more complexly outside of the kind of binaries that have stalled "yes s/he is–no s/he isn't" debates. In Norman Bates's case, you have to ignore or downplay too much in order to formulate an argument about his character that works within the established binaries of heterosexual-homosexual and masculine-feminine. Referring to Norman as bisexual might work, but only in the sense that his character is not clearly coded as homosexual or heterosexual, not because of any suggestions that he is attracted to both men and women sexually. When we add the gender "confusions" the film attaches to Norman, it would appear that "queer"—at least in relation to the definition above—best describes someone like Norman. Tania Modleski has remarked:

> As the figure of Norman Bates suggests, what both male and female spectators are likely to see in the mirror of Hitchcock's films are images of

ambiguous sexuality that threaten to destabilize the gender identity of protagonists and viewer alike.[7]

Psycho has long been held up as the prototype of all sorts of films, including those in which a sexual "perversion" of some sort serves as the final narrative surprise or shock. Even on first viewing, however, anyone with an eye for queerness will not be all that surprised when Norman appears at the fruit cellar door in his ill-fitting wig and housedress. For while the narrative has him being shyly flirtatious and sexually suggestive with Marion as he checks her into her room—touching the "soft" mattress, being unable to say the word "bathroom," inviting her to share dinner with him in his parlor, and nervously offering up some subconscious Freudian sexual symbolism with "Uh, y-you get yourself settled, and—and take off your wet shoes, and I'll be back . . . with my trusty umbrella"—certain aspects of Anthony Perkins's performance, as well as what seem to be the intrusions of his jealous mother, are also working to establish Norman as "effeminate" and mother-dominated.[8]

These initial attempts to confuse, or, as I would have it, to queer Norman in terms of his sexuality and gender are echoed later in the film when detective Arbogast questions Norman about Marion after asking him if he spent the night with her:

Arbogast: Let's just say for the uh—just for the sake of argument—that she wanted you to gallantly protect her—you'd know that you were being used—that uh—you wouldn't be made a fool of, would you?
Norman: Well, I'm—I'm not a fool.
Arbogast: Well, then—
Norman: And I'm not capable of being fooled! N-not even by a woman!
Arbogast: Well, it's not a slur on your manhood. I'm sorry.
Norman: Now let's put it this way. She might have fooled me—but she didn't fool my mother.

This brief exchange is riddled with sexuality-related gender tensions. Arbogast suggests that one conventional straight cultural and narrative position for men—the gallant protector of women—is somehow not really masculine enough, indeed it might be understood as a weakness. Even though he apologizes to Norman, it's clear to both Norman and the viewer that Arbogast is indeed trying to "slur" Norman's "manhood" with his insinuations. For his part, Norman first attempts to assert his masculinity by insisting that he can't be fooled "even by a woman," then admits that Marion may have fooled him, "but she didn't fool my mother." So he is, in effect, admitting that he is less than conventionally masculine because a woman did fool him—and that another woman (his "invalid" mother) was actually more intelligent than he. Within the context of this discussion, he has placed himself, culturally and narratively, in a feminine position (foolish, unperceptive, gullible, weak), while putting his mother in a more masculine one. Soon, mother also will reveal a "masculine" physical strength that belies Norman's comments about her when she rushes from her bedroom to attack and kill a snooping Arbogast.[9]

Even when we discover "mother" is within Norman, she is represented as the dominant/masculine one, with the boyish Norman as the weaker/feminine (or effeminate) aspect of a split personality. Long before the revelations of the final scenes, however, the film asks us to understand Norman as (ef)feminized by his strong mother, and, in relation to this cross-gendered narrative space, to question his heterosexuality to some extent, even if on a subconscious level. As Raymond Bellour and others have pointed out, the troubling questions about Norman begin with his name: "Nor-man: he who is neither woman ... nor man, since [as we discover later] he can be one in the place of the other, or rather one and the other, one within the other."[10] To this I would add that "Norman" is a letter away from "normal," and that within "Norman" is "Norma" (what his mother personality is called in the Robert Bloch novel) and "ma."

Norman and Marion's famous dinner in the parlor is, perhaps, the sequence that causes most first-time viewers to consciously think there might be something "wrong" with Norman. Again at the center of this discomfort is Norman's mother. When Marion asks if he goes out with friends, Norman responds, "Well, uh—a boy's best friend is his mother." Commenting upon the death of his mother's boyfriend, Norman observes that "a son is a poor substitute for a lover." The parlor sequence is where incest is most clearly put forward as the explanation for why Norman acts so tentatively around a woman he seems to desire.[11] One way of understanding Norman is as someone whose incestuous desires are constantly in conflict with his "normal" heterosexual urges. Hence his alternating awkward flirting and voyeurism with statements about how he needs to stay with his mother as she is his "best friend" and because he serves as a substitute (albeit a "poor" one) for her dead lover. However, as suggested earlier, what complicates this already complex psychosexual situation is that in patriarchal cultural discourses and representation mother-son closeness and incest is almost always connected with homosexuality.

This was a particularly potent—and virulent—connection to make at the time of the film's original release, as many Americans were still in the thrall of a dominant ideology that linked Communism to homosexuality, and both to doting mothers. As Robert J. Corber notes in his analysis of *North by Northwest* and *Psycho*,

Philip Wylie, who coined the term *momism* in his best-selling book *A Generation of Vipers* (1942), argued that American society was rapidly becoming a matriarchy in which domineering and overly protective mothers disrupted the Oedipal structure of the middle-class nuclear family by smothering their sons with "unnatural" affection.... In vilifying domineering mothers, Wylie helped to lay the foundation for the identification of homosexuality and lesbianism as threats to national security. Although he did not explicitly link momism to homosexuality and lesbianism, Wylie identified communism as a form of political deviance directly related to incompetent mothering; in doing so, he reinforced the association in the nation's political imaginary between communism and same-sex eroticism. After all, contemporary psychiatric discourse had located the source of homosexuality and lesbianism in incompetent mothering.[12]

It might seem surprising that after talk like this, Corber argues that "Norman is coded as neither a Communist nor a homosexual. He dresses in his mother's clothing because he overidentifies with her, not because it excites him sexually."[13] But Corber's final point about Norman appears to be a queer one: "Norman ... cannot be adequately explained by the available postwar discourses of identity."[14]

Despite the reservations or outright denials of critics like Corber and Robin Wood, however, part of a case for Norman as homosexual, or, rather, of a case for some of Norman's coding as being taken from dominant cultural discourses about homosexuality, can be made on the evidence of the mother-son dynamics in the film—and this is the case for initial as well as subsequent viewings.[15] Along with Norman's comments about his mother being his "best friend" and his being a "poor substitute for a lover," first-time viewers are confronted by what they understand as the sexually jealous outburst of Mrs. Bates:

> No! I tell you! I won't have you bringing strange young girls in here for supper. By candlelight, I suppose, in the cheap erotic fashion of young men with cheap, erotic minds! ... And then what after supper? Music? Whispers? ... "Mother, she's just a stranger!" As if men don't desire strangers! Ah! I refuse to speak of disgusting things because they disgust me! Do you understand, boy? Go on! Go tell her she'll not be appeasing her ugly appetite with my food, or my son! Or do I have to tell her 'cause you don't have the guts? Huh, boy? You have the guts, boy?

As Arbogast does later, Mrs. Bates casts doubts upon her son's "manhood," even as she describes straight sex as "cheap" and "disgusting." After a few tentative attempts to explain things, Norman is reduced to screeching "Shut up! Shut up!" when his mother wonders about how much "guts" he has, that is, how "manly" he is. As is the case elsewhere in the film, this episode both evokes the possibility of Norman's "normal" heterosexual desires, while simultaneously undermining such a possibility with its suggestion of an incestuous relationship—one that first-time viewers understand as being perpetrated by a monstrous mother.

After the psychiatrist's explanations at the end of the film, a somewhat different picture of the mother-son relationship emerges, but one that still works within certain conservative psychoanalytic and popular notions about the sources of male homosexuality. A too protective or too domineering mother might cause a son to remain stuck in an early infantile or immature, an oral or anal, stage of sexual development. A son who (over)identifies with his mother—with the "feminine"—might pervert the classic Oedipal trajectory and place himself in the position of his mother desiring the father/men.

Along these lines, David Sterritt's analysis of *Psycho* focuses upon "the film's preoccupation with anal-compulsive behavior, which recurs throughout the narrative in thinly disguised form."[16] However, Sterritt's subsequent linking of the film's welter of anal references with "Norman's confusions about sexual difference and appropriate sexual behavior" merely hints at the homosexual or the queer, while it uncritically explains things by citing "Freud's assertion that during the 'pre-genital' phase (to which Norman has regressed)" there is no distinction between the "masculine" and the "feminine," just between the "active" and the "passive," with the passive being connected with the eroticization of the rectum.[17] Extrapolating from Sterritt on Freud, since the mother side of Norman becomes associated with the active, which is, in the later adult genital stage, tied to the masculine, and the boyish side of Norman is associated with the passive, later understood as the feminine, Norman suffers those "confusions about sexual difference and appropriate sexual behavior." Sterritt does come close to calling Norman either homosexual or queer, however, when he says that Norman gives a "flamboyant" performance as mother, that we first see this performance "through a window of the house, behind which he parades in his mother's dress," and that, later, Norman will present his "buttocks . . . swaying effeminately" to the camera/viewer.[18]

Diana Fuss works out these ideas about Freud and anality with specific reference to the demonization of male homosexuality in "the popular imaginary," although she finally concentrates her discussion on how male homosexuality has also been popularly, and pejoratively, linked with Freud's other early phase of sexuality, the oral. Although her article uses *The Silence of the Lambs* and Jeffrey Dahmer as examples, Fuss might well have used Norman Bates, surrounded as he is in *Psycho* by references to "appetite" and to the anal:

If, in the popular imaginary, gay male sexuality can be said to have an ero-togenic zone of its own, its corporeal "repository" may well be the spec-tacularized site of the anus.... I would like to suggest that alongside the scene of intercourse *per anum* between men, modernist culture offers quite another spectacle of male homosexuality, one based on oral, rather than anal eroticism.... Notions of anal incorporation cannot help but invoke tropes of orality.[19]

Fuss also notes that the classic "slippery-slidey slope" psychoanalytic model "for the so-called sexual perversions" often results in the medical and pop-ular connection of oral-anal homosexuality with such things as necrophilia and cannibalism.[20] More specifically, Fuss's account of this model in relation to what it has to say about the "oral-cannibalistic" is chillingly spot on in terms of much of *Psycho*'s presentation of Norman-as-"mother" ("Go tell her she'll not be appeasing her ugly appetite with my food, or my son!"):

[M]ale homosexuality is represented as fixated at the earliest stage of the libidinal organization—the oral-cannibalistic stage—in which the recalci-trant subject refuses to give up its first object (the maternal breast and all its phallic substitutes). Instead, the male homosexual *ingests* the (m)other, "puts himself in her place, identifies himself with her, and takes his own person as a model in whose likeness he chooses the new objects of his love." Oral-cannibalistic incorporation of the mother not only permits a homo-sexual object choice but unleashes sadistic impulses.[21]

Sterritt also briefly invokes *Psycho*'s oral-anal connection, while making the kind of conventional equation of it with "arrested development" that Fuss critiques:

Eating is the first step in the alimentary process that ends with defecation; the film's early food references are a kind of foreplay, drawing us toward the realm of anal anxiety where much of the movie will take place.[22]

Since he doesn't eat with her, however, Norman's heterosexual "foreplay" with Marion before dinner is really a cover for the queer "anal anxiety" to come. It is an anxiety that is finally, and horrifyingly, represented by that dou-ble superimposition of Mrs. Bates's mummified skull over Norman's mad face over a shot of the car with Marion's body in it being pulled from the swamp. "Everything piles up in the swamp—and is dredged up again," Raymond Durgnat comments. "The film is not just a sick joke and a very sad joke, but a lavatory joke."[23] Indeed, one audacious moment in the preview trailer has Hitchcock leading the audience into cabin 1's bathroom. "A very important clue was found here," he tells us as he lifts up the toilet seat. Directing his gaze toward the (offscreen) toilet bowl, he informs us that the "important clue" is "down there."

The first part of the psychiatrist's analysis of Norman is careful to cover almost all of the conservative pop Freudian bases regarding the family romance and male homosexuality. What we discover at the end of the film is that Norman "was already dangerously disturbed . . . ever since his father died," that "for years" after Mr. Bates's death "his mother was a clinging, demanding woman," and that "the two of them lived as though there was no one else in the world." But after his mother met and fell in love with another man, "it seemed to Norman that she 'threw him over' for this man," so Norman killed them both. Stricken with guilt and longing, Norman digs up his mother's remains, preserves them, and begins to "split" his own personality to accommodate his mother's, or at least his version of mother: "Now he was never all Norman, but he was often only mother." Since Norman "was so pathologically jealous of her, he assumed that she was as jealous of him. Therefore, if he felt a strong attraction to any other woman, the mother side of him would go wild." In a film that exploits vagueness and contradiction, it is not surprising to find that the psychiatrist finally seems to exonerate Mrs. Bates, even after he has condemned her moments earlier as a "clinging, demanding woman." So Mrs. Bates is and is not guilty of perverting her son from normative heterosexuality, while Norman later complicates this per-version through a spectacular (over)identification with one aspect or version of his mother—the sexually jealous, castrating woman.

However, while there is plenty in the psychological stew Dr. Richman offers to bolster arguments that Norman could be read as a homosexual char-acter, based upon conventional analytic and popular paradigms of the time (including homosexuality as a mental illness), the film finally seems to want to have things both ways, or, perhaps, neither way, where Norman is concerned. To a certain extent, the film represents his relationship to Mar-ion as normatively heterosexual and conventionally masculine, as he maneu-vers her into his parlor for supper and then peeps in on her as she undresses (yes, the latter is well within representations of the normative and the con-ventional for straight men). But the shadow of his mother, whether we understand her as a real person or as Norman internalizes her, hangs heavy over his every potentially heterosexual move. Since he is "never all Norman," even his moments of heterosexual desire are immediately queered by the incestuously jealous mother elements in him. One might even wonder why Norman takes on this particular version of his mother and then allows it to become omnipresent. Could it be he really doesn't want to have sex with women, that he wants someone to stop him and them? Through the mother side of him, Norman casts women like Marion as sexually appetitive (as the film does to some extent, actually) and depraved. "Mother" hates these women's appetites for "her son" and kills them because of this.

Psycho's narrative does not definitively connect Norman's psychological situation with either heterosexuality or homosexuality, though. It could be called heterosexual if we understand Norman as being disturbed by his "normal" desires for these women, then projecting these desires onto the women, whom he punishes in the guise of his nonnormative heterosexual partner, "mother." However, what we have here could be feeding into another classic cultural stereotype of homosexuality: homosexual men are jealous of, and therefore hate, (straight) women. Theodore Price links what he calls Hitchcock's "misogyny theme" to "woman-killer" characters like Norman, and both to homosexuality:

> [M]any of Hitch's Jack the Ripper figures are homosexuals. And in Hitchcock films—something that must never be overlooked—is a convention that all homosexuals (or nearly all) hate women on general principles, or, at the very least, are hostile to women because they cannot make love to them effectively.[24]

Within this scenario, Norman uses the mother side of him as a cover for his homosexual dread and hatred of straight woman and their sexuality. As his homosexuality has been both developed and repressed by his relationship with his mother, and continues to be by the "mother" within him, it is Norman-as-"mother" who finds these women "disgusting," and it is Norman-as-"mother" who gets rid of them as Norman goes through the motions of being heterosexually boyishly nervous in these women's presence. Since the woman-hating, "mother" side of Norman is always there, whereas his boyish persona is not, how can we be certain that the gaze through that peephole in the wall is fully heterosexual? After all, the "mother" side of Norman, with all its potential for a cross-gender homosexualizing or queering of his character, is watching these women, too.

From an auteurist perspective, one could point out that the suggestive connection of intense mother-son bonds with homosexuality, bisexuality, or less sharply defined queerness was nothing new in Hitchcock films. Corber and others discuss *North by Northwest* (1959) in terms that suggest it can be read as a film in which a mother-dominated ad man learns self-reliant All-American masculinity by facing his foreign (Communist?) bisexual (Vandamm) and gay (Leonard) demons, and through this process, forging a successful heterosexual relationship (after two divorces) while saving the United States.[25] Earlier Nazism, mother-domination, and bisexuality were

featured in *Notorious* (1946), with Alex Sebastian wooing Alicia Huber-
mann even as he points out to her what "attractive" men American agents
Devlin and Paul Prescott are. As the keeper of the mansion keys, Alex's
mother is set up as a jealous woman who consistently ruins his relationships
with other women. Mother is proven right about Alicia, however, and
mother and son are reunited in mother's bedroom when Alex discovers Alicia is an American agent. *Shadow of a Doubt* (1942) presents a slight varia-
tion on the mother-son incest theme, as a maternal older sister is set up as
the long-standing family romance for her not-quite-straight "Merry Widow
Murderer" brother. But the most pointedly homosexual among Hitchcock's
mama's boys is Bruno Anthony of *Strangers on a Train* (1951). Pampered and
indulged by his slightly dotty mother (who, among other things, gives him
manicures), Bruno is attracted to tennis star Guy Haines and kills Haines's
wife as a sign of his affection. Bruno wants Guy to kill his father in return,
which would leave the family mansion to him and his mother. Along with
Phillip and Brandon in *Rope* (1948), Bruno is Hitchcock's most "out" male
homosexual character. Is it just a coincidence that he is also represented as
psychopathic?

In discussing Hitchcock "plot formations," Robin Wood includes *The
Lodger* (1926), *Murder* (1930), *Shadow of a Doubt*, *Rope*, *Strangers on a Train*,
Psycho, and *Frenzy* (1971) in his entry for "the story about a psychopath."[26]
In all but one case, the psychopath in question, at one time or another, has
been understood by some critics and audience members as homosexual/gay.
The Lodger is the exception, perhaps only because we never get to see the
killer. However, the lodger, his wrongly accused stand-in, as played by out
homosexual actor Ivor Novello, has been read as possibly homosexual or
bisexual partly as a result of a *Psycho*-like combination of incest suggestiveness and the feminine-coded/effeminate performance style of the male lead.
In addition, up to the revelation that Novello's character is not the Jack the
Ripper–like Avenger, the narrative does everything it can to make us see the
lodger as forbidding and strange: as two intertitles put it, he is a "queer" gen-
tleman who "doesn't like the girls," besides which he knows how pick out a
fabulous evening gown for the daughter of the house.

I am willing to concede that not all of Hitchcock's psychos are clearly or
consistently coded as homosexual, largely as a result of cultural and film censorship practices in England and America, but I defy anyone to point to a
Hitchcock psychopath who is clearly and consistently presented as a conventionally masculine heterosexual. No, I am not confusing gender and
sexuality here. Within a traditional patriarchal perspective, to be question-
ably "masculine" is almost always to be sexually "suspect" to some degree.
Even in less pejorative cultural contexts, gender fluidity/gender fucking is

generally associated with some kind of nonheterosexual position. Strangely enough then, censorship and pop Freudianism come together in Hitchcock's films about psychopaths to create a compelling collection of men who often are neither cut-and-dried "gay villains" nor just heterosexual men in "gender crises," as their stories are presented from within the less binary-fixed queer spaces of gender and sexuality.

Again, what I'm suggesting in this chapter is that we look at characters like Norman Bates for how they can open up—can "queer"—the representation of gender and sexuality, even if the filmmakers' intentions were to avoid censorship while playing around with half-baked, popularized conventional psychoanalytic notions of gender "dysfunction" and sexual "perversion." In discussing *Psycho*, James Naremore finds that it is the film that most "openly" throws together Hitchcock's favorite themes of "[i]ncest, latent homosexuality, voyeurism, [and] necrophilia."[27] While the onscreen results might be called (and have been called in Norman's case) "incoherent" and "muddled," and even dangerously so, one possibly constructive effect of the gender and sexuality vagueness and confusion in a film like *Psycho* is to challenge various binary-based understandings and analyses of the representation of gender and sexuality. As I mention above, this theoretical and critical opening up to queer possibilities does not excuse filmmakers, films, or characters from rigorous ideological analyses. Norman might still be understood as a pejorative and culturally suspect representation, but for less clear-cut "gay images" reasons. Or, from a feminist perspective, Norman (and the filmmakers) might be criticized for indulging in voyeurism and sexual objectification, but not necessarily within those classic paradigms that situate the straight man as the sole possessor of the sadistic, objectifying gaze.

In a passing reference, Tania Modleski tellingly links *Psycho* to *Murder*. While she does not use the term, her work on *Murder* often moves into queer critical areas. This is most evident in a discussion of cross-dressing circus trapeze performer Handel Fane that contains observations that could be applied to Norman Bates:

> The full complexity of Fane's characterization is seldom acknowledged in Hitchcock criticism. Many critics claim, for example, that Fane is a homosexual, disregarding the fact that the most disturbing thing about this character is his defiance of any simple categorization. Fane not only impersonates women but also takes them as objects of his desire.... Fane, instead, and much more radically, challenges the categories, boundaries, and dichotomous structures that sustain patriarchal culture.[28]

Since Modleski mentions it, and as it hasn't been discussed yet in this chapter, let's consider the most provocative bit of gender coding in both films—men wearing women's clothes—as another example of how labels like "homosexual," "heterosexual" or even "bisexual" won't really do for characters like Norman and Fane.[29] Outside of certain broad comic contexts, men's wearing women's clothes is connected with homosexuality by most people. Yet we also know that there are heterosexual men who like to dress in women's clothes. However, most of these men would call themselves "transvestites," and they wear women's clothes for personal, not professional, reasons. Fane is not a transvestite, but an actor who also does a circus act in drag. The idea of drag (or "female impersonation") is even more readily associated with homosexuality. Yet Fane is also narratively presented as Diana Baring's lover and as a romantic rival to Sir John.

Norman wears women's clothes for personal reasons, but Dr. Richman's analysis of this at the end of the film does little to fix Norman's gender or sexual identities:

Sam: Well, why was he—dressed like that?
District Attorney: He's a transvestite!
Dr. Richman: Ah, not exactly. A man who dresses in women's clothing in order to achieve a sexual change, or satisfaction, is a transvestite. But in Norman's case, he was simply doing everything possible to keep alive the illusion of his mother being alive. And when reality came too close—when danger or desire threatened that illusion—he dressed up, even to a cheap wig he bought. He'd walk about the house, sit in her chair, speak in her voice. He tried to be his mother! And, uh, now he is. Now that's what I meant when I said I got the story from his mother. You see, when the mind houses two personalities, there's always a conflict, a battle. In Norman's case, the battle is over, and the dominant personality has won.[30]

The novel is clear about Norman being a transvestite, and suggests that he was one "long before Mrs. Bates died."[31] But, finally, as Sam explains things to Lila, the novel still leaves Norman's sexuality in the queer zone: "Transvestites aren't necessarily homosexual, but they identify themselves strongly with members of the other sex."[32] Of Dr. Richman's analysis of Norman in the film, Robert J. Corber notes, "the psychiatrist's reductive use of Freudian categories seems to multiply rather than fix the potential meanings of Norman's behavior."[33] Actually it's more a case of Richman's being vague in his use of psychiatric terms, rather than "reductively" employing "Freudian categories," that results in the gender and sexuality complications surrounding Norman. For example, what does Richman mean when he says the Norman is "not exactly" a transvestite? Albeit in a muddled manner, the psychiatrist does acknowledge that there are both homosexual and heterosexual transvestites. Does "sexual change" mean a gender change that might be related to homosexuality, but not necessarily? Does sexual "satisfaction" mean receiving heterosexual satisfaction from wearing women's clothes, or does it mean a homosexual's satisfaction in thinking himself feminine or (like) a woman?

However, Richman implies that Norman's case is somewhat different from that of either a homosexual or heterosexual transvestite. Are we to understand, then, that Norman is a transvestite to the extent that he wears women's clothes, but "not exactly" one in that his cross-gender dressing is not clearly connected with any particular sexual identity label, or, perhaps, might be connected with them both in certain ways? That is, Norman's cross-dressing is not clearly being done in conjunction with homosexual or heterosexual desires, but his desire to embody a straight woman's personality? But Richman also mentions that when Norman feels heterosexual desire, as appears to be the case with Marion, he dresses as mother and "becomes" her. According to Richman, it would appear that Norman's *heterosexual* impulses result in his crossing gender lines. Queer enough for you yet? If not, also consider that many transgendered and pre-op transexual men talk about being a "woman trapped in a man's body," a "feminine man," or words along these lines. If Norman is "not exactly" a transvestite, maybe he might also be "sort of" transexual or transgendered, particularly in the final scene of the film, where his male body now houses only "the dominant personality" of his mother.

It should be clear by this point that the presentation of Norman's relationship with his mother (and the "mother" within him) is the most important and complex means by which *Psycho* queers Norman's character. But Norman's relationship with the film's other major character, Marion Crane, is presented in a way that often parallels and reinforces the queerness of the Norman-mom pairing. Like Mrs. Bates, Marion is presented as both the object of Norman's desire and as his double: both the other and the twin. "When we watch the film," James Naremore comments, "Marion and Norman somehow *evoke* one another."[34] More than one critic has observed that the character of "Mary" in Robert Bloch's original novel was changed to "Marion" for the film, "so that it would suggest the mirror image of Norman."[35] *Psycho's* narrative consistently counterpoints and compares these two characters. Both are sexual outlaws as they are involved in "illicit" sexual situations, both have internalized dead mothers who watch over their sex lives, and both are guilty of "crimes of passion." But whereas Marion's crime is, in part, committed in order to make her heterosexual relationship with Sam more conventional, more in line with what she feels her mother would have wished, Norman's crimes cement his queer relationship with his mother (and the "mother" within him).

There are many moments when Norman and Marion are simultaneously yoked together and placed in opposition to each other through visuals or dialogue. Once they take refuge in the motel office to escape the "dirty night" outside, Marion and Norman are caught together reflected in a mirror for a moment. It is when he is separated from Marion by the registration desk, with his back turned to her, that Norman decides to give her cabin 1, the room next to the office, the one he can peep into from his parlor. Facing her across the desk again, they appear at once different and similar:

> One is female, the other male; one is fair, the other dark. Yet they have aquiline profiles, wide shoulders, and slender, bird-like bodies.[36]

In a later sequence, birds become an important source for contrasting and connecting Norman and Marion, as well as linking both of them to Mrs. Bates. During the dinner in the parlor, Marion notices the stuffed birds all around the room. Norman compares her to a bird ("You—you eat like a bird") as a prelude to discussing taxidermy. "It's a strange hobby. Curious," Marion replies. For the rest of the sequence, as Marion and Norman talk about his mother and the "private traps" they have been born in or have stepped into, birds are carefully integrated into shot compositions. Early on, Norman stands before an owl with outstretched wings so that his head replaces that of the nighttime bird of prey. Later, when discussing his mother, a low angle shot will place Norman under the same owl, as if he were the prey. At certain points in the sequence, both Norman and Marion have a bird's beak pointed at their head. After Marion returns to her room, Norman's peephole reveals her undressing next to pictures of small birds. Let's also state the obvious: Marion's last name is Crane.

On first viewing, the birds appear to signal the victim status of both Marion and Norman. At the same time, certain uses of birds suggest Norman may be dangerous to Marion. The peephole scene seems to reinforce this. But Marion's murder in the shower leads us to see the birds as Mrs. Bates's stand-ins. Both Marion and Norman appear to be the victims of her sexual jealousy. By the end of the film, however, we come to realize that in a certain ways Mrs. Bates is one of the victimized birds (she has been killed and preserved like them), while Norman has internalized a version of his mother as bird of prey in order to continue to wreak vengeance on sexual women like his mother who elicit desire even as they scare him. Norman is like Marion, who is like mother in certain ways, who Norman, in turn, becomes like in other ways.

All roads lead to mother, and as far as Norman is concerned, all these roads lead to "disgusting" straight female sexuality, which returns us to the popular notion that loathing, fear, and hatred of straight women are certain signs of male homosexuality. Put in more conservative psychoanalytic terms, homosexual men are unsuccessful in turning women into fetish objects in order to overcome the castration fears women's penis-lacking bodies represent. This could describe Norman at the peephole. He tries to make Marion a fetish object, but the part of him that is "mother," the feminine part of him, or the part of him that represents his repressed homosexuality (as it has been transferred onto a figure connected with both femininity and transgressive sexuality) frustrates the process, leaving Norman impotent and "mother" furious.

This misogynistic vision is one that the film does not fully separate itself from.[37] In certain ways, *Psycho* presents both Mrs. Bates and Marion in a manner that feeds into Norman's understanding of heterosexuality as a dirty business perpetuated by women with "ugly appetites." In part, the psychiatrist's revelations picture Mrs. Bates as a woman who first encouraged Norman's incestuous closeness, then ignored him the first time an opportunity for a sexual relationship with a man presented itself. At the beginning of the film and during the peephole and shower scenes, Marion is displayed in classic sex object style for the audience, if more complexly for Norman. In part, these scenes are constructed to register as naughty turn-ons (whether this is the effect on all viewers or not), with Marion as the tease.

The sense that heterosexuality is a rather futile and pathetic activity—although one that is not fully the woman's fault—becomes even more pronounced if you watch the film from outside a normative straight male position. Indeed, part of the queerness of *Psycho* has to do with its dour representation of heterosexuality, as well as its striking refusal to construct a conventional central straight couple during the course of the film. The one exception to all this is the sheriff and his wife, but they are minor, ineffectual figures. Of course, *Psycho* is not the only Hitchcock film to represent heterosexuality as a less-than-desirable arrangement, especially for women. Indeed, the delusions and anguish that feed straightness are major preoccupations in almost all of the director's work: from the adulterous triangle in *The Ring* (1927), to the disintegrating bourgeois marriage in *Rich and Strange* (1932), to the sadomasochistic couples in *Notorious*, to the painful deconstruction of heterosexual romance in *Vertigo* (1958). But in these films, and many others, there is a central heterosexual couple the audience is asked to identify or empathize with to some degree, for all their problems. Or, as is the case with a film like *Shadow of a Doubt*, a sympathetic, if not perfect, heterosexual couple is formed as a response to the spectacle of queer destruction and chaos. With the exceptions of *Vertigo* and *Frenzy*, at the end of the films central heterosexual couples remain to provide some sense that the patriarchal status quo will be reestablished. But, then, to a great degree, *Vertigo* is as caught up in evoking the tragedy of heterosexual romantic loss as it is in deconstructing heterosexual romance. *Frenzy* is perhaps the only film in Hitchcock's canon to rival *Psycho* in the ruthlessness by which it denies the central convention of dominant culture and its narratives: that the formation of a heterosexual couple is both desirable and necessary, and that this couple will survive all challenges to make the world (of the narrative) a better place.

The first potential central heterosexual couple *Psycho* offers is Sam and Marion, but, as Leo Braudy notes of their secretive hotel tryst, they "have a melancholic relation[ship] in which sex and money are the prime topics of conversation."[38] Christopher Sharrett finds that the initial "tenderness" in the opening scene "is quickly deflated by the puritanical constraints of Marion's life and the dismal financial legacy Sam inherits from his father."[39] Marion and Sam do discuss making their relationship more conventional, but, finally, Marion tells Sam he makes "respectability sound disrespectful." Returning to her office job, Marion talks with a woman coworker who offers her "something—not aspirin" for her headache: "My mother's doctor gave them to me the day of my wedding. Teddy was furious when he found out I'd taken tranquilizers!" Here is yet another mother intimately involved with her child's sex life. Soon after this, the narrative more strikingly moves into heterosexuality and/as incest territory with the arrival of Mr. Cassidy, who is buying a home as a wedding present for his daughter, an eighteen-year-old he calls "my baby" and "my sweet little girl": "And tomorrow she stands her sweet self up there and gets married away from me." Suggestively sitting at the edge of Marion's desk and flashing around forty thousand dollars, Cassidy talks about "buying off unhappiness" for "his baby," while simultaneously using the money as a crude come-on to attract the much-younger Marion. Later, as she drives off with the money, Marion will smile weirdly, like Norman, when she imagines Cassidy's anger: "Well, I ain't about to kiss off forty thousand dollars! I'll get it back, and if any of it's missin', I'll replace it with her fine, soft flesh!"

While Marion seems to have stolen the money as a way to ease Sam's financial problems so they can get married, she also appears to have stolen it as some sort of revenge against the sleazy Mr. Cassidy and "his baby"'s wedding plans. But we sense almost immediately that Marion's crime will neither affect the relationship of Mr. Cassidy and his "sweet little girl," nor result in Marion and Sam's being united as the "respectable" couple at the center of the narrative. Enter Norman Bates, a figure that some critics and viewers see, on first viewing, as a potential heterosexual match for Marion.

As discussed earlier, the film encourages us to make strong connections between Marion and Norman, especially in the parlor sequence. "They face each other," Danny Peary says, "two friendly people with secrets, false identities, guilt and paranoia, crimes in their pasts."⁴⁰ Besides, Marion has half-jokingly told Sam she's "thinking about" going out and finding "somebody available." Perhaps Marion will save Norman from his overbearing, jealous mother:

Marion: Sometimes we deliberately step into those traps.
Norman: I was born in mine. I don't mind it anymore.
Marion: Oh, but you should. You should mind it!
Norman: Oh, I do—but I say I don't.
Marion: You know—if anyone ever talked to me the way she spoke to you—
Norman: Sometimes, when she talks to me like that, I feel I'd like to go up there and curse her—and-and-and leave her forever! Or at least defy her!

But Marion's heterosexual rescue of Norman is not to be. Declining Norman's offer "to stay just a little while longer," Marion decides to go back to Phoenix in order to try and pull herself out of the "private trap" she stepped into there. With all that talk earlier about Norman's restrictive relationship with his mother as the trap he was "born in," one wonders if Marion's stagnant relationship with Sam is part of the "private trap" she refers to here.

Marion's murder not only leaves the film without a central identification figure, but also without the chance that Marion and Sam will work out their problems and become the conventional central young heterosexual couple in the narrative. The appearance of Marion's sister, Lila, at Sam's doorstep opens up the possibility that she will step in for her sister. While Lila "represents the return of the indispensible heroine," she is also narratively calculated to trigger a knee-jerk audience response: she could be Sam's new love interest.⁴¹ However, Lila's brisk, no-nonsense demeanor must finally defeat even the most conventional viewer's hopes for the (re)constitution of the heterosexual couple in her and Sam. Finally, she and Sam form what Raymond Bellour calls the "shadow-couple," who "mimic" the traditional central diegetic heterosexual couple, thereby "marking out its absence": "Sam and Lila, pretending to be married—as Sam and Marion were intended to be—approach the motel where Marion first met Norman on the path that was supposed to lead her to Sam."⁴² Or, as Barbara Klinger puts it:

The narrative initially represents a sexualized romantic couple in Marion and Sam. The reformulation of the couple in the second part, Lila and Sam, is in totally asexual, nonromantic terms.⁴³

Psycho does leave us with a central "romantic" couple, however: Norman and his mother, Mr. and Mrs. Bates. Looking back over the narrative, it seems inevitable that a sexualized parent-child couple would dominate the film. Normative heterosexuality never really had a chance in *Psycho*. During the opening sequence, Marion's dead mother is evoked during Sam and Marion's hotel tryst. Marion wants Sam to come to her house "with [her] mother's picture on the mantel" for a dinner date. Sam wonders if they will then have to "[t]urn Mama's picture to the wall" when they have sex. Marion's coworker receives competing calls from her mother and her husband during the work day, and talks about the time her mother gave her tranquilizers for her wedding night. Mr. Cassidy goes on and on about keeping his daughter, his "baby," his "sweet little girl," happy as she prepares to get married. Norman and his mother, who "lived as if there was no one else in the world," become the terrifying summation of these parent-child pairs.

Norman kills his mother-lover, but a version of her remains as Norman's personality "splits" itself. The final shot of the film reveals that this couple has mutated yet again, as "mother" takes over Norman's mind, but still resides in his body. We hear "her" voice, but see Norman's face.[44] In *Psycho*, the queer couple endures whereas straight female sexuality and normative heterosexual coupling are methodically eliminated from the narrative. But while this situation might give certain queerly positioned viewers some measure of perverse narrative pleasure, this is more than counterbalanced by the disturbing quality and uses of queerness in this narrative. Based as it is in incest and in punishing transgressive (for the time) female desire, the gender and sexuality queerness surrounding Norman and his mother is hardly a cause for celebration in the film, although Hitchcock and his scenarist Joseph Stefano do invest some of it with dark humor.

Speaking of the final scene of the film, R. Barton Palmer notes that it gives us "a constitution of the couple, but this couple, based on psychopathology and Oedipal failure, cannot serve as the microcosm of a restored social order."[45] Not that all viewers necessarily want to see heterosexuality restored as part of the "social order" of things, but what appears to be *Psycho*'s queer alternative is even more bleak. "Apocalyptic," "nihilistic," "despairing"—words like these have become critical commonplaces to describe *Psycho*'s final shots and its final effect upon viewers. For a moment at the end of the film, Mrs. Bates's mummified face is superimposed over Norman's face (with "mother"'s voiceover), and then both of these are placed over a shot of the trunk of Marion's car, with Marion's body in it, being pulled out of the muck of a swamp. The queer couple presides over the death of both female (hetero)sexuality and the possibility of establishing a central diegetic heterosexual couple who could return the film to straight, patriarchal cultural and narrative spaces. It is a narrative theme Hitchcock plays with in earlier films like *Shadow of a Doubt*, *Rope*, *Strangers on a Train*, and *North by Northwest*, but in these earlier films, he always held back a bit, allowing the possibility that a heterosexual couple would survive the threats of homosexuality or queerness.

But take another look at *Psycho*. There is an important character who seems to survive the apocalypse. She is positioned as outside the "dangerous" and fetishized straight female sexuality of Marion, the ultimately futile heterosexual coupling of Sam and Marion, and the queer psychosis of Norman. Largely forgotten or denigrated by critics and viewers, Lila Crane can take on a major, and a positive, role in a queer reading of *Psycho*. Lila, as noted earlier, appears in the narrative not to become Marion's replacement in forming a central heterosexual couple, but to become her sister's avenger, a role even Marion's lover, Sam, seems slow to take on.

It's telling that Hitchcock and scenarist Joseph Stefano removed all the indications of the budding romance between Lila and Sam that are in Robert Bloch's novel, thereby working against long-standing heterocentrist narrative and cultural conventions. Stefano and Hitchcock, with the help of Vera Miles's performance, also make Lila more brusque than she is in the novel. Taking on both Sam and Arbogast during her first appearance in the film, Lila is not concerned with being conventionally feminine, culturally or narratively. Outspoken—"I don't care if you believe me or not," she shouts at Arbogast—and persistent in the presence of men, Lila is ready to investigate the Bates Motel herself when Arbogast doesn't return with his report as promised:

Lila: Sam, he said an hour—or less.
Sam: Yeh. It's been three.
Lila: Well, are we just going to sit here and wait?
Sam: He'll be back. Let's sit still and hang on, okay?
[Lila gets up and moves to the door.]
Lila: How far is the old highway?
Sam: You want to run out there, don't you? Bust in on Arbogast and the old lady—
Lila: Yes, yes!
Sam: —and maybe shake her up? That wouldn't be a wise thing to do.
Lila: Patience doesn't run in my family,
Sam. I'm going out there.
Sam: But Arbogast said—
Lila: An hour—or less!
[Sam turns away.]
Lila: Well, I'm going!

Shamed by Lila's determination, Sam finally says he'll go, forcing a reluctant, argumentative Lila to stay behind in case Arbogast comes back. The scene's final medium close shot of Lila with rake heads sticking up behind her dissolves into a shot of Norman looking out over the swamp that has just swallowed the car with Marion's body in its trunk. For a moment during the dissolve, Lila is staring at Norman's back, and the rakes are clawing at him and at the swamp. Even as she is left behind, Lila is being set up as the hero of the film, as the one who will expose Norman and find Marion.

To a great extent, Lila will take over the narrative functions of both the lover and the law (Sam, Arbogast/the Sheriff)—functions almost always fulfilled by heterosexual male characters. In qualifying the charges of misogyny against Hitchcock, though not exonerating him, James Griffith points to Lila saying that she "shows more strength than the men," and that she "carries out most of the detective work, leaving Sam to distract Norman while she goes ahead to try the door to cabin 1 and later to search the house."[46] In all this, Lila is connected to the character in some contemporary slasher films that Carol Clover calls "the Final Girl," who remains to confront the killer at the end of the film. While Clover doesn't feel that Lila is fully the prototype for this Final Girl, her description of the Final Girl does fit Lila (and her position in relation to Norman) in many ways:

> The Final Girl is boyish, in a word. Just as the killer is not fully masculine, she is not fully feminine—not, in any case, feminine in the way of her friends. Her smartness, gravity, competence in...practical matters, and sexual reluctance set her apart from the other girls. [47]

Also, while Lila isn't in the entire film, once she appears, the film does in large part "restructur[e] the narrative action from beginning to end around her progress in relation to the killer."[48] William Rothman calls the dissolve from Lila in the hardware store to Norman at the swamp "the first suggestion of a magical connection between Norman and Lila."[49]

Beyond this, Lila's active narrative position in the last half of the film also carries with it some degree of audience empathy and identification. Somehow this has escaped most commentators, who talk about *Psycho* as if the viewer's empathy and identification completely passes from Marion to Norman until the revelation in the fruit cellar. Lila's exploration of the Bates home is just the most spectacular instance of how the last half of *Psycho* invests her with a narrative strength unusual for women characters. So I'll have to disagree with Clover and, using her words, again say that Lila finally does take on, "in varying degrees, the function of Arbogast (investigator) and Sam (rescuer)," and *is*, therefore, the prototype for the Final Girl of slasher films.[50] Perhaps the greatest difference between her position and that of contemporary Final Girls is that Sam does rush in to disarm Norman-as-"mother" when he threatens Lila in the fruit cellar. However, this is the least Sam can do after stupidly goading Norman into anger while Lila was still in the Bates house.

Not exactly "boyish," Lila, in her tailored outfit, is decidedly not the conventional erotic feminine figure that Marion represents. As Barbara Klinger puts it, "Lila is depicted as prim, a severely restricted counterpart to Marion in terms of sexual iconography."[51] Julie Tharp offers a less heteronormative account of Lila's gender position by comparing her to *The Silence of the Lambs'* Clarice Starling who, "[a]lthough small and frequently wearing dresses . . . is not especially 'feminine.' "[52] Noting another difference between Lila and her sister, William Rothman finds that whereas Marion talks with Sam about getting married, "there is no indication that Lila even thinks of marrying."[53] Later, in analyzing Lila's search of the Bates house, Rothman will remark that "[w]hat Lila sees," when she looks pensively at Mrs. Bates's bed, is "the mark of a single body in a bed made for two," which becomes "a poetic image of [her own] solitude and absence, of sexuality denied."[54]

If you are a lesbian, gay, or queerly positioned reader, you might begin to see where I am going with this discussion of Lila. Yes, Lila might be understood as a nonconventional straight woman, but, like her contemporary counterpart, *The Silence of the Lambs'* Clarice Starling, she could also be a dyke.[55] Lila's narrative, visual, and verbal coding do nothing to definitely fix her as heterosexual. If anything, the film's coding indicates that she is different from the film's straight woman lead character, Marion. Marion's hotel room scene with Sam is all sex and tension; Lila's motel room scenes with Sam are all business. Marion's one independent action leads to her death; Lila's independence from cultural and narrative norms for women leads her to uncover the film's mysteries before she is supplanted by the male psychiatrist in the final section of the film. Granted, as many of the critics I quote above indicate, some of the ways in which Lila might be understood as a dyke could be based upon negatives and absences—"not feminine," "sexuality denied," "prim," "[hetero]sexual reluctance," "severely restricted" sexually. But stepping outside of these pejorative and heterocentric positions, it is possible to see Lila's lesbianism as being more positively, and subtly, coded narratively, visually, and verbally through her appearance and attitude, her outspokenness, and her independence from men. This appears to be the reading of Lila that Julianne Moore used to play her in the 1998 remake directed by Gus Van Sant: "Moore, too, stands out as Lila, whom she says she portrayed as a lesbian. . . . [I]t's not difficult to imagine her hunting for her sister by herself. Moore's Lila is independent, and capable of taking on Norman single-handed."[56]

Understanding Lila, as Moore and Van Sant seem to, as the lesbian hero of *Psycho* helps counterbalance possible readings of Norman as a "crazy-because-he's-gay/queer" psycho killer. Lila uncovers the truth about the murders of two women—Marion and Mrs. Bates—who were being punished, in part, for being sexually desiring and active. Lila, as a lesbian, would have some empathy for these female sexual outlaws. But, as might be expected in a Hitchcock film, the working out of Lila's lesbianism is also troubled by two related things: repression and incestuous desires. In order to attach these things to her lesbianism, the narrative finds opportunities to link Lila with Norman's mother-based queerness, something that is most evident during her exploration of the Bateses' bedrooms. During her search, Lila seems both moved and disturbed by what she encounters. William Rothman suggests that in her progress through Mrs. Bates's bedroom Lila discovers things that remind her of her own dead mother: the bronzed crossed hands of a woman, the bed with the indentation of a body.[57] Between these reminders, however, Lila is startled by her own reflection in Mrs. Bates's full-length mirror. "Lila occupies the mother's place," William Rothman notes. "In Lila's vision and in her reflection, Mrs. Bates momentarily comes to life." However, placed where it is between the folded women's hands and the mother's bed with the body indentation, Lila's fright before the mirror might also be understood as representing Lila's (over)identification with her own dead mother—the very thing the film connects to Norman's gender and sexuality problems.

Both Norman and Lila have stood before mother's mirror and seen themselves and/as mother in it. However, whereas Norman's intense connection to his mother leads to his dangerous, infantile, effeminate queer or gay mama's boy narrative status, Lila's implied connection with mother can be understood within either conservative/pejorative or celebratory discourses that find strong mother-daughter connections an important source or "cause" of lesbianism. Read as regressive, like Norman's queerness, Lila's mother-centered lesbianism would be understood as being defined by those negatives or absences mentioned above: she's never progressed to normative feminine adult heterosexuality. Lila's fright before the mirror—thinking she sees Mother Bates—would seem to indicate a narrative preference for this reading. But Lila is hardly portrayed as being infantile or dependent, quite the opposite—she is perhaps the most adult character in the film. So her exclusive emotional attachment to mother(s), as well as to her sister, rather than to men, would most accurately be considered the basis of her strength. Lila goes where conventional straight women characters fear to tread.

However, the final effects of Lila's search for the mother are mixed, like so much else in the film: she appears both eager and anxious about encountering mother in her bedroom or in the fruit cellar. Besides this, Lila's interlude before Mrs. Bates's bed is simultaneously poignant and creepy, especially as the film cuts from this scene to a scene in which Norman shrilly insists to Sam, "This place happens to be my only world. I grew up in that house up there. I had a very happy childhood. My mother and I were more than happy." Then, again, maybe Lila's case is supposed to represent the more positive effects of strong mother-child bonding when the child is a girl. This would certainly appear to be what the film is suggesting, by contrast, during Lila's search of Norman's room, which has been kept as it was when he was a child, with the addition of Beethoven's "Eroica" (commonly misread as, or reminding critics and viewers of, "Erotica") on the record player, and an untitled bound volume that looks as if it could be a family photo album, but which in the original book is filled with pornographic pictures. Considering the disturbed look on Lila's face as she opens it, the quick cutaway from Lila, and what we learn of Norman and his mother, the photos in this volume could be both types simultaneously.

For Lila, however, the film's insinuations about family romance and homosexuality are not limited to her mother. As noted earlier, in many ways Lila shares or takes over the traditional narrative position of the lover-rescuer in relation to her sister. She wants to save her sister "before she gets in this too deeply." In such a role, Lila becomes the rival for the man's position in two triangles involving her sister: Sam-Marion-Lila and Norman-Marion-Lila. Recall along these lines that in the opening bedroom scene, Sam has set up Lila, along with her mother, as an impediment to his having sex with Marion: "[D]o we send sister to the movies?" Lila's narrative placement as a potential rival to Sam in relation to her sister also marks Lila's lesbianism as adult and not "regressive." Another way of looking at Lila's position in *Psycho* is to see her as the "forbidden love" in the Sam-Marion-Lila triangle, just as Mother Bates (who Lila momentarily "becomes" in the mirror) is in the Norman-mother–mother's lover triangle.

It makes sense that lesbian Lila forces straight Sam to stall Norman while she goes into the house. She wants to talk with Mrs. Bates alone, and, in doing this, perhaps reconnect with her own dead mother while discovering something that will allow her to find her sister. But mother isn't in her room, she's in the fruit cellar, a site so compelling that it draws Lila away from making her escape from Norman. John Hepworth, with reference to Robin Wood's work on the film, discusses the possible homosexual meanings of the fruit cellar and "mother"'s "No I will not hide in the fruit cellar. Ha! You think I'm fruity, ha!":

> Of *Psycho*'s Norman Bates, Wood did write, "The cellar gives us the *hidden sexual springs of his behavior* (my italics): there Lila finds Mrs. Bates. It is the

fruit-cellar (his italics)—the fruit is inisisted upon in the mother's macabre joke about being 'fruity': the source of fruition and fertility become rotten."... Along with "homo," "faggot," and "queer," the word "fruit" has long been a popular appellation for a homosexual.[58]

In response to Wood's contention that he did not understand "fruit" and "fruity" as necessarily being connected with male homosexuality, Hepworth wonders, "What *non*-homosexual 'hidden sexual springs' Wood had in mind in his statement."[59] I can understand Hepworth's frustration in the face of what he sees as stubborn heterocentrism (even though Wood is gay himself), but I am with Wood in one sense: the fruit cellar and the reference to fruitiness is not necessarily limited to, or even clearly about, male homosexuality. It might be in Norman's case, but, then again, it is "mother" who is the fruity one in the cellar, so we might be dealing with a less specific type of queerness here.

Then there is lesbian Lila. The entire last half of the film has been moving her toward this encounter with the dead mother and Norman in the fruit cellar. After being frightened by Mother Bates's mummified body, Lila finds herself in the thrall of the spectacle of Norman in drag, Norman as "mother." As Rothman describes this moment:

> Lila, who undertook to penetrate the most private recesses of this place, has been singled out for this theatrical gesture.... Like Handel Fane when he enters Sir John's view at the circus, like Charles when he reveals his true face to Charlie on the train, the being standing unmasked before Lila demands acknowledgment.[60]

I wonder of it's just a coincidence that Rothman compares Norman in this moment to two other murderous queer-coded characters in Hitchcock films (*Murder*, *Shadow of a Doubt*). In any case, the scene is filmed to appear as if Lila has conjured up Norman. For a moment before he appears, Lila looks at an empty doorway, then Norman-as-"mother" makes his entrance. He pauses to let Lila gaze at him. Caught between the dead mother and the spectacle of mother-related queerness, Lila responds with a combination of fear and fascination. In the sight of Norman-as-"mother," Lila has finally confronted the figure she had mistaken herself for in Mrs. Bates's mirror. Norman-as-"mother" finally becomes Lila's dark doppelgänger within a queer narrative of incestuous desire and (possible) homosexual repression.

There is a moment during the psychiatrist's analysis of Norman when Lila reveals that she might understand and sympathize with Norman. Sam, with a repelled look on his face, asks Richman why Norman was "dressed like that." At this, Lila looks over at Sam as if she were appalled by him and his question. The novel expands upon this suggestion of Lila's empathy for Norman. "Then the horror wasn't in the house," Lila tells Sam, "It was in his head." A few moments later, Lila says, "And right now, I can't even hate Bates for what he did. He must have suffered more than any of us. In a way I understand. We're all not quite as sane as we pretend to be."[61] But the film only leaves us with Lila glancing askance at Sam. Otherwise, as with *The Silence of the Lambs*, *Psycho* finally pits the lesbian against the queer man, with straight men ready to burst in to help subdue the queer monster. Though queerness has the penultimate word and image, the final shot of Marion's car-coffin being pulled out of the muck, underlined by Bernard Herrmann's ominous score, is there to remind us of the horrors of queerness.

It's no wonder that Lila, sitting in a room full of straight men, remains silent, except for making a brief reference to her sister, during the psychiatrist's explanation of Norman's mental illness. As Julie Tharp remarks, much of the psychiatrist's "theatrical description" of Marion's death and queer Norman's schizophrenia is "sadistically addressed" to a "stunned" Lila.[62] The only two close-ups of her during the sequence remind us of why Lila might be so guarded now when she has been nothing but outspoken and active before this: she has been made to feel that she is hiding "shocking" secrets similar to those that are being exposed about Norman. The first close-up of Lila's concerned face occurs early in the sequence at the moment Dr. Richman says "He only half-existed to begin with," while the second is timed to Richman's pointing at Lila and saying, with reference to Norman's desire for Marion, "He wanted her." Norman's queer repressions and incestuous desires are, perhaps warningly, being associated with Lila.

Queerly speaking, *Psycho*'s last half is, to a great extent, the story of a brash, heroic dyke who is subdued when the narrative forces her to encounter the perils and terrors of queerness as she sets out "to penetrate the most private recesses" and "the hidden sexual springs" of the Bates home. The inquest at the end of the film begins with the sheriff saying, "Even I couldn't get to Norman, and he knows me." With no transition, but associatively suggesting a connection, the script has the sheriff turn to ask Lila if she is warm enough (she is). As the inquest comes to a close, however, Lila is sitting rigidly and quietly among the men as a police officer brings Norman- as-"mother" a blanket because s/he feels "a little chill." Reduced by the narrative to a scream that blends with Norman-as-"mother"'s, then to speechlessness, and, finally, to near silence, Lila becomes the immobilized link between the dead mother and the queer psycho, while, by physical force or conventional psychiatric discourse, straight men—Sam, Dr. Richman—subdue the frightening figure Lila discovers she has mistaken herself for in the bedroom mirror.[63] I guess even Lila doesn't escape *Psycho*'s queer apocalypse after all.

NOTES

1. *Psycho* (1960, Paramount: Alfred Hitchcock). All dialogue and descriptions of shots are taken from the 1997 widescreen video print of the film.
2. In his stuttering, Norman joins other gay- and queer-coded characters in Hitchcock films like Brandon (*Rope*) and Bruno (*Strangers on a Train*), a point made by William Rothman, without the queer connection, in *Hitchcock—The Murderous Gaze* (Cambridge, Ma., and London: Harvard University Press, 1982), 271.

    The "crazy" quote is from John Hepworth, "Hitchcock's Homophobia," in *Out in Culture: Gay, Lesbian and Queer Essays on Popular Culture,* ed. Corey Creekmur and Alexander Doty (Durham, N.C., and London: Duke University Press, 1995), 188.

    Other readings of *Psycho*, not cited in subsequent notes, that call Norman gay, imply he's straight, or avoid the issue of sexuality are found in Neil P. Hurley, *Soul in Suspense: Hitchcock's Fright and Delight* (Metuchen, N.J., and London: Scarecrow Press, 1993); and Donald Spoto, *The Art of Alfred Hitchcock: Fifty Years of His Films* (Garden City, N.Y.: Doubleday, 1976), 355–81. Hitchcock himself never had much to say in public about Norman's gender and sexuality; the closest he gets are statements such as his observation that the stuffed owls in Norman's parlor are "like symbols," as they "belong to the night world; they are watchers, and this appeals to [Norman's] masochism." (In François Truffaut with Helen G. Scott, *Hitchcock* [New York: Simon and Schuster, 1985], 282.) In response to Andrew Sarris's comment that "the psychiatrist's explanation . . . isn't given much weight," Hitchcock replies, "Possibly the details would have been too unpleasant. I think that perhaps we're skimming over. . . ." Hitchcock leaves his comment here suspensefully open-ended: what "unpleasant details" of Norman's personality were they "skimming over" in the film? (In *Interviews with Film Directors* [New York: Avon, 1967], 245.)
3. Robin Wood, "The Murderous Gays: Hitchcock's Homophobia," in *Hitchcock's Films Revisited* (New York: Columbia University Press, 1989), 336–57. In this chapter, Wood asks "which, in fact, *are* Hitchcock's gay characters," and wonders whether claims that certain characters like Norman Bates are homosexual "largely rest upon heterosexist myths about homosexuals" (345). He does admit, though, that Hitchcock may "have shared" these myths.
4. *The Silence of the Lambs* (1991, Orion: Jonathan Demme). A comparative analysis of *Psycho* and *The Silence of the Lambs* is made in Julie Tharp's "The Transvestite as Monster: Gender Horror in *The Silence of the Lambs* and *Psycho*," *Journal of Popular Film and Television* 19:3 (Fall 1991): 106–13. This interesting article links Norman's gender troubles to homosexuality via the film's use of codes of transvestism.
5. Made a year after *Psycho*, in an attempt to cash in on its popularity, *Homicidal* (1961, Columbia: William Castle) is another film that could be discussed more accurately by using the term "queer." While the final explanations by a doctor and a police detective try to make the killer and the killings less connected to

queer psychosis than to an elaborate scheme to inherit a patrilineal fortune, the narrative consistently evokes queerness of one sort or another. *Homicidal* begins queerly, and like Hitchcock's television series, with producer-director William Castle stitching a needlepoint sampler while discussing his earlier shock films. The sampler is then turned toward the camera—it spells out the title of the film.

Homicidal's major narrative queerness involves a mother and a nurse raising a girl as a boy, without the father's knowledge, so that s/he can inherit the family fortune. After the parents' deaths, the nurse takes the child to Denmark, the land of Christine Jorgensen's then-recent sex change operations. "What happened there, we don't know," the police detective intones during the film's final explanations. What we are told during the course of the film is that the child has been harshly treated by the father and the nurse (acting on the father's directions) in order to "make [him] more of a man," and to "toughen [him] up." So even though the killer supposedly murders only those people who knew about the inheritance ruse (the county clerk–turned–justice of the peace and the nurse), the narrative suggests s/he could have killed these people because they had some part in forcing the girl to become conventionally masculine. For example, before killing the nurse, Emily/Warren reminds her of the beatings she administered at her/his father's command to make her/him more manly. It's only poetic justice, then, that the ex-clerk and the nurse die at the hands of the now tough and heartless queer monster they helped to create. So what is monstrously queer here is, for once, something that is connected with patriarchy and conventional masculinity.

One possible less progressive understanding of the ideological messages about gender in *Homicidal*, however, is that the film reinforces the idea that girls should be raised to be feminine—or else look at what can happen. On the other hand, when masculinity is defined as it is in *Homicidal*, perhaps it is better that everyone, not only girls, should be raised to be feminine. After all, Castle opens the film placidly doing needlepoint. While initially this moment seems queerly comic, if we consider the story that follows, maybe *Homicidal* is suggesting that such traditionally feminine pursuits as needlework could be preferable for men as opposed to the violent masculinity the rest of the film critiques.

6. For more on the *The Silence of the Lambs* debates, see Douglas Crimp, "Right On, Girlfriend!" *Social Text* 33 (1992): 2–18, and Janet Staiger, "Taboos and Totems: Cultural Meanings of *The Silence of the Lambs*, in *Film Theory Goes to the Movies*, ed. Jim Collins, Hilary Radner, and Ava Preacher Collins (New York and London: Routledge, 1993), 142–54.

7. Tania Modleski, *The Women Who Knew Too Much: Hitchcock and Feminist Theory* (New York and London: Routledge, 1988), 5.

8. Much has been made about what a "risk" it was for "a late-fifties fan magazine cover boy to play a transvestite." Perkins himself is quoted as commenting: "The question was 'Was it a wise thing to rush into in the sixties.' Probably less so than in the eighties, when it seems to me people get away with anything. Look at Vanessa Redgrave in *Second Serve* [in which the actress played a tennis pro who undergoes a sex change], just as an example.... Hithcock agreed that it was a

gamble." (In Stephen Rebello, *Alfred Hitchcock and the Making of Psycho* [New York: HarperCollins, 1991], 59–60). Both Rebello and Perkins seem ready to queerly mix Norman in with transvestites and transsexuals.

Perhaps unwittingly, Perkins's son, Osgood, also suggests that Norman is not straight: "[My father] was typecast into very straight villains or very straight madmen who didn't have the layers of Norman." (In Janet Leigh, with Christopher Nickens, *Psycho: Behind the Scenes of the Classic Thriller* [Harmony Books: New York, 1995], 160). Perkins's own rumored homosexuality and bisexuality have added to Norman's aura as a queer character for some viewers. For more on Perkins, see in particular Wayne M. Bryant, *Bisexual Characters in Film: From Anais to Zee* (New York and London: Harrington, 1997), 128–29, and the 1997 episode of "E! True Hollywood Story" that narrativizes the actor's life as one that moves "from closet case to loving husband battling AIDS." This episode also appears to have used Norman Bates as the model for discussing Perkins's own family life, as it discusses his "super-close" relationship with his mother, his "classical Oedipal" rivalry with his father, and his mother's being "needy and demanding" before his father's death—and even more so afterwards. Queering things further, photographer Christopher Makos, one of Perkins's lovers, says that Perkins was "not a gay man posing as a heterosexual, [but] a sexual being."

9. Sunny Bavaro, a student in one of my Hitchcock courses at Lehigh University, pointed out that Norman's confused queerness is encapsulated in the film's two stabbing-as-a-substitute-for-sex "rape" sequences. Marion's takes place in a shower, while Arbogast is attacked by someone rushing from a bedroom. Arbogast falls down the stairs, after which his attacker jumps on top of the detective and straddles him in a moment filmed to suggest a rape. So masculine-feminine Norman-as-"mother" "rapes" and kills a woman and a man during the course of the narrative.

10. Raymond Bellour, "Psychosis, Neurosis, Perversion," *Camera Obscura* 3–4 (Summer 1979): 125.

11. Stephen Rebello notes that an earlier draft of the script submitted to the Motion Picture Association of America for a censorship code check was filled with even more material that established an incestuous relationship between Norman and his mother. Included in this script were "Mrs. Bates's" reference to Norman as "ever the sweetheart" and "aflame with the 'fantasy of making love,'" along with the psychiatrist's description of Norman and his mother's relationship as "more that of two adolescent lovers." Needless to say, the MPAA suggested this material be toned down (77).

12. Robert J. Corber, *In the Name of National Security: Hitchcock, Homophobia, and the Construction of Gender in Postwar America* (Durham, N.C., and London: Duke University Press, 1993), 197–98.

13. Ibid., 214–15. In this chapter I will modify the term "overidentification" to read "(over)identification" as it refers to males psychically connecting themselves to what is conventionally considered the "feminine" (and once, in relation to Lila's lesbianism, to refer to women's close psychic connections with their mothers).

I do this because, while using the common psychoanalytic term, I don't want to suggest, as it does, that male connections with the feminine (or lesbian connections with the mother) need to be understood as problematic or "too much." While Norman's case in *Psycho* is extreme, I have a feeling that for many viewers the film reinforces the idea that any identification between male children and their mothers (or other women) can easily lead to "perversion" and other tragedies (in the case of *Psycho*, psychotic madness).

14. Ibid., 215.
15. See Robin Wood's letter in response to John Hepworth's criticism of him in "Hitchcock's Homophobia," reprinted in *Out in Culture: Gay, Lesbian and Queer Essays on Popular Culture* (Durham, N.C., and London: Duke University Press, 1995), 194–95. Wood also expresses his reservations about understanding Norman (and a number of other characters in Hitchcock films) as gay in "The Murderous Gays: Hitchcock's Homophobia," 336–57, cited in an earlier note.
16. David Sterritt, *The Films of Alfred Hitchcock* (Cambridge, Ma., and New York: Harvard University Press, 1993), 100.
17. Ibid., 101–2.
18. Ibid., 111, 113–14.
19. Diana Fuss, "Monsters of Perversion: Jeffrey Dahmer and *The Silence of the Lambs*," in *Media Spectacles*, ed. Marjorie Garber, Jann Matlock, and Rebecca L. Walkowitz (New York and London: Routledge, 1993), 181–82, 184.
20. Ibid., 187–88.
21. Ibid., 188. In this passage, Fuss quotes Sigmund Freud's *Leonardo Da Vinci and a Memory of His Childhood* (1910), standard ed., 100. Some of Robert Bloch's remarks about his use of Ed Gein as the basis for Norman in the novel echo Fuss's comments here, and, perhaps, they might be seen as offering a peek into the film's "unconscious":

    > In my novel, following on Freudian precepts, I made Norman Bates a transvestite who dressed up as his mother with a wig and dress whenever he committed these crimes. Much to my surprise, I discovered that the actual killer dressed up also, but he allegedly wore the breasts and skins of his mother.... He was a necrophiliac and a cannibal.... He had a fixation on his mother, who had died twelve years previously. He kept her room inviolate and untouched since that time and the gentleman was also given to perversions in the time-honored tradition of the Nazi death camps (Rebello, 13).

    The novel also has Norman involved in the occult—something that often is culturally associated with homosexuality and other sexual "perversions."
22. Sterritt, 102.
23. Raymond Durgnat, "Inside Norman Bates," in *Focus on Hitchcock*, ed. Albert J. LaValley (Englewood Cliffs, N.J.: Prentice-Hall, 1972), 135. Although not directly associated with Norman, two often noted aspects of the "lavatory" humor of *Psycho* are a close-up of the license plate of one of Marion's cars, ANL-709, and the Production Code battles Hitchcock and scenarist Joseph Stefano had to fight in order to keep the shot of Marion flushing a toilet. As John

Russell Taylor puts it in *Hitch: The Life and Times of Alfred Hitchcock* (New York: Berkley, 1980):

> The very sight of a toilet, [the censor] said, was offensive. Here, too, Stefano did battle and won—since the very intention Hitch and he had with that scene was to be offensive. They reckoned that . . . if you actually show a toilet on screen and a close-up of something being flushed down it, you would already have knocked the underpinnings out from under 90 per cent of an American audience, so deeply did the neurosis of toilet-training go, and you would have them just where you wanted them (261).

24. Theodore Price, *Hitchcock and Homosexuality: His 50-Year Obsession with Jack the Ripper and the Superbitch Prostitute—A Psychoanalytic View* (Metuchen, N.J., and London: Scarecrow Press, 1992), xiii.
25. Corber, 191–203.
26. Wood, 241.
27. James Naremore, *Filmguide to Psycho* (Bloomington and Indianapolis: Indiana University Press, 1973), 18.
28. Tania Modleski, *The Women Who Knew Too Much: Hitchcock and Feminist Theory* (New York and London: Routledge, 1988), 36.
29. Modleski does label Normal bisexual at one point in her book, however, when she remarks that "[female bisexuality] reminds a man of his *own* bisexuality (and thus his resemblance to Norman Bates), a bisexuality that threatens to subvert his 'proper' identity" (8).
30. Unlike most critics who feel the film undermines Dr. Richman's analysis by making the character pompous and smug, I think the narrative sets him up to explain Norman to confused viewers. Not that Richman's analysis is without its problems, but I think we are meant to take it seriously as an explanation of Norman's illness. Actually, Richman's vagueness and contradictoriness about certain psychosexual points helps create the sense of uneasy queerness surrounding Norman's character.
31. Robert Bloch, *Psycho* (Greenwich, Conn.: Fawcett, 1961), 151.
32. Ibid., 151.
33. Corber, 189.
34. Naremore, 46.
35. Naremore, 46. See also Bellour, 125.
36. Naremore, 46.
37. In the film's preview trailer, Hitchcock constantly calls Mrs. Bates "the woman" and tells us she is one of the "weirdest" people, as well as a dominating, "maniacal woman." It appears that any "blame the woman/mother" readings of the film can begin with its trailer.
38. Leo Braudy, "Hitchcock, Truffaut, and the Irresponsible Audience," in *Focus on Hitchcock*, ed. Albert J. LaValley (Englewood Cliffs, N.J.: Prentice-Hall, 1972), 121.
39. Christopher Sharrett, "The Myth of Apocalypse and the Horror Film: The Primacy of *Psycho* and *The Birds*," *Hitchcock Annual* (1995–96): 43.

40. Danny Peary, *Cult Movies 3* (New York: Simon and Schuster, 1988), 192.
41. Bellour, 124.
42. Bellour, 107, 124.
43. Klinger, 337.
44. Accounts of the film's production by both Janet Leigh, with Christopher Nickens, 81–83, and Stephen Rebello, 131–33, reveal that "mother"'s voice was achieved through the combined efforts of a gay man and two straight women, which is of more than passing interest considering what the film suggests about Norman's queerness.
45. R. Barton Palmer, "The Metafictional Hitchcock: The Experience of Viewing and the Viewing of Experience in *Rear Window* and *Psycho*," *Cinema Journal* 25:2 (Winter 1986): 18.
46. James Griffith, "*Psycho*: Not Guilty As Charged," *Film Comment* (July–August 1996): 77.
47. Carol Clover, *Men, Women and Chainsaws: Gender in the Modern Horror Film* (London: BFI Publishing, 1992), 40.
48. Ibid., 40.
49. Rothman, 315.
50. Clover, 40.
51. Barbara Klinger, "*Psycho*: The Institutionalization of Female Sexuality," in *A Hitchcock Reader*, ed. Marshall Deutelbaum and Leland Poague (Ames: Iowa State Press, 1986), 337.
52. Tharp, 108.
53. Rothman, 321.
54. Rothman, 323.
55. Elizabeth Young discusses "the lesbian possibilities" in Clarice's character, based on narrative cues and Jodie Foster's star image, in "*The Silence of the Lambs* and the Flaying of Feminist Theory," *Camera Obscura* 27 (1991): 5–35. Julie Tharp compares *The Silence of the Lambs* and *Psycho* in a number of ways, including the narrative functions of Lila and Clarice Starling: "[Clarice] is truly the New Woman, a modern, professional counterpart to Lila Crane, the dauntless female of *Psycho* who insists on taking Arbogast's place as investigator, and even sidelines Sam Loomis into stalling Norman so that she can search the house. Like Lila, Clarice has to fight to be taken seriously as an investigator, but Clarice at least has the sanctioned right to do so. Both women feel themselves to be operating on behalf of their missing and mutilated sisters—Lila her blood sibling, Clarice her sisters in spirit (108)." While Tharp does discuss Starling's "masculine" qualities, she does not compare Lila to her in this respect, and the discussion of these women remains within a straight feminist position.
56. *Psycho* (1998, Universal: Gus Van Sant). Kevin D. Melrose, "Van Sant Keeps Suspense in Controversial 'Psycho'," *Philadelphia Gay News* 23:8 (December 11–17, 1998): 32. At least one journalist reporting on Moore's interpretation of the part, felt that Lila's "lesbo tendencies were...alluded to in the original" (Howard Wilmont, "Hollywood Gossip," *Boyz* [May 12, 1998]: 14). Writer Michael Musto found Moore's "decision to play Lila as a lesbian stereotypically consists

of her being tough, irritable and bossy." ("La Dolce Musto," *Village Voice* XLIII [December 22, 1998]: 14).

57. Rothman, 320–21, 323.
58. Hepworth, 195–96.
59. Hepworth, 196.
60. Rothman, 328.
61. Bloch, 155–56.
62. Tharp, 107.
63. Though implicitly negative about "camp," Danny Peary's comments about *Psycho*, especially Norman's appearance in the basement, suggest that more recent audiences find the film "campy," rather than "scary" or "lurid" (187). Even if this is so, the message that queerness is something negative would still register on audiences who understand Norman as a big, ugly, ridiculous drag queen with a knife. I tend to see Norman's appearance in the fruit cellar door as both shocking and campy in its effect. Like Peary, I find the rest of the film's humor darkly comic, but not campy—with the possible exception of the sight of Norman's hip-swinging ascent of the stairs to "mother"'s room.

The author and the publisher would like to thank the following for permission to reprint certain material in this book, some of which appears here in revised versions:

Duke University Press for " 'My Beautiful Wickedness': *The Wizard of Oz* as Lesbian Fantasy," originally in *Hop on Pop: The Pleasures and Politics of Popular Culture*, ed. Henry Jenkins, Tara McPherson, and Jane Shattuc, 2000, and for "The Queer Aesthete, the Diva, and *The Red Shoes*," originally in *Out Takes: Essays on Queer Theory and Film*, ed. Ellis Hanson, 1999.

The American Film Institute for "Queerness, Comedy, and *The Women*," in *Classical Hollywood Comedy*, ed. Kristine Brunovska Karnick and Henry Jenkins, 1995.

Steven Angelides and Craig Bird, editors, and Brett Farmer, interviewer, for "Seeing Queerly: Going to the Movies with Alexander Doty," originally in *Critical inQueeries* 2:1, June 1998.

Kevin Macdonald for the use of letters and other material in the Emeric Pressburger Collection at the British Film Institute, London.

Photo credits: All stills in this book are courtesy of the Museum of Modern Art Film Stills Archive.